EARLY CHILDHOOD DEVELOPMENT AND ITS VARIATIONS

EARLY CHILDHOOD DEVELOPMENT AND ITS VARIATIONS

KRISTINE L. SLENTZ
SUZANNE L. KROGH
WESTERN WASHINGTON UNIVERSITY

LEA

LAWRENCE ERLBAUM ASSOCIATES, PUBLISHERS
2001   MAHWAH, NEW JERSEY   LONDON

Lawrence Erlbaum Associates, Inc., Publishers
10 Industrial Avenue
Mahwah, New Jersey 07430

Cover design by Kathryn Houghtaling Lacey

Library of Congress Cataloging-in-Publication Data

Slentz, Kristine.
  Early childhood development and its variations / by Kristine L. Slentz and Suzanne L. Krogh.
    p.   cm.
  Includes bibliographical references and index.
  ISBN 0-8058-2884-2 (pbk. : alk. paper)
    1. Child development.   2. Child psychology.   I. Krogh, Suzanne.   II. Title.

  HQ772 .S534 2001
  305.231—dc21
                                                                      00-027286
                                                                      CIP

Books published by Lawrence Erlbaum Associates are printed on acid-free paper,
and their bindings are chosen for strength and durability.

Printed in the United States of America
10 9 8 7 6 5 4 3 2 1

To our families, friends, and colleagues who supported
and motivated us, and tolerated our occasional
preoccupation—you know who you are

Contents

To Our Readers and Their Instructors:
An Introduction to the Series   xiii

Preface   xv

1   Understanding Early Childhood Development   2
    Chapter Objectives   2
    Vignette 1.1: "I Don't Believe in Child Development"   3
    Who Is a Child and What Is Child Development?   3
    Early Childhood Educators and the Need to Know About
        Development   4
        The Concept of Development   5
        Resiliency and Vulnerability   6
        Common Ground   8
    Typical and Atypical Development   9
        Developmental Milestones and Stages   10
        Individual Differences   11
    Vignette 1.2: The Story of the Pie Man   12
        Developmental Delay and Disability   13
        Cultural Diversity   14
    Theories of Early Development   15
        Heredity and Maturation: An Emphasis on Internal Processes   16
        Maturational Theory   17
        Psychoanalytic Theory   17
        Environment and Behavior: An Emphasis on External Factors   19
        Classical Conditioning   19
        Operant Conditioning   20
        Social Learning Theory   21
        Interactive Theories   21
        Synactive Theory   21

Cognitive Development Theory   23
Transactional Theory   23
Ecological Theory   24
Origins of Developmental Problems   25
Prenatal Influences   26
Perinatal Influences   27
Postnatal Influences   27
Developmental Screening   28
Translating Theory Into Practice: Common Principles   29
Extending Your Learning   31
Vocabulary   32
Internet Resources   35
Reading Resources in Developmental Psychology   36
References   36

2   **INFANCY: FROM CRADLE TO PLAY GROUP**   40

Chapter Objectives   40
Vignette 2.1: What's Wrong With Cara?   41
Family Context   42
The Newborn   43
Physical Growth and Motor Development During Infancy:
    Reflexive and Rudimentary Movement   45
Reflexive Movement and Brain Development   45
    Survival Reflexes   45
    Primitive Reflexes   46
    Brain Development   47
Gross Motor Development: Moving Against Gravity   48
    Head Control   49
    Prone Lying   50
    Sitting   51
    First Controlled Maneuvers   51
    Moving on All Fours   52
    Walking   53
Fine Motor Development: Reaching and Grasping   54
    Reaching   55
    Using the Hands   56
    Early Grasping   56
Variations in Motor Development   58
Vignette 2.2: Motor Development in an Alaskan Village   60
Infant Cognitive Development: Learning About the World   63
The Nature of Infant Intelligence   63
Infant Sensory Capabilities   64
    Vision   64
    Hearing   65
    Other Senses   65
Becoming Intentional   66
    Reflexive Activity (Birth to 1 Month)   67
    Primary Circular Reactions (1 to 4 Months)   68

Secondary Circular Reactions (4 to 8 Months)   69
Coordinated Circular Reactions (8 to 12 Months)   69
Variations in Infant Cognitive Development   70
Infant Social-Affective Development: Becoming a Social Partner   71
Sleep–Wake States   71
Vignette 2.3: Newborn Sleep–Wake States   74
Caregiver–Infant Interactions   74
Infant Social Skills   77
Social Smile   77
Stranger Anxiety   77
Proximity Seeking and Separation Anxiety   78
Social Referencing   78
Prelinguistic Communication   79
Crying   79
Early Vocalizations   79
Babbling   80
Transition to Symbolic Communication   80
Variations in Infant Social-Affective Development   81
Implications for Caregivers of Infants   83
Eating and Sleeping   84
Crying   84
Child Care   84
Concluding Remarks   85
Extending Your Learning   85
Vocabulary   86
Internet Resources   90
References   90

3   TODDLERHOOD: FROM PLAYGROUND TO PLAYGROUND   94

Chapter Objectives   94
Vignette 3.1: Excerpts From a Toddler's Diary (Written by His
    Mother)   95
Family Context   97
Physical Growth and Motor Development During Toddlerhood:
    Late Rudimentary–Early Fundamental Phase   98
Physical Growth   98
Gross Motor Development: Refining Basic Skills   99
Walking   99
Climbing   101
Play Skills   101
Fine Motor Development: Using the Hands   102
Variations in Toddler Motor Development   104
Toddler Cognitive Development: Becoming a Symbolic Thinker   105
Tertiary Circular Reactions (12 to 18 Months)   106
Internal Representations (18 to 24 Months)   107
Imitation   107
Spatial Relationships   108
Problem Solving   108

Means for Obtaining Ends: Tool Use   109
Cause and Effect   109
Early Preoperational Thought   110
Vignette 3.2: A 2-Year-Old on the Telephone   110
Language and Communication   112
First Words   112
Beyond Single Words   114
Language and Concepts   115
Vignette 3.3: Give It to Me!   116
Variations in Toddler Cognitive Development   116
Toddler Social-Affective Development: Becoming Independent While
Learning the Rules   117
Temperament   119
Social Games   121
Variations in Toddler Social-Affective Development   121
Implications for Caregivers of Toddlers   122
Safety   122
Mealtimes   123
Toileting   124
Tantrums   125
Concluding Remarks   126
Vignette 3.4: Final Entry in a Toddler's Diary (Written by His
Mother)   126
Extending Your Learning   126
Vocabulary   127
Internet Resources   128
References   129

4   **PRESCHOOLERS: FROM PLAYGROUND TO PEER GROUP**   132

Chapter Objectives   132
Vignette 4.1: Moving Day   133
Family Context   134
Physical Growth and Motor Development During the Preschool
Years: Mastering Fundamental Movements   135
Physical Growth   135
Gross Motor Development: Coordinated Motor Play   136
Ball Play   137
Active Play   138
Fine Motor Development: Proficient Use of Hands   139
Manipulating Objects   140
Using Tools   141
Drawing and Writing   141
Variations in Preschool Motor Development   143
Preschool Cognitive Development: "I Think It, Therefore It Is"   144
Preoperational Thought   145
Vignette 4.2: Clouds and Tea   145
Literal Interpretations   146
Egocentrism   147

Transductive Reasoning   147
Irreversible Thinking   147
Vignette 4.3: Selena and the Gorilla   148
Animism   148
Language and Literacy   149
Phonology and Syntax   149
Semantics and Pragmatics   151
Emergent Literacy   153
Variations in Preschool Cognitive, Language, and Literacy Development   154
Preschool Social-Affective Development: Self and Others, Friends
and Family   156
Preschool as a Period of Initiative   157
Emotional Development   157
Knowledge of Self   158
Gender Identity   159
Ethnic Identity   160
Peer Interactions   161
Variations in Preschool Social-Affective Development   162
Implications for Caregivers and Teachers of Preschoolers   163
Child Care   164
Teaching Across Languages and Cultures   165
Teaching Children of Diverse Abilities   165
Concluding Remarks   166
Extending Your Learning   166
Vocabulary   167
Internet Resources   169
References   169

5   **PRIMARY SCHOOL: FROM PEER GROUP TO ACADEMICS**   174
Chapter Objectives   174
Vignette 5.1: Cutting the Cake to Make More   175
Vignette 5.2: New Rules on the Playground   175
Family Context   176
Physical Growth and Motor Development During the Primary
Years: The Late Fundamental and Early Sports Phases   177
Physical Growth   178
Hands and Eyes   178
Social Aspects of Physical Growth   179
Gross Motor Development: Games and Sports   179
Fine Motor Development: Manipulatives and Academics   181
Perceptual Motor Development   182
Variations in Primary Motor Development   182
Primary Cognitive Development: Perception Gives Way to Inference   183
Making the Transition: The Piagetian Perspective   183
Concrete Operations   184
Conservation   184
Perspective Taking   185
Classification and Categorizing   185
Transductive to Inductive Logic   186

Vignette 5.3: Staying Dry at the Beach   186
   Alternate Views of Cognitive Development   187
      Vygotsky's View   188
      The Information-Processing Model   190
      Howard Gardner's Multiple Intelligences   191
   Achievements in Language and Literacy   194
      Language   194
      Literacy   196
   Variations in Primary Cognitive Development   197
      Growing Up Gifted   198
      A Fuller View of Giftedness   198
      Students With Disabilities   199
Primary School Social-Affective and Moral Development:
   Intrapersonal and Interpersonal Growth   200
   Affective Development   201
      Self-Concept and Self-Esteem   201
      Maslow's Hierarchy of Human Needs   202
      Industry and the Development of Self-Esteem   203
      Motivation   203
      Fears   204
   Social Development   205
      Interpersonal Development: Friendships   205
Vignette 5.4: Making Friends   205
      Interpersonal Development: Sibling Relationships   207
   Moral Development   207
   Variations in Primary School Social Affective Development   209
Implications for Caregivers and Teachers of Primary School Children   210
Concluding Remarks   211
   Extending Your Learning   212
   Vocabulary   212
   Internet Resources   214
   References   215

AUTHOR INDEX   217

SUBJECT INDEX   223

To Our Readers and Their Instructors: An Introduction to the Series

The book you are now beginning is one of a series of four interrelated texts. Taken together, they provide an introduction to the broad field of early childhood education. Usually, such introductions are provided to students in one large survey textbook. Over the years, however, our knowledge of early development as it relates to education has increased enormously at the same time that legislative and cultural issues have grown in number. Add to that the fact that more and more early childhood centers and classrooms include youngsters who would once have been segregated in self-contained special education classes and it becomes evident that now all teachers of young children need to understand development and education across a broad spectrum of abilities. We thus are faced with a problem: Introductory textbooks must either get much longer and heavier, or simply skate across the surface of their topics.

Meanwhile, college and university instructors must decide how to fit this expanded knowledge and information into their courses. The answers they arrive at are many and various, making the traditional all-purpose textbook a source of frustration for many.

This series of textbooks has been designed to alleviate the frustration by offering four modules divided by general subject areas:

- an overview of history and the current field of early education;
- typical and atypical growth and development, infancy through the third grade;
- models and methods of teaching and guiding behavior; and
- curriculum, with a focus on preschool and the primary grades.

By creating this modular scheme, we have been able to treat each topic in more depth and incorporate discussions of abilities and needs across all levels, including developmental delays and giftedness. Instructors are invited to mix and match the texts as appropriate to their own interests and needs.

The titles of the four books in the series are:

Volume I: Early Childhood Education: Yesterday, Today, and Tomorrow
Volume II: Early Childhood Development and Its Variations
Volume III: Teaching Young Children
Volume IV: The Early Childhood Curriculum

We hope you find this new approach to early childhood courses a useful and refreshing one. We welcome your feedback and ideas.

—Kristine Slentz   —Suzanne Krogh
 Special Education   Elementary Education
 Western Washington University   Western Washington University
 Kristine.Slentz@wwu.edu   Suzanne.Krogh@wwu.edu

PREFACE

Never again in our lifetimes do we learn so much so quickly and in so many different areas as during the early childhood years. All these remarkable early accomplishments are anticipated as part of the process of growing from baby to child, even as we notice the individual differences among children in rate, sequence, and emphasis of developmental achievement. Parents and other caregivers of infants, toddlers, preschoolers, and primary-age children are deeply concerned with the outcomes of development: interactions, activities, behaviors, skills, personalities. A thorough understanding of the processes of development, however, is an important foundation for making sense of age-related changes in behavior and an important knowledge base for anyone involved in the education and care of children from birth through eight years old. The purpose of this book is to examine the ways in which development unfolds from birth through the primary years from the perspective of *what* happens (outcomes, milestones) as well as *how* things progress (processes, variables, factors).

Who Should Read This Book and Why

Anyone who has an interest in learning more about how children grow and change from infancy through the primary years could benefit from knowledge of the information contained in this book. Perhaps you are a community college student preparing for a career in child care or are headed for a 4-year university to major in early childhood or early childhood special education. The ideas presented in these pages will assist you in understanding the origin and impact of individual differences among youngsters of similar ages. If you are studying to be a certified teacher of preschool or primary school children, the information will improve your ability to design curricula that address the developmental needs of your students. You might be studying to become a home educator, infant specialist, or early interventionist, in which case investigating the foundations of typical development will provide a context for understanding the impact of developmental disabilities and delays. Maybe you are planning to become the director of an early childhood program and want to know more about the impact of physical and social environments on all domains of early development. You could be the parent or caregiver of an infant, toddler, preschool, or primary-age child who is seeking to better understand the continual evolution of a child's behavior.

Whatever your intent or career goals, it is a good bet that your future includes working with young children and their families. You presumably share the authors' excitement and fascination with the early years and have a vested interest in being able to have a positive and constructive influence on the lives of the boys and girls you encounter. We hope you are also interested in exploring the full range of early development, including risk and protective factors, cultural issues, and the many unresolved issues in the field.

Organization of the Book

The organization of this book into chapters deserves mention, because it reflects both the necessity and the difficulty of dividing the concept of early development into workable units of study. Child development research and early educational programs are usually organized by domain or age or both. In the professions of early childhood education (ECE) and early childhood special education (ECSE), there are people who work with and study infants, toddlers, preschoolers, and primary school children and their families. Most of these youngsters are developing within expected norms; others are at risk for delay and yet others have identified disabilities. The professional literature reflects a focus on development in and facilitation of motor, social, cognitive, language, and adaptive domains. There are focused academic areas of practice, research, and inquiry as diverse as early intervention, values education, self-concept, and parenting support.

Development by its very nature is multifaceted, dynamic, interactive, and variable, so pulling it apart by ages or domains seems arbitrary no matter how it is partitioned. This particular book is organized primarily by age. The first chapter addresses theories, issues, principles, and assumptions of early development. Subsequent chapters progress from infancy through primary school in order, with each chapter covering the specific domains of motor, cognition, and social–affect. We hope this organizational scheme will impart the notion that each age range is characterized by certain processes, tasks, and milestones. The skills and abilities of infants, toddlers, preschoolers, and primary school children are not mutually exclusive, however, and the age ranges designated by each term are arbitrary and overlap. Technically, infants become toddlers when they begin to walk. In reality, walking is a skill that emerges for most children between 9 and 14 months. For this book, infancy covers the months from birth to 18 months, and toddlers are considered to be those children between 18 months and 3 years old. The preschool years, as the term is used in this book, includes youngsters from ages 3 to 5, even though many 5-year-olds have already entered kindergarten.

It is important to remember, also, that children grow and develop as individuals in a holistic fashion. They do not develop in the motor domain for 5 minutes and then switch to the social–affective domain. When a toddler pulls on a parent's pant leg and points to something new and exciting, all domains of development are operating simultaneously as the child communicates information through a motor action in a social interaction with a predictable response from the parent. Throughout the chapters in this book, you will see references to other chapters that reflect developmental precursors and sequels as well as discussion of the interrelationships among motor, cognitive, and social–affective domains.

Chapter Content

In addition to age-related developmental expectations, each chapter contains information about differences in rates and patterns of development for the age range covered. As anyone who works with young children is aware, there are wide variations in the rate and patterns of early development. Some infants seem intent on becoming mobile and are upright and moving around by 9 months of age. Other babies have greater interest in manipulating and examining toys and are content to sit in one place filling and dumping containers and communicating their accomplishments with their caregivers. Many developmental variations reflect differences in cultural and family expectations. Certain patterns of development, however, cause concern for caregivers and require assessment, therapy, or specialized instruction. Early childhood professionals often spend many hours of the day observing, caring for, and educating young boys and girls and are in an excellent position both to capitalize on the existence of diversity and to identify possible developmental delays or the presence of undiagnosed disabilities. Specific developmental disabilities are discussed in this book in the chapters reflecting the age at which they are most commonly diagnosed and in the context of the domains of development most significantly affected.

The information in this book and subsequent volumes is intended to prepare early childhood teachers who are comfortable and confident in their abilities to work with a wide variety of children and families, including:

- Understanding the developmental expectations for infancy, toddlerhood, preschool, and primary years.
- Learning about family and cultural patterns different than your own.
- Performing developmental observations and screenings.
- Making referrals and participating collaboratively as team members with special services personnel.
- Working as partners with parents of all infants and toddler, preschooler, and primary-age youngsters.

In this book, therefore, we explore both individual differences and specific developmental variations that fall outside the range of typical development as well as the expected norms and milestones. The intention is to convey the belief that all young children are valued and important and to view the full range of developmental patterns as falling within the responsibility of the early childhood profession. The hope is to cultivate an appreciation of the complexity and beauty of early growth and development while at the same time acquainting the reader with the myriad related biological and social forces that shape the lives of young children.

Additionally, chapters 2 through 5 end with a section that applies knowledge and information about development to care and education of children in the age range being addressed. Implications for how youngsters learn at different ages, working with families and incorporating home environments into early education, and current issues in the early childhood profession are discussed in this section. Internet resources are listed at the end of each chapter to direct readers to current information and organizations related to early development. Presenting the application section as the final one is designed to suggest direct connections between chapter content and the everyday roles of early childhood professionals, very important people in the lives of young children.

ACKNOWLEDGMENT

This book could never have been completed without the enthusiastic, competent, and ever accessible assistance of Amanda Stempel.

EARLY CHILDHOOD DEVELOPMENT AND ITS VARIATIONS

1

UNDERSTANDING EARLY CHILDHOOD DEVELOPMENT

Children are the living messages we send to a time we will not see. . . .

Neil Postman

▼ *Chapter Objectives*

After reading this chapter, you should be able to:

- ▼ Identify important concepts and processes of early development, including risk, resilience, vulnerability, and protective factors.
- ▼ Compare and contrast a variety of theoretical perspectives on early development.
- ▼ Describe causes of disability and developmental delay during the early childhood years, using "people-first" language.

As you think about and apply chapter content on your own, you should be able to:

- ▼ Refine and clarify your own views on diversity in early childhood settings, including consideration of individual differences in gender, culture, race, ethnicity, and ability.
- ▼ Use a variety of developmental theories to explain and understand the behavior of young children.

Vignette 1.1: *"I Don't Believe in Child Development"*

A thorough understanding of the development of young children is not a desirable mission for everyone. I have a relative who once said, "I don't believe in child development." Initially, I took the statement to mean that he did not really want to hear my advice about his 2-year-old son's willful behavior. In many retellings of this story, I have always emphasized the abrupt ending to the conversation and my puzzlement as a child development specialist that any parent could overlook the significance of early learning and maturation.

As I began to think about an introductory chapter for this text, however, a more impartial interpretation of the comment came to mind: My brother-in-law is just not interested in understanding the academic theories and patterns of child development. He would rather simply observe and experience the surprise and mystery of my nephew's life unfolding, instead of striving to make logical sense of each change in his son's behavior. The inherent enigma of the growth process is more meaningful to him than any scientific, medical, educational, or developmental explanation.

I can easily accept the appreciation of mystery over understanding when I think of my own resistance to my father's attempts to teach me about wave action. Ocean waves are a phenomenon I would rather watch than know about, appreciate rather than analyze. I want to experience the thrill and surprise of not being able to predict and to preserve the intense wonderment of not knowing how or why the waves behave the way they do.

Readers of child development texts, however, do not have the luxury of relying solely on romantic, poetic, or mysterious explanations of early growth. Early childhood professionals have a responsibility to each and every child they serve that requires acquisition and application of knowledge about the process of development. (Kris Slentz)

WHO IS A CHILD AND WHAT IS CHILD DEVELOPMENT?

A child's existence has as many different meanings as there are people involved in his or her life. To parents, children might be the culmination of careful planning or the surprise of a lifetime; dreams come true or shattered; reflections of themselves and entirely puzzling personalities. Grandchildren provide new opportunities for grandparents to make use of parenting expertise, new roles for themselves and their own children, and the promise of ongoing youth during the aging years. Peers become instigators, pals, and confidants. Each boy or girl brings another perspective and ingredient to group interactions: sometimes a calming and comforting influence, sometimes an element of risk and creativity. Neighbors can see young children as a special connection in the community or as surrogate family members or perhaps develop a "Dennis the Menace" relationship.

Likewise, studying the growth and development of children can be undertaken from many perspectives. Developmental psychology, for example, applies theory and research to understanding the causes and effects of age-related changes in children's behavior. Child neuropsychology is a scientific perspective on the influence of brain structure and function on behavior, whereas pediatrics emphasizes the unique medical needs of young people. Child advocates focus their energy on laws that relate to minors and on the legal process as it involves children in the court system. Religious leaders attend to the spiritual and moral aspects of children's lives, and teachers strive to support physical, cognitive, and affective growth through the educational system. Family and friends come to know and love individual children through the daily routines of home and community life and promote independence through caregiving and nurturing. All this and more frames the development of each child, providing a backdrop and an organizing scheme for evolution of the person the child eventually becomes.

People who influence the lives of children have preferred methods, areas of authority and influence, resources, current recommended practices, and often strong beliefs and opinions. Professional disciplines have related but distinct content areas for training, research, and literature. In the everyday lives of young girls and boys, however, there is no objective "truth" about child development from any one perspective. The events and interactions of each child's days create a rich mosaic, a work in progress. The intent of this book is to integrate research, theory, and practice as they relate to children from birth to 8 years old and apply the resulting knowledge to school, home, and community environments. As a result, you should find the presentation of the information to be objective, professional, and grounded in the daily routines and activities of young children and the adults who are responsible for their well-being.

EARLY CHILDHOOD EDUCATORS AND THE NEED TO KNOW ABOUT DEVELOPMENT

For most parents, the changes in young children's lives are more meaningful as an ongoing process of growing up than as a field of study. Parents' beliefs, opinions, and explanations of development evolve from unique experiences with their own children, as illustrated in Vignette 1.1. Nothing could provide a better foundation for parent–child relationships.

On the other hand, it will one day soon be your job to provide care, instruction, and guidance to babies, toddlers, preschool, or primary school boys and girls. The field of early childhood education and the people who represent the profession are often underestimated and undervalued in our society and in educational circles. Many of us have heard how nice and patient we must be, to spend time with young children all day. We are too often considered by many to be glorified baby-sitters, who "just play" with children, as opposed to the "real teachers" of academic content. Wages in child-care programs reflect the sentiment that the only qualifications required are enjoying children, mothering, and being older than those in your charge (Howes, 1987; Cost, Quality & Child Outcomes Study Team, 1995). Few people outside the profession acknowledge the intelligence, competence, and creativity necessary to design and implement curricula across such widely divergent ages and skill levels. Such attitudes exist despite the fact that a number of the more progressive educational practices currently being promoted in public schools originated in early childhood settings. Multiage groupings, team teaching, integrated curricula, activity-based instruction, and multicultural curricula have for decades formed a strong foundation for working with young children in groups.

Teachers occupy an important role in the lives of young children, especially during the early years when adults have more influence than peers. Those of us who have chosen careers in early childhood have a responsibility to recognize the general age-related changes in children's behavior, analyze and explain deviations from expectations, and support ongoing learning. Knowledge of child development, rather than just personal opinion and experience, is a critical foundation for working with youngsters, their families, and other professionals. The information contained in this book provides you with clear expectations for early development, but the knowledge will only be meaningful if applied to understanding the behavior and guiding the learning of each individual girl and boy you encounter. The best early childhood professionals are those who understand child development as a process that all children undergo, while retaining an appreciation of the beauty and mystery of every child's life as it unfolds within unique family and cultural contexts.

The Concept of Development

The development of young children during the first 8 years is an elaborate passage that ordinarily proceeds on its own without much attention to the subtle and complex aspects of the process. We take it for granted that in the short space of one year, newborn infants will become upright, mobile, and able to communicate. We expect toddlers to develop a sense of self and a working knowledge of the world around them. It does not surprise us that by kindergarten, most youngsters have mastered a majority of the fundamental motor, language, social, and self-care skills required for successful life as adults. Primary school curricula are organized on the presumption that children will become literate and able to use reading and writing as a foundation for subsequent learning.

Although we speak generally of development as a necessary and anticipated component of growth and learning, it is a concept worth discussing in more detail. For purposes of this book the term *development* refers to the gradual, cumulative, and orderly changes, both physical and psychological, that result in increasingly sophisticated behaviors and interactions during the course of a person's lifetime. This book covers development from birth to the age of approximately 8 years. The reader is referred to any of the many excellent developmental psychology texts listed at the end of the chapter for a thorough discussion of reproduction, prenatal development, and the birthing process, as well as later childhood and adolescence.

An understanding of child development is often equated with knowledge of developmental theory or research, with a focus on the changing behaviors, attitudes, and abilities of boys and girls over time. Young children, of course, grow and learn within the context of families and communities, so the concept of development is far more complex than a simple list of milestones that describe individual functioning of children (Katz, 1996). There is a variety of contrasting opinions about the factors that control development and even concerns about the usefulness of the concept as a knowledge base for early childhood educators (Goffin, 1996). In this chapter we explore some of the issues basic to a more expansive and inclusive concept of development. The more you read about and work with young children, the more refined your own thinking about early development will become.

Resiliency and Vulnerability

Central to the notion of development are the related concepts of *resilience* and *vulnerability*. These terms describe the complex combination of biological makeup and environmental conditions that establish the relative balance between positive (resilient) and negative (vulnerable) developmental outcomes. Resilient children tend to do well in life and develop skills, attitudes, and behaviors that allow them to be successful even in the face of adverse life experiences. Vulnerability implies a less advantageous course of development, especially in the event of biological or environmental hardship. Vulnerable children are more likely to struggle for achievement and experience less success at home, in school, and in the community. Bee (1997) describes vulnerable children as those who can thrive only in optimal, supportive settings, whereas resilient children seem able to prosper across a range of supportive and nonsupportive life circumstances.

A number of researchers have studied vulnerability and resilience (Henderson, Benard, & Sharp-Light, 1999; Burns, 1994; Horowitz, 1990; Werner, 1989). Resilient children of all ages have been characterized as those who are socially competent, have good problem-solving skills and a sense of their own future goals, and operate autonomously in their daily environments (Benard, 1999). A synthesis of the research strongly supports the conclusion that resilience is promoted by specific *protective factors* in children's home, school, and community environments. In particular, children whose daily lives include care and nurturing, high expectations, and meaningful opportunities to participate are more likely to be successful than peers with similar life circumstances who lack such opportunities (Western Regional Center for Drug-Free Schools and Communities, 1991).

Protective factors are operational in a child's environment from before the moment of conception. Family history most commonly contributes healthy genes from both mother and father and good models for parenting and family life. The availability of competent prenatal care and childbirth education classes makes pregnancy a joyous and meaningful experience for most couples. In a majority of homes, adults provide for continual physical well-being and attend to the changing emotional needs of their offspring. Pediatricians see little boys and girls from infancy for well-child care, and childhood illnesses are treated promptly. Adults make it a priority to monitor their children's activities and moods, becoming intimately acquainted with the unique personalities, preferences, and outlooks of individual sons and daughters. Expectations for happy and positive adult–child interactions, satisfying peer relationships, and successful academic performance support a myriad of opportunities for children to participate in recreational, artistic, athletic, and self-directed activities at home, in school, and in the community.

Developmental vulnerability, on the other hand, presumes the negative results of risk factors that compromise the course of development. Children's lives are filled with risk, most often transient and situational aspects of new learning opportunities. Babies learning to roll over may surprise their caregivers by falling off the table or couch; toddlers manipulating toys might pinch their fingers; preschoolers can expe-

Caring adults who include young children in the activities of home and community are providing an important foundation for early development.

rience frustration when learning to talk and listen; primary school students risk having their feelings hurt when attempting to join peers in play. Illness and accidents also pose risks for young children. Some sources of risk are, however, more permanent and pervasive and pose potentially serious threats to long-term development.

Tjossem (1976) proposed three major categories of risk that are liable to compromise early development: environmental risk, biomedical risk, and identified risk. *Environmental risk* factors are those that exist in the context of the child's life and include the most frequently occurring threats to early development. Poverty, for example, is associated with a myriad of conditions hazardous for young boys and girls: hunger, homelessness, unsafe neighborhoods, very young parents, dropping out of school, and lack of adequate health care. Young lives are endangered by substance or child abuse or both. Children from families whose language and life ways differ from the majority culture may encounter bias and discrimination, resulting in social or academic difficulties or both. All of these factors fall into the category of environmental risk; protective factors to counter environmental risk are provided by early education programs such as Head Start, primary health care programs such as Public Health, a myriad of social service agencies, and sensitive, caring family members.

Biomedical risk exists when children are born prematurely, undergo trauma during birth, or have serious neonatal illness or other biological or medical problems early in life. The full range of biomedical risk factors is evident in neonatal intensive care nurseries. Modern neonatal medicine has advanced to the point that the majority of infants who endure biomedical risk early in life recover fully. Furthermore, they resemble their healthy peers developmentally by the time they are 3 years of age (Kopp & Parmelee, 1979). The earlier babies are born, the smaller, weaker, and more stressed they are, increasing the likelihood of subsequent developmental problems.

Identified risk refers to diagnosed disabilities and recognizable delays in early development. Genetic conditions such as *Down syndrome, Williams syndrome, phenylketonuria*, and *Fragile X syndrome* are most often identified at birth or early in life. Disabilities that originate in the central nervous system (brain, spinal cord) such as *autism* and *cerebral palsy* are also usually diagnosed during infancy or toddlerhood. Early intervention services for infants, toddlers, and their families are designed as protective factors to remediate and compensate for risk associated with diagnosed disability and identified developmental delay.

The three categories of risk just described are not mutually exclusive. Because the effects of risk are cumulative, the risk of developmental problems increases in proportion to the number of risk factors that are present in children's lives. Poverty and disruptions in family caregiving environments, for example, compound the effects of biomedical risk. The best developmental outcomes for infants born at risk due to biomedical factors are associated with informed, supportive parenting environments and family financial stability (Gorski & VandenBerg, 1996). Families struggling daily with a lack of employment, education, food, shelter, and social support may not have the financial or personal resources necessary to provide specialized care for infants born too soon or with medical complications, chronic illness, or disabilities.

Risk and opportunity form a delicate balance in the lives of all young children and their families. Early childhood professionals occupy powerful roles in terms of being in positions to identify and counteract risk in the lives of the youngsters with whom we work. One longitudinal study of resilience and vulnerability found that the presence of one caring adult for even a relatively short period of time was enough to make the difference between positive and negative outcomes in a child's life (Werner, 1990). That person might be an older caregiver, a neighbor, a friend, or quite often a teacher. Your role as an adult in early education can literally provide a life preserver for any child whose life contains multiple risk factors. Sometimes the least appealing child in your care, perhaps the lethargic little one with the dirty hands and face, tight clothes, and shaggy hair who takes food from others and hides it in his pockets, is the one who will benefit most from your attention and support.

Common Ground

Early childhood education in the Western hemisphere is grounded in commonly held beliefs and expectations about the processes of growth and learning, despite considerable variability among expert perspectives and specific theories. The views that frame our understanding of early development are summarized here as principles that guide early educators in their teaching, developmental psychologists in their research, pediatricians in their practice of medicine, parents in their caregiving interactions, and authors in the content and organization of their books. However, not all families share the predominant view of development that guides early childhood education. It is our hope that common principles of professional practice will help early educators clarify their own assumptions and values and thus increase sensitivity in recognizing and adjusting services for diverse groups of families.

First, professionals most often view development as a continuous, orderly process that supersedes individual differences and variations within the course of growth and learning. The skills and behaviors children exhibit are considered to evolve from simple to complex interactions within physical and social environments. Vocalizations develop into speech sounds and word approximations, which are later refined as recognizable words and combined into rudimentary sentences. Initial ways of knowing about the world are concrete and exist within the youngster's immediate context of activity. Babies who do not yet understand the meaning of the word *dinner*, for example, know nonetheless that it is mealtime by the sounds and odors of cooking, activity in the kitchen, time of day, and people who are present. First graders can talk about food in a much more abstract sense, discussing favorite foods, recalling associated memories, comparing menus and recipes, and planning celebrations outside an immediate mealtime context.

Developmental test items reflect this orderly progression of simple to complex skills and concrete, contextual thinking to abstract, decontextualized thinking. Parenting and teaching practices also demonstrate consistency with developmental principles of simple to complex behaviors and concrete to abstract thinking and learning. Parents and teachers alike talk in short, simple phrases to young children, emphasizing the immediate context. Primary school children are instructed for much longer periods and expected to learn new information from listening as well as from hands-on activities.

A second principle is that development follows a pattern from global to differentiated, or general to specific, activity. This principle is illustrated in descriptions of early prenatal development from a fertilized egg cell to multiple cells; differentiation of the placenta, umbilical cord, and embryo; and subsequent emergence of unique organ systems, limbs, and features. The diffuse, reflexive physical movements of a newborn in response to light, touch, and body position are likewise refined over time into distinct voluntary actions like reaching, grasping, and walking. Cognitive theorists have documented early patterns of reflexive to *volitional movement* as sequences for teaching and learning skills such as motor and speech imitation, cause and effect, and object permanence (Dunst, 1981). Neurodevelopmental treatment, a popular model for physical therapy, also has its basis in the integration of reflexive behavior into voluntary movement patterns.

TYPICAL AND ATYPICAL DEVELOPMENT

Although the course of most children's early growth and learning can be depicted as "normal," there is tremendous variation in the timing and sequence with which youngsters acquire specific skills. Understanding the development of infants, toddlers, preschool, and primary school children requires knowledge of two concepts that may at first glance appear to be in opposition: developmental milestones and individual differences.

Developmental Milestones and Stages

Developmental milestones refer to the similar sequences of behaviors, skills, and knowledge that groups of children are expected to acquire at certain ages. For example, in the first year of life we expect babies to learn how to stand upright and communicate using words. Walking and talking are two important milestones in the development of young children in our culture. As family members, school personnel, and professionals observe changes over time in the behavior of youngsters, expectations are formed based on the developmental patterns and sequences of a majority of children. Research in infant development has identified *norms* for the ages at which children without identified disabilities or delays acquire a myriad of skills, from tracking objects visually, to pointing at objects, and identifying emotional states. Pediatricians use developmental milestones as a foundation for well-baby checkups and authors use them for creating early childhood assessment instruments. Milestones of infant, toddler, and preschool development are also included in most popular parenting books. Teachers and curriculum specialists use norms and milestones to determine curriculum content for particular grade levels. Describing the similarities among children seems to be applied most often in the areas of early motor, cognitive, and language development.

A word of caution is warranted when discussing, or using developmental milestones. Developmental milestones represent averages across large numbers of children for acquisition of specific skills, without regard for the important relationships, activities, and lifestyles of individual children. Sources will differ in the precise ages at which particular milestones are expected to occur, causing worry for parents and confusion for teachers when observing the development of specific children. In this book, you will read about patterns, sequences, and processes of development in the various domains, but references to ages will most often be presented in a range or as an approximation. For each of the youngsters you encounter, the influence of family and social and cultural environments are likely to prove as powerful as any predetermined maturational timetable (Goffin, 1996).

If we were to listen in on discussions of people who live and work with young children, we would no doubt hear the term *stages* used often. "He is just going through an ornery stage"; "She is in the 'Why?' stage"; or "They are both in the stage of saying 'No' to everything." Professionals who study child development disagree about whether development is continuous and sequential in nature or discontinuous and occurring in stages. One opinion is that small, gradual changes accumulate to result in significant developmental change over a period of time. This perspective views development as continuous, with differences in behavior as children mature reflecting more sophisticated and novel combinations of skills. Another view is that there are key points at which a child's entire way of thinking, learning, and applying skills changes, resulting in a new and entirely different stage of development.

Helen Bee (1997) described developmental change as continuous, with alternating periods of rapid change (transition) and calm (consolidation). In her explanation, transition refers to developmental advances that pile up to effect major change in the entire system, whereas consolidation occurs during calmer times of more gradual

The study of child development includes knowledge of
predictable changes from infancy through the primary school
years, as well as an appreciation of individual differences
among children.

change. This perspective accounts for both major changes in children's approaches to learning over time and slower, more sequential acquisition of new skills and abilities.

Individual Differences

Probably, no single child grows and develops in the specific sequence or on the exact timeline as published milestones. The development of infants follows a more predictable course than does that of preschoolers, because very early skills are more heavily dependent on maturation of the central nervous system and other physiological processes. Even so, some babies are walking at 9 months whereas others take their first independent step at 14 months of age. By the time children start school, their individual interests and experiences seem to contribute significantly to both what they learn and how they learn. The primary explanation for variations in early development lies in the notion of individual differences. *Individual differences* include the unique biological makeup, environmental circumstances, and personality of each child. Individual differences are critical features of studies in personality and social competence.

For professionals working with young children, it is important to balance knowledge of developmental expectations for groups of children with attention to the individual characteristics of each boy and girl. Information about developmental expectations for a given age can provide a meaningful framework for understanding the uniqueness of each child. Periodically, however, we encounter youngsters whose development seems so unusual that caregivers are concerned for the children's continued well-being. When do individual differences indicate a delayed course of development or a disability? Vignette 1.2 illustrates a unique perspective on the identification of disability within a framework of developmental norms.

Vignette 1.2: *The Story of the Pie Man*

Once there was a father whose two young daughters attended an integrated early childhood program at a large university. He was involved in a Parents as Partners project. The role he chose for himself in the program was to orient new parents to the program: terminology, assessment procedures, and the approach to early education. After working for a time with staff and observing their presentations, he developed his first orientation session, using a handout of the graphic in Fig. 1.1. The man brought two pies to the session and explained the program to new parents in the following way (paraphrased and edited).

"Our children are like these two cream pies. For the most part, they are more alike than different. They are all basically the same shape and appearance, and we are going to want to do the same things with each of them. Yet each little pie has its own combination of unique ingredients that makes it special and different from all the others. We could describe and understand each pie by listing each specific ingredient. This one here has eggs, milk, sugar, chocolate, flour, butter, whipped cream. This other one has a lot of the same ingredients but has strawberry and not chocolate, less sugar, no vanilla, and so on. The list of ingredients is too time consuming to list in conversation, so we have names for each one: These pies are 'chocolate cream' and 'strawberry cream.' But what really makes them different is the specific ingredients; the names are just a shortcut.

"We also give names to describe children as a shortcut—labels that describe certain sets of ingredients: 'shy,' 'active,' 'hyper,' 'moody.' Some of the children in this program have labels that describe other conditions: 'cerebral palsy,' 'this syndrome,' 'that syndrome,' 'noncompliant.' Some of us aren't sure of all the ingredients of our little pies, but we know they are somehow not the kind of pies we expected.

"What the teachers here try to do before anything else is to get clear on each child's specific 'ingredients,' to understand all the elements that make up each of our individual pies. That is called assessment and you will be asked to help them understand your child. In this program they will cut your little pie up into six pieces to describe the ingredients. Those pieces are called gross motor, fine motor, cognitive, self-care, social, and communication.

"Now, I am a mechanic, so when I hear about gross and fine motors I think of dirty and well-tuned engines. But here they are talking about large-muscle movements like walking, running, balance, and stuff for gross motor, and small-muscle movements like writing, hand–eye coordination, and manipulation for fine motor. 'Cognitive' doesn't have anything to do with cogs, either, unless you think of what goes on between a child's ears as cogs turning. Cognitive means thinking, problem solving, and the like."

The dad went on to describe all the other developmental content areas, preparing other parents to understand the jargon and procedures of the program. He answered more and better questions than staff had ever been asked at orientation and concluded: "Now, the thing to remember

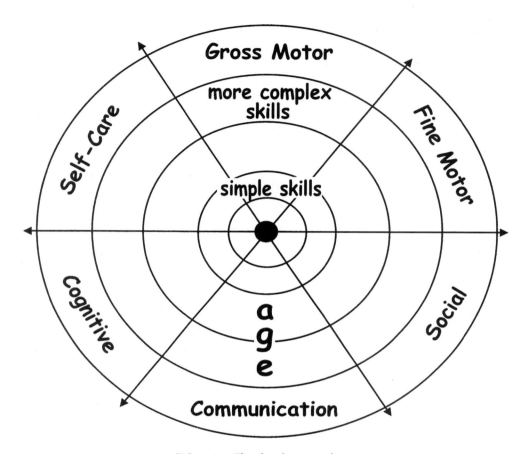

FIG. 1.1.   The developmental pie.

is that what is important in all this is your child's specific combination of abilities, interests, and experiences. Other programs might cut your little pie up into only four pieces, or five, or call the pieces different names. Maybe just 'motor, problem-solving, and social-communication.' But your child is still the same child, with the same 'ingredients,' just like these are the same pies, no matter how we slice them. And the people who make the pies usually understand them best, because even if someone else is slicing them up to see what's in there, we know the ingredients. Let's eat!"
And he sliced up and served the pies and they all enjoyed them immensely.

Developmental Delay and Disability

Not all children develop according to expectations or follow typical patterns and timelines as they grow and learn. Early identification of developmental delay and disability was recognized years ago as being associated with earlier and more successful interventions for young children (McNulty, Smith, & Soper, 1983; Shonkoff, Hauser-Cram, Krauss, & Upshur, 1992). A solid understanding of developmental delay and disability is, therefore, central to the study of early development and an important base of knowledge for professionals in early childhood.

One of the great myths of early childhood is that children with and without disabilities constitute two separate groups of children. Legal definitions of disability and substantial developmental delay are designed primarily to determine eligibility for special services but do little to describe the development or needs of individual youngsters. Specific disability labels such as Down syndrome, cerebral palsy, autism, and learning disability include groups of children whose behaviors and abilities vary immensely. In reality, children with identified disabilities often have more in common with their typically developing peers than with other children who might share a particular diagnosis or disability label. For these reasons, it is impossible to determine appropriate educational outcomes or strategies for young children based on the presence or absence of a disability label. Preschool children with diagnosed disabilities, in fact, often achieve higher levels of social, communication, and cognitive skills in inclusive settings than in segregated special education settings (Guralnick, 1990).

Norman Kunc (1994) described a disability as only one aspect of the person, similar to eye color, gender, interests, temperament, and family attributes. A disability becomes a handicapping condition only when others allow the disability to become the defining characteristic of the child, resulting in limited interactions and expectations.

Readers of this book are encouraged to consider the full range and variations of development, including disability and delay, as normal elements of the human condition, part of the possible range of life circumstances. For this reason, you will encounter the terms *typical* and *atypical* rather than the more disparaging *normal* and *abnormal* in descriptions of early development. The meaning of the term *typical* in this context should be taken as the developmental course followed most often by young children; *atypical* patterns are those observed less frequently. In addition, words used to designate disabilities are used to describe rather than to label children: "the girl with Down syndrome" rather than the "Down syndrome girl" or "the boy who has autism" rather than "the autistic boy." Using "people-first" terminology acknowledges a child as being more important than the disability and helps avoid pejorative language.

The use of respectful terminology should in no way be interpreted as an attempt to discount the impact of disability or delay on development. The presence of certain disabilities may limit a child's ability to acquire new skills in specific areas, requiring adaptive equipment or alternative ways to reach early educational goals. Sometimes the presence of a specific disability such as Down syndrome slows the usual rate of development, so that young children learn new skills and behaviors in a fairly typical sequence but more slowly than the majority of their peers. Many disabilities carry the risk of secondary effects, as when children with hearing impairments struggle to learn the spoken language and experience social problems as a result. Subsequent chapters address the specific disabilities most commonly identified during the infant, toddler, preschool, and primary years.

Cultural Diversity

The culture within which a young child grows is one individual difference that has a significant impact on developmental expectations. Obviously, culture is more than how people dress, what they eat, the holidays they celebrate, and the languages they speak. Culture is an important foundation for each child's understanding of self, family, society, and the world. In many cultures, it is not unusual to have strong bonds and loyalty to family members who have not lived under the same roof for many years, whereas other cultures value physical proximity. Youngsters are cared for by certain people and in particular ways in every culture. For example, in Western cultures, parents have primary caregiving responsibilities for infants. It is most appropriate in some cultures for grandparents to be primary caregivers of young children; in other cultures, older siblings expect to assume this role. In North America, we expect preschoolers to participate in groups with peers, but in many parts of the world, children spend time almost exclusively with caregivers until they are 6 or 7 years of age. In some families, young children are allowed to play only with items available from nature or the household instead of having commercially purchased toys.

Early childhood programs of all sorts are currently experiencing an increase in the cultural and linguistic diversity of children served. Although the majority of elementary programs nationwide have focused on academic instruction in English, early childhood education has traditionally emphasized a pluralistic approach (York, 1991; Diaz Soto, 1991). Nonbiased curricula and multicultural approaches honor diverse backgrounds and abilities rather than view cultural and linguistic differences as deficits. The emphasis on family participation in early intervention programs for infants and toddlers has also increased the importance of viewing children's development within the contexts of diverse home environments.

Ideally, early childhood professionals accept responsibility for all young children and work as partners with specialists and parents to provide appropriate instruction, design accessible environments, prevent secondary disabilities, and support participation in age-appropriate activities. Children of diverse languages, cultures, and abilities stand to benefit from learning together. Peer models and supportive adults motivate youngsters by maintaining high expectations for their success. Boys and girls from the majority culture who are developing typically grow up with an enhanced appreciation of individual differences and a strong basis for becoming adults who are tolerant and accepting of diversity as neighbors, employers, family members, and friends.

THEORIES OF EARLY DEVELOPMENT

What accounts for the similarities we observe in the development of young children? How do individual differences in biology and culture affect developmental outcomes? Why are some children resilient in the face of adversity, whereas others seem vulnerable in spite of relatively advantageous circumstances? Many different theories have been presented over the years to explain the intricacies and variations of early development. Theories are presented here only as a framework for thinking about the behavior of young children. Every theory springs from, and is limited by, the knowledge, experience, and particular sociocultural perspective of its author. Later chapters, for example, present theories that address temperament, attachment, cognition, and social competence.

In general, theories reflect the relative extent to which nature and nurture are considered to control the course and outcomes of development during the early years. The influences of heredity and maturation represent the *nature* viewpoint, and investigations of environmental and behavioral factors designate the *nurture* position. In addition, a third group of theories emphasizes the role of interactions among child characteristics, caregiver circumstances, and community variables. Although no one would argue that only heredity or only the environment controls development, each theoretical orientation emphasizes a different set of conditions in an attempt to explain changes in children's behavior over time. Familiarity with the major categories of theory in the study of development is desirable for professionals who work with young children and families, because general classroom approaches as well as specific teaching methods, curricula, materials, and styles of interaction in early childhood programs often derive from a particular theoretical perspective. Theories of development usually provide little in the way of practical suggestions for teaching young children (Stott & Bowman, 1996). The organization of theoretical positions presented in Table 1.1 is admittedly artificial and is intended to provide you with many different perspectives from which to organize your thinking and observations, inform your explanations, and enhance your interactions with young children.

Heredity and Maturation: An Emphasis on Internal Processes

The role of internal variables in explaining age-related changes in children's behavior is emphasized in both maturational and psychoanalytic theories. Development is considered to be an expression primarily of inborn predispositions and invariant innate processes. Like a plant, a child's growth and learning proceed according to a fixed biological plan that is determined at the moment of conception. Individual differences in personality, physical and cognitive abilities, talents, and preferences are considered to reflect differences in genetic characteristics. This group of theories can be viewed as an extension of the early theories of Jean Jacques Rousseau (1712–1778), a Swiss man who argued that early education should follow children's interests rather than a prescribed curriculum. His writings emphasized the inherent goodness of infants, developed the notion of development as a natural phenomenon,

TABLE 1.1

Developmental Theories: An Organizational Framework

Emphasis in Explaining Development	Internal Processes and Factors Inherent in the Child	External Factors in the Child's Life	Interactions Between the Child and the Environment
Representative theories	Maturational theory, psychoanalytic theory	Behavioral theory, social learning theory	Synactive theory, constructivist theory, transactional theory, ecological theory
Associated names	Gesell, Freud, Erikson	Pavlov, Watson, Skinner, Bandura	Als, Piaget, Sameroff and Chandler, Bronfenbrenner
Associated terms	Inborn, innate, genetic, inherent, growth, maturation, internal, stages, readiness	Behavior, learning, stimulus, response, reinforcement, observable, measurable	Responsive environments, caregiving interactions, systems, risk factors, protective factors

and promoted a child-directed process of learning over specific educational outcomes for young children.

Maturational Theory

Researchers who study the development of young children from a maturational perspective most often describe similarities in the behaviors of typically developing children. Arnold Gesell (1880–1961) is one of the most widely recognized *maturational theorists* of the 20th century. He observed thousands of young children and documented the precise timing and sequence of milestones in motor, language, cognitive, and social domains (Gesell & Ilg, 1949). Gesell's studies of early growth and maturation initially were published for both professional and popular audiences (Gesell, 1929; Gesell, 1945). The Gesell Institute of Human Behavior continues to this day to conduct research and publish materials depicting norms for typical development at specific ages and associated implications for teachers, pediatricians, and parents. Products of Gesell's work include tools for pediatric well-child assessment and diagnosis of developmental disabilities (Knobloch & Pasamanick, 1974), a series of books describing and explaining the behavior of children year by year for parents and teachers and methods for screening children's readiness for kindergarten. Milestones in physical, cognitive, and social development are included in subsequent chapters of this book for infants, toddlers, preschoolers, and primary school children.

Psychoanalytic Theory

Other examples of theories that explain developmental changes by emphasizing systematic variation in internal variables are the *psychoanalytic theories* of Sigmund Freud (1856–1939) and Erik Erikson (1902–1994). The dramatic impact of Freud's psychoanalytic theory warrants a place among the first theories to be reviewed in this chapter. Freud was a Viennese neurologist who worked to identify the causes of mental illness in adults. The absence of physiological factors in many cases led him to hypothesize a fixed sequence of psychosexual stages in early childhood: oral (infancy), anal (toddlers), phallic (preschoolers), latency (school age). Freud's theory held that the emotional health of adults is shaped by key interactive experiences during the first 5 years of life. Trauma in any given stage was seen to result in related problems in later life. For example, traumatic experiences in weaning for infants, toilet training during toddlerhood, or disciplinary interactions for preschoolers were associated with subsequent eating disorders, compulsive behavior, and personality disorders, respectively (Freud, 1923/1960).

Freud viewed early childhood as a period of intense inner conflict between the pleasure of fulfilling instinctual drives and the reality of getting along in the world. He described a three-part psychological structure as central to the development of personality: the id, ego, and superego. The id was interpreted as an unconscious repository of urges and desires from birth onward, whereas the ego developed during the early years as a control mechanism that allowed the child to delay gratification.

The internalization of parental and societal values, rules, and norms in the form of the superego was considered an important process during the early childhood years.

Erikson's theory of emotional development emphasizes stages of internal crises that must be resolved in order for children to acquire healthy self-concepts and become competent social participants. He accepted and extended many of Freud's theoretical concepts but emphasized the active role of children in shaping their own experiences and responses and the roles of family members, teachers, and peers as agents of social change. Erikson hypothesized stages of emotional development during the entire life span, the first four of which include the early childhood years (see Table 1.2). Erikson (1963) believed that during the first year of life infants are in a stage of developing a basic sense of trust or distrust in the world and in themselves, primarily as a result of interactions with caregivers. Between the ages of 1 and 3, toddlers negotiate a stage in which they either develop feelings of autonomy and competence commensurate with developing independence or learn to feel shame and doubt about their own abilities. The third stage of Erikson's theory includes an emotional crisis of initiative versus guilt, spanning the years from 3 to 6. At about 6 years, children enter the fourth stage, in which industry and achievement become primary social goals to offset feelings of inferiority. Erikson's theory describes well the social behaviors of young children, but does not really explain the causes or origin of his stages (Shaffer, 1994).

Theories that emphasize internal biological factors as primary determinants of early development have traditionally been categorized as explanations on the nature side of development. Maturational theories have contributed significantly to our understanding of the similarities among young children as they grow and learn. Norm-referenced tests, profiles of developmental milestones, and awareness of behaviors that commonly occur in combination are all applications of theories that emphasize heredity and maturation. Studies of identical twins and recent research in behavioral genetics and social biology hold the promise of further increasing knowledge about the precise genetic and biological mechanisms that control behavior.

Criticism of biologically based theories addresses the relative disregard of important external influences such as social class, culture, and family variables. Studies of risk and protective factors in particular suggest that maturation alone is an overly

TABLE 1.2

Psychosocial Development: Erikson's Stages I to IV

Stage	Key Experiences
1. Trust vs. mistrust (birth through 1 year)	Attachment to caregiver; nursing, weaning.
2. Autonomy vs. shame/doubt (2 and 3 years)	Walking and using hands, toilet training, emerging independence.
3. Initiative vs. guilt (4 and 5 years)	Goal-oriented activities, early peer interactions, independence in self-care.
4. Industry vs. inferiority (6 to 12 years)	Academic performance, peer friendships.

simplified explanation. Norms for the emergence of specific skills at any given age, in addition, represent a hypothetical composite average and most probably do not reflect the actual developmental profile of any particular child. Perhaps of greatest relevance to early childhood professionals is the implied lack of significance ascribed by maturational theories to teaching and parenting practices. If changes in children's behaviors are understood to originate primarily from inborn sources, the role of adults is mainly to observe and understand age-related similarities, provide appropriate conditions based on correct interpretations, and cope in a sensitive manner. Many professionals in education, medicine, therapy, and psychology pursue early childhood careers rooted in the belief that parenting, teaching, counseling, and specialized services can have a significant impact on the course of young children's development.

Environment and Behavior: An Emphasis on External Factors

At the opposite end of the nature–nurture continuum from maturational theories are explanations that emphasize the predominant influence of factors external to the child. Behavioral theories highlight the importance of environmental events and analyze the effects of specific contextual conditions on developmental outcomes. Age-related changes in the performance of children are viewed as a function of learned behavior rather than of inborn characteristics, refining the original theories of John Locke (1632–1704). Locke believed that the newborn mind is like a blank slate on which daily circumstances write a life story, with an emphasis on the quality of the child's educational, social, and physical environment.

Classical Conditioning

Studies of animals early in the 20th century revealed the power of learning in developing new behaviors. The Russian psychologist Ivan Pavlov (1878–1958) taught dogs to salivate on hearing a bell ring, even though sound typically has nothing to do with salivation. Food, however, elicits a reflexive response of saliva production in dogs. By consistently pairing the presentation of meat with the formerly neutral sound of a bell, Pavlov was able to teach his dogs to salivate in response only to the bell. This type of learning was called *classical conditioning* and provided an important initial foundation for modern behavioral psychology. Classical conditioning relies on the pairing of a stimulus that elicits a response involuntarily with a stimulus that is initially neutral; the learned behavior is an involuntary response to the formerly neutral stimulus.

John Watson (1849–1936) studied with Pavlov and applied principles of classical conditioning to the study of child development and parenting practices in the United States. Watson, in a now famous experiment, taught a baby to be afraid of a white rat by making a loud noise each time the boy curiously reached for the little animal. Baby Albert quickly learned to fear the rat despite his initial eager curiosity and lack of hesitance, because the animal was consistently associated with a frightening sound. Watson generalized the results of his study with Baby Albert to recommend a structured and unemotional approach to raising children (Watson, 1928). He felt that too much pampering led to unhappy and inept children, as illustrated by the dedication of his parenting book, "To the first mother who brings us a happy child." Although Watson's approach seems overly controlling and rigid today, modifications of his ideas exist still as staples of parenting wisdom. For example, consistent bedtime rituals for young children are recommended as a way to help children unwind and calm down at the end of the day. Perhaps the most important classical conditioning takes place in infancy, whenever caregivers are consistently paired in the infant's mind with intrinsically pleasurable events like eating and physical comfort.

Operant Conditioning

B. F. Skinner (1904–1990) shared Watson's view that psychology in general, and the study of child development and parenting specifically, needed a more scientific foundation than that provided by psychoanalytic theory. He expanded on the study of conditioning to emphasize learning that occurs as a result of events that follow spontaneous behavior. Skinner's theory of *operant conditioning* included principles of *reinforcement, extinction*, and *punishment*. His experiments showed that when a specific behavior is followed consistently and immediately by reinforcement the behavior will increase in frequency; conversely, if a behavior is ignored, it will eventually diminish and, if punished, will be performed less often. Skinner designed many experiments in carefully controlled conditions, with both animals and children, to test his behavioral theories of learning (Skinner, 1953).

The laws of behavior originally defined by Skinner have been modified and refined with great success for application to both teaching new skills and weakening undesirable behaviors over the years in classrooms, child-care centers, and the homes of young children. Reinforcements of praise ("You've worked really hard at that"); free time ("As soon as you finish your illustration you can go play"); special activities ("If every group has their projects completed, we'll have a popcorn party on Friday"); and stickers are commonplace in the teaching of new social and academic skills. Professionals and parents alike know that often the best way to get rid of an annoying behavior, such as interrupting, is to ignore it altogether. Although Skinner demonstrated clearly the effectiveness of punishment in decreasing animal behaviors in controlled laboratory settings, he was opposed to its use with children (Skinner, 1983). The ongoing debate about the use of spanking with young children clearly reflects different perspectives on the application of Skinner's research.

Behavioral theories emphasize the gradual changes in young children's behaviors over time rather than developmental stages. Observable behaviors that can be counted and studied directly are viewed as more important than internal feelings that must be inferred and interpreted. Behaviorists analyze and study the behaviors of young children as meaningful indications of development rather than as mere clues to internal states. In busy environments, however, it is difficult for parents and teachers to exert adequate control over interactions with young children. As a result, behavior modification techniques involving punishment are often reserved for serious inappropriate behaviors such as physical aggression. Additional criticisms of theories of behavior see the focus on observable and measurable behaviors as depersonalizing the processes of development, as well as discounting of the roles of both emotion and cognition in learning.

Social Learning Theory

One behaviorist whose more recent theory emphasized social and cognitive aspects of learning new behaviors was Alfred Bandura (1925–). Bandura observed that children appeared to learn many skills quickly and without apparent reinforcement. His *social learning theory* introduced the cognitive concept of *modeling*, the process of learning new skills by watching someone else perform them. Modeling is a complex process that requires a multitude of cognitive competencies on the part of the learner: perception, attending, memory, interpretation, and reproduction of the behavior at the right time and place (Bandura, 1977). In later publications, Bandura described his own theory as a "social cognitive theory" (1986).

Social interaction behaviors seem to lend themselves particularly well to social learning. Bandura (1973), in his best-known work, studied the effects of social models on aggressive behavior, showing that children who viewed aggressive behavior were more likely to act aggressively in similar circumstances. These studies demonstrated quite effectively that children do not always require direct reinforcement in order to learn new behaviors. For educators, Bandura's work highlights the importance of demonstration in teaching, the significance of teachers as role models for the development of positive behaviors and attitudes, and the contribution of children's developing cognitive skills to changes in learning strategies over time.

Interactive Theories

Both maturational and behavioral theories explain certain aspects of development but seem to disregard the significance of either environmental contexts or individual differences, respectively. The most compelling research to many professionals investigates the combined effects of both child and environmental factors over time. In one study, the combination of child status and environmental variables predicted developmental outcomes with four times as much power as either child or environment variables alone (Lewis, 1996)! Since teachers are concerned with both understanding individual children and designing supportive, nurturing environments, *interactive theories* provide an important contribution to early educational practice.

Synactive Theory

Heidi Als and her colleagues (1982, 1986, 1994) demonstrated the importance of considering both child and environmental variables in efforts to improve outcomes for babies in intensive care nurseries. *Synactive theory* asserts that there is a delicate, constantly evolving balance between prenatal and neonatal physiology and the immediate environment. Typically, a baby is sheltered from sound, touch, light, and movement before birth by the uterine environment, which supports optimal development of the sensory and motor behaviors typical of full-term newborns. When babies leave the womb and enter the world prematurely, the result is low birth weight, an imma-

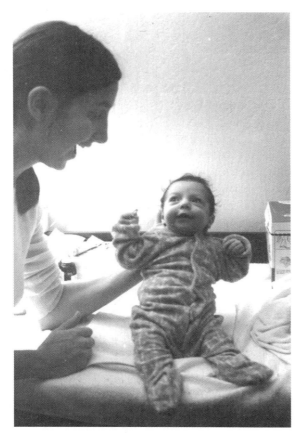

Interactive theories of development emphasize the impor-
tance of the continual interplay
between young children and
the people, objects, and events
in their immediate environments.

ture central nervous system, trauma, and life-threatening illness. Consequently their movements, sleep–wake cycles, and responses to social and physical stimulation are likely to be less organized and adaptive than those of full-term newborns.

Instead of a dim, quiet, and undulating place, the intensive care nursery is a setting where infants hear monitors and voices, see many lights, and are handled, frequently in an invasive and painful manner, for caregiving and medical reasons. Synactive theory has promoted comprehensive and detailed assessments of central nervous system maturity, gestational age, and response to specific environmental stimuli for premature babies. Appropriate, parallel practices in nursing and caregiving are matched to each baby's individual pattern of behavior. Assessment of the abilities of ill and very low birth weight babies to respond to sensory stimuli results in an individualized plan of care that protects immature babies from becoming overly stimulated and provides evolving supportive interventions to match the changing needs of infants once they become more physiologically stable and behaviorally organized. Premature infants whose care has included careful attention to both developmental status and environmental characteristics spend less time in the hospital and experience fewer medical complications than those whose care is solely medical

(Als, Lawhon, Brown, Gibes, Duffy, McAnulty, & Blickman, 1994). Synactive theory emphasizes risk that accrues from biomedical sources and potential protective factors in the caregiving environment of the intensive care nursery.

Cognitive Development Theory

Jean Piaget (1896–1980) was a Swiss psychologist who worked with Alfred Binet on standardized testing of intelligence. Piaget became interested in the incorrect answers of younger children on intelligence tests and began trying to describe their thought processes. Piaget conducted meticulous observations of his own children engaged in everyday activities and designed miniexperiments to test their comprehension of objects, actions, and concepts from infancy onward. He concluded that young children construct knowledge of the world through interactions with the environment and suggested detailed explanations of the processes and sequences of cognitive development.

Piaget's theory emphasizes the importance of interactions between youngsters and objects in the physical environment in the development of increasingly complex cognitive structures. He hypothesized distinct stages of cognitive development for infants, preschoolers, and school-aged children. Piaget's sensorimotor stage is addressed in detail in chapters 2 and 3, covering infancy and toddlerhood, respectively. The chapters on preschool and primary school years address the preoperational and concrete operational stages.

Transactional Theory

A theory that extends the description of interactions between biological status of the child and the caregiving environment is *transactional theory*. Years ago, Sameroff and Chandler (1975) undertook an ambitious study to explain why some children born with multiple biological risk factors experienced better developmental progress than others who grew up with fewer risk factors in their lives. They reviewed the results of multiple assessments of child functioning over time as well as numerous parent and family variables. When the data were analyzed, however, there was no evidence of any one main effect on developmental outcomes. Neither the biological status of the child nor characteristics of the caretaking environment alone seemed to account for how well the youngster functioned over time. The best predictor turned out to be the "continual and progressive interplay" (Sameroff & Chandler, 1975, p. 234) between biological risk at birth and the quality of care the young child receives. The resulting theory describes a series of transactions between the child and the environment over time, in which the child plays an active role in altering the physical and social environment and vice versa. Transactional theory addresses directly both biomedical risk and the immediate caregiving environment and has been applied directly in early intervention programs that emphasize the quality of parent–child interactions for young children at risk of developmental delay or disability. For example, parents of a child born prematurely might be taught special techniques for feeding and holding an irritable baby, or preschool teachers of a blind child might learn to use auditory and tactile methods to teach new skills.

Ecological Theory

Another theory that examines the interaction of child and environmental factors is Bronfenbrenner's *ecological theory* (1979). Ecological theory emphasizes the interactive impact of all aspects of a child's environment on developmental outcomes. The concept of environment includes cultural and societal values (macrosystem); neighbors, community services, places of work, and media (exosystem); extended family, systems of health care, and education (mesosystem) as well as the immediate daily environments of home, classroom, church, park, and doctor's office (microsystem). Bronfenbrenner's model viewed these systems as concentric, with the child in the center of a dynamic interplay among the complex and interrelated contexts of his or her life. Figure 1.2 is a simplified representation of Bronfenbrenner's ecological theory.

In ecological theory, each child is viewed as an individual, and each aspect of the environment is seen as contributing to developmental outcomes. Thus, the character-

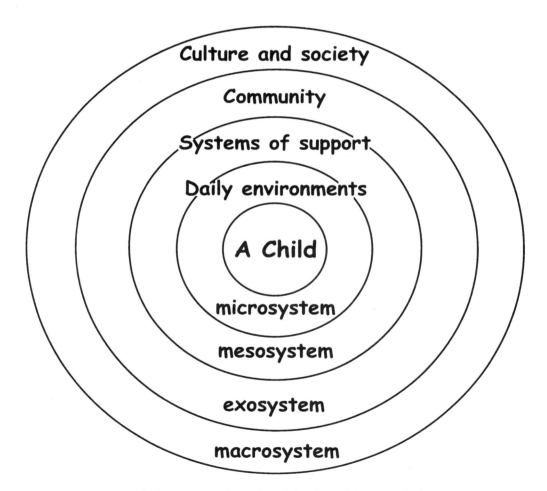

FIG. 1.2.   Bronfenbrenner's ecological model. Adapted from Bronfenbrenner, 1979.

istics of both the child and multiple environmental contexts are considered in attempts to support growth and learning. Head Start programs provide a good example of the application of ecological theory to the provision of early education services. Each child is assessed and has an individualized learning plan based on his or her unique developmental, physical, academic, and social status. Children are eligible for Head Start because of the family variable of low income, and services are comprehensive, including health, nutrition, family support, transportation, and education. Head Start curriculum varies from classroom to classroom, reflecting the geography, composition, and livelihood of surrounding communities and cultural practices and values of the children enrolled. Ecological theory addresses risk and protective factors that exist because of child biomedical or disability-related conditions in combination with family, community, and societal services and supports.

ORIGINS OF DEVELOPMENTAL PROBLEMS

Throughout this book, variables internal and external to the child are discussed as having an impact on the growth and learning of babies and young children. An additional consideration is the timing of the various factors involved. Biological and environmental circumstances that originate before, during, and after the birth of a child can all influence the course of developmental progress in different ways. Prenatal, perinatal, and postnatal conditions are summarized in the following sections, and subsequent chapters address in more detail the effects on early development. Table 1.3 summarizes causes of atypical development across time periods.

TABLE 1.3

Origins of Developmental Delay & Disability: Examples

	During the Prenatal Period	*During the Perinatal Period*	*During the Postnatal Period*
Chromosomal	Down Syndrome (Trisomy 21) Tay-Sachs Disease Klinefelter' Syndrome (XXY) Turner's Syndrome (XYY)		
Teratogens	Drugs (prescription and illegal) Alcohol Radiation		Lead Mercury
Infection	Sexually transmitted diseases (HIV/AIDS, syphilis) Cytomegalovirus (CMV) Toxoplasmosis Rubella	Herpes HIV/AIDS Respiratory distress syndrome Gonorrhea	Meningitis Encephalitis
Trauma	Maternal accidents Abuse of pregnant mother Prenatal stroke	Breech delivery Anoxia (oxygen deprivation) Use of forceps during delivery Stroke	Accidents Injury Child abuse
Other	Maternal nutrition Heart complications Cleft lip and/or cleft palate Spina bifida	Prematurity Lack of oxygen Complications during delivery	Malnutrition Sudden infant death syndrome (SIDS) Parental use of drugs Extreme, chronic poverty

Prenatal Influences

From the point of conception until birth, there exist a host of potential risks and protective factors. Prenatal risks to development often result in significant and sometimes life-threatening disabilities that are often identified at birth or within the first 3 years of life. Mothers who are well nourished; get adequate rest and competent prenatal care; and live in safe, comfortable environments provide conditions that promote healthy fetal development. Conversely, the uterine environment is compromised when mothers ingest *teratogens*, substances that pass to the fetus through their shared blood supply and act directly to disrupt the development of the baby. Drugs, both illicit and prescription, and alcohol are two of the most frequently identified causes of prenatal problems. The prescription drug thalidomide has been directly linked to limb deformities, for example. When pregnant women drink alcohol, the developing baby is put at risk for fetal alcohol syndrome and associated cognitive and physical disabilities. Other factors such as maternal stress or radiation also can threaten the uterine environment.

Because the health of the unborn child is dependent on the health of the pregnant woman, *maternal infections* often infect the fetus too, especially if the cause is a virus or bacterium that is small enough to cross the placenta and enter the bloodstream of the fetus. Examples of prenatal infections that pose risks to future development include sexually transmitted diseases such as herpes, HIV and AIDS, and syphilis, as well as conditions such as toxoplasmosis, cytomegalovirus (CMV), and rubella that the mother may contract during the prenatal period. Infections are most likely to have pervasive effects during the first trimester, when basic neurological and motor systems are developing.

A child's genetic make up is determined at conception, with the mother's egg and father's sperm each contributing 23 *chromosomes*. The resulting 46 chromosomes are ordered in pairs, composed of *DNA (deoxyribonucleic acid)*. DNA contains the unique combination of *genes* that control the design of each person's unique characteristics. Powerful microscopes allow physicians to directly examine and compare the 46 chromosomal pairs of any given child to the expected chromosomal patterns for all humans.

It is at this earliest point in development that chromosomal causes of disability and delay operate. An increase, decrease, or difference in the number or configuration of chromosome pairs usually has a significant impact on development throughout the child's life. *Down syndrome*, for example, results when there are three chromosomes rather than a pair in the 21st position, accounting for the alternative diagnostic label of *trisomy 21*. Other identified trisomies have been linked to pervasive and severe disabilities at birth (e.g., trisomy 18). Many early disabilities and delays appear to stem from genetic causes, but the specific chromosomal differences are not always identifiable. Some inherited diseases are associated with the genetic makeup of particular racial and ethnic groups. *Tay-Sachs* disease occurs most often among Jewish families of Ashkenazic descent, *phenylketonuria* is more common among Caucasian families, and sickle cell anemia is diagnosed most frequently among families with African ancestors. Other genetically determined risks involve problems of metabolism such as hypothyroidism, phenylketonuria (PKU), or Tay-Sachs disease that are inherited from the parents.

Atypical development of the face, brain, and spinal cord also occur during the prenatal period, although the exact mechanisms controlling these areas of fetal development are unknown. Cleft lip and palate result from openings in the skin and bone in the center of the upper lip or inside crest of the mouth or both. A *cleft lip* can cause obvious disruptions in newborns' appearance, and parents most often elect to schedule surgery to close the opening as soon as possible. *Cleft palate* is associated with difficulties in nursing and subsequent problems in eating and development of speech. Multiple surgeries may be necessary during the early childhood years to repair serious clefts, restructure placement of teeth, and even reconstruct bone in the jaw and mouth. *Anencephaly* is a rare condition characterized by the absence of a cerebral cortex; babies born with such a severe disorder in brain development usually do not survive for more than a few days. *Spina bifida* describes a range of conditions caused by openings in the skin or bone that usually cover the spinal cord. Lesions and the resulting protrusions of the spinal cord can be located between the neck and the lower back, requiring immediate surgery to repair the wound and minimize subsequent nerve damage.

Perinatal Influences

Although the birth of a child usually proceeds in a predictable and sound fashion, there are at times particular risks associated with the birthing process itself. Certain maternal infections, for example herpes and HIV or AIDS, can be transmitted to the baby during passage through the birth canal. Infants whose genetic or physical conditions have been compromised during the prenatal period, or who are born too soon, may be less robust in tolerating the stress of labor and delivery. Long labors and difficult deliveries sometimes require the assistance of forceps or suction to complete the birth, posing the threat of injury to the newborn's head. Premature separation of the placenta from the uterine wall or the umbilical cord's becoming wrapped around the baby's neck during delivery can result in the baby's being deprived of oxygen. Although modern obstetrical practices have greatly decreased the chances that traumatic births will result in lasting problems, on occasion young children have developmental delays associated with a difficult entry into the world. Having professional care and attendance during pregnancy and birth are probably the best protective factors against risk associated with the perinatal period.

Postnatal Influences

We would like to assume that all infants go home to nurturing environments in which they are supported physically and emotionally to develop to their fullest potential, and in fact this is the fortunate case for many families. Increasingly, however, early childhood professionals are seeing biologically sound youngsters whose early development is being compromised by negative circumstances in their homes and communities. Families with very low incomes may not be able to provide sufficient food, permanent shelter, or appropriate care. Newborns who live in crowded, stressful, and unsanitary conditions are at increased risk for illness and disturbances in critical basic functions of eating and sleeping. Child abuse and neglect, as well as violence among adults, threaten children's emotional and physical well-being. Research on risk and resiliency strongly suggests that infants are spared negative long-term effects of mild and moderate birth complications if they have responsive and nurturing caregiving environments. Even mild birth trauma, however, can be enough to disrupt development if a baby goes home to an environment full of risk factors (Werner & Smith, 1982).

Even in the most affluent homes, accidental injury poses a significant threat to toddlers who are mobile and curious but not very sophisticated about recognizing danger in their environments. Falling down stairs, wandering away from parents, hurting oneself on hot or sharp objects, ingesting toxic substances, running into traffic or water, and choking are all very real risks in the lives of toddlers. Lack of adequate supervision and unsafe living conditions place infants and young children in further danger of unintended injury.

As indicated in previous paragraphs, some disabilities are identified at or even before birth. Conditions that are usually identified very early in life often have a pervasive impact on early development, and are discussed in chapter 2, "Infancy." Many other special needs are not identified until children are expected to move around to explore their environments independently and interact competently with adults and peers. Diagnoses of problems in sensory abilities and social–emotional development are addressed in chapter 3, "Toddlerhood." More subtle cognitive delays and diagnoses of communication and learning problems are discussed in the chapters on preschool and primary school-aged children.

Developmental Screening

Early educators are often involved in the identification of developmental delays and disabilities through developmental screening activities. Screening is a type of assessment that evaluates a large number of children with a relatively quick test, to identify those who might need further assessment. Many communities sponsor screening clinics for young children through school districts or public health agencies. Pediatricians regularly conduct developmental screenings in the process of well-baby checkups. Head Start programs are required to screen the development of each enrolled child annually. Kindergarten and primary school students are often given screening tests if they are referred to special education.

Screening assessments are relatively short and inexpensive to administer. The level of information that screening tests yield is fairly global, answering questions such as, "Is this child developing within expected norms?" or "Does there seem to be a developmental problem?" Because the questions are so general, even the best screening tests can only sort children into three categories:

1. *Reassure*: Results indicate that children in this group are developing as expected. Parents are reassured and may be given information on parenting and what to expect from their children as they continue to grow and change.

2. *Refer*: Results indicate that children in this group are developing more slowly or quite differently than other children of the same age. Parents of children in this group are encouraged to schedule more thorough and detailed evaluations of their children. Most screening programs refer families directly to other professionals for further testing. This is an aspect of screening that requires sensitivity to the feelings of parents, who are facing the possibility that their children may have developmental delays or disabilities.

3. *Reschedule*: Results are equivocal for children in this group, without a clear indication of whether or not there is a developmental problem. Parents are advised to take the child back in a few months to be tested again. Questionable results on a screening test indicate the need for a sensitive approach to helping parents monitor their child's development more closely than usual.

The results of screening tests are too general to assist teachers in selecting learning goals, developing curriculum, or evaluating the progress of children in early education programs. The results of screening, as in all assessments, can be especially misleading for children from social and cultural groups that are not represented in the original construction of the test. Screening tests do provide an efficient and cost-effective method for identifying those children who would benefit from a more thorough and comprehensive developmental evaluation.

TRANSLATING THEORY INTO PRACTICE: COMMON PRINCIPLES

Applying developmental theories and principles to the care and education of infants and young children may seem complicated and confusing after reading a chapter full of divergent and sometimes conflicting viewpoints. How does knowledge of an individual child's characteristics inform curriculum development? How can teachers gather and use information about children's home environments? How can early childhood programs promote resilience and provide meaningful experiences for each and every child?

An analysis of current behavioral, developmental, and biomedical models of development reveals an important set of values and practical implications that are common across the full range of theoretical perspectives (Mallory, 1992). These five convergent principles are offered here as a framework for thinking about the desired outcomes for early childhood programs: independence, adaptation, social competence, responsive environments, and individualized approaches.

The first common principle for early childhood education is an emphasis on promoting independence as youngsters develop and grow. Much of what children learn in the first 8 years of life enables them to operate increasingly on their own in the world. For sick and traumatized newborns, independence may at first mean surviving outside the enclosed and heated isolette without the aid of a respirator. For most babies, independence takes the form of moving about separately from their caregivers and making their own needs known. Preschoolers generally become independent in

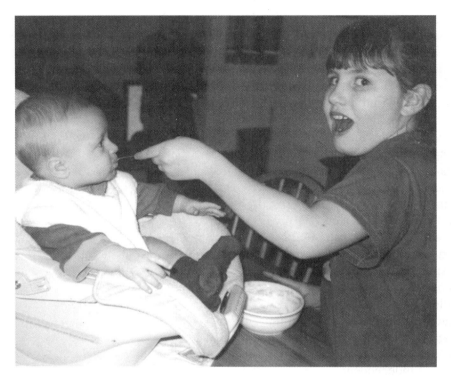

Early childhood professionals can apply developmental theories to create responsive environments, and to design curricula tailored to meet the needs of individual infants, toddlers, preschoolers, and primary school children.

creating their own learning experiences, interacting with peers, and communicating with familiar adults. Children in primary school spend more time away from their homes and family members and become adept at altering their behavior to match the demands of different places and people.

Central to the notion of independence is the common principle of adaptation. Early childhood programs strive to support the development of strategies that allow children to participate effectively and with confidence in many different environments as they grow and learn. Rather than simply teaching facts and skills in isolation, early childhood educators encourage progressively sophisticated methods of problem solving and interaction that are useful at home, in classrooms, and in the larger community. Infants develop routines for exploring new play materials, and toddlers learn to use their new vocabulary words. Preschoolers find that sharing and turn-taking skills learned at school work well at home and in the neighborhood, too. Primary school girls and boys begin to use the perspectives of other people in evaluating and making choices about their own behavior.

Supporting young children in the development of social competence is another commonality across a variety of early childhood theories. As youngsters grow, their sphere of influence and interaction expands outward from a primary caregiver to multiple adults and other children in any number of settings. Encouraging positive interactions between young children and caregivers and among peers, identifying and responding accordingly to emotions, sharing and taking turns, and resolving conflicts are important activities in almost all classrooms and parent education programs.

Critical to the common values of independence, adaptation, and social competence are early childhood environments that are responsive to the needs of each child. Working with families to interpret infant cues and ensure safe, comfortable, and predictable caregiving routines promotes responsive home environments. Careful attention to schedules and routines, traffic patterns in the classroom, selection of toys at the appropriate developmental levels, the creation of learning centers, and interactions among adults and children contribute to responsive classroom environments.

Individualized approaches are a necessity if learning and caregiving experiences are to be equally responsive for all children. For example, a responsive teacher might wait for a child with a high level of self-directed behavior to select from among available activities but structure options for a peer whose tendency is to move around the room without making choices. Some babies will provide clear and frequent cues (fussing, crying, smiling) for comfort, discomfort, hunger, boredom; others require a responsive caregiver to initiate interactions or interpret ambiguous cues. Infants and toddlers with vision impairments, for example, are less likely than their sighted peers to catch a caregiver's eye and smile when they want attention. Independence for some preschoolers means the opportunity to solve their own disputes over toys. For a child who uses a wheelchair, rearranging furniture to allow freedom of movement might facilitate independence.

Taken together, the principles of independence, adaptability, social competence, responsive environments, and individualized approaches form a practical framework for the care and education of young children in Western cultures. Developmental theories, risk categories, disability labels, and protective factors can each be explored in detail for deeper understanding of issues, controversies, research, and opinion in the area of early development. The task for you as an early childhood educator is to draw on theoretical information and academic knowledge as a backdrop for the ongoing responsibilities, challenges, and rewards of working with diverse groups of young children and families. In the foreground will be the dynamic interplay of daily events, observations, interactions, and reflections that will ultimately shape your personal ideas and applications of the concepts and principles of early development.

EXTENDING YOUR LEARNING

1. Write a one-page paper that describes why early childhood educators should be knowledgeable about child development.

2. Write a case study of a young child, describing in detail the risk and protective factors existing in his or her home, school, and community, as well as in society at large.

3. Select a theory of early development that especially interests you, and read more about it. Apply the theory to explain specific aspects of development for young children during infant, toddler, preschool, or primary years.

4. Identify a specific disability or diagnostic label described in the section on prenatal, perinatal, and postnatal influences, and research the exact mechanism through which development is affected. Write about the impact on infant, toddler, preschool, and primary behaviors and associated family issues.

5. Interview a genetic counselor or an intensive care nursery nurse. Find out about the rewards and stresses of their jobs. Try to arrange an observation in the intensive care nursery.

6. Observe a classroom that serves children with and without identified disabilities. Identify the major similarities and differences you see among the young children you observe.

7. Without having the children with disabilities or delays identified ahead of time, note the children you would be most concerned about developmentally. Were those children in fact the ones eligible for special services? (Be careful to observe rules of confidentiality.)

8. Spend the day with (or interview) the parents of young children with and without special needs. Describe similarities and differences in caregiving demands and parent–child interactions.

9. Spend time with a family with young children whose cultural background differs from your own. Identify specific differences in family membership, child-rearing practices, the role of adults and children, and ideas about early childhood education.

10. Visit a classroom that serves children of diverse cultural and linguistic backgrounds. Observe and describe classroom routines, materials, interactions, and teaching strategies that facilitate inclusion of children's native languages, parent involvement, and community resources.

VOCABULARY

Anencephaly.　　Condition characterized by the absence of a cerebral cortex.

Autism.　　A pervasive developmental disorder characterized by impairments in social interaction and communication skills, believed to be caused by differences in brain function.

Atypical development.　　A set of developmental patterns and sequences that vary considerably from those followed by most young children.

Biomedical risk.　　Biological conditions (prenatal, perinatal, or postnatal) that can compromise the course of early development (premature birth, neonatal illness).

Cerebral palsy.　　A non-progressive neurological disorder caused by an abnormality of the immature brain, of teratogenic, genetic, infectious, or traumatic origin. Results in a range of movement difficulties.

Chromosomes. Strings of DNA arranged in 23 pairs, made up of individual gene segments; genetic material contained in the nucleus of each cell in a person's body.

Classical conditioning. Learning that occurs through pairing a stimulus that is initially neutral with a stimulus that elicits a response involuntarily.

Cleft lip and palate. Openings in the skin and bone in the center of the upper lip or inside the crest of the mouth or both.

Development. Gradual, cumulative, and orderly changes (physical and psychological) resulting in increasingly sophisticated behaviors and interactions across the course of a person's lifetime.

Developmental milestones. Similar sequences of behaviors, skills, and knowledge that groups of children are expected to acquire at certain ages.

DNA. Deoxyribonucleic acid; long strings of chemical molecules that contain a person's entire genetic blueprint.

Down syndrome. Condition resulting from an additional chromosome with the 21st pair; characterized by mental retardation and recognizable facial features. Also called Trisomy 21.

Ecological theory. Emphasizes the impact of all aspects of a child's environment on developmental outcomes as a basis for understanding early development.

Environmental risk. Negative conditions that exist in the context of a child's life (i.e., poverty, hunger, unsafe neighborhoods).

Extinction. Ignoring, or lack of consequence for a behavior, with the effect of causing the behavior to decrease ("Ignore it and it will go away").

Fragile X syndrome. A condition in which the bottom of the X chromosome in the 23rd pair of chromosomes is pinched off, causing a range of physical anomalies and cognitive disabilities.

Genes. Segments of chromosomes that appear in consistent locations on chromosomes and control particular individual characteristics (height, weight, hair and eye color, blood type, facial features, body type, elements of intelligence, etc.).

Identified risk. Diagnosed disabilities and recognizable delays in early development (Down syndrome, Fragile X syndrome).

Individual differences. Unique qualities possessed by a person.

Interactive theories. Emphasize the joint effects of child-related factors and elements of the social and physical environment as a basis for understanding early development.

Maternal infections.   Viral or bacterial agents that cross the placenta and infect the fetus.

Maturational theories.   Emphasize physiological growth as a basis for understanding early development.

Nature (as a determinant of developmental change).   Elements inherent and internal to an individual; heredity, genetics, maturation.

Norms.   Average ages at which children achieve developmental milestones.

Nurture (as a determinant of developmental change).   Elements an individual is exposed to in his or her social interactions and physical environment.

Operant conditioning.   Learning that occurs as a result of positive, negative, and neutral consequences of behavior.

Phenylketonuria (PKU).   An inherited condition in which the body is unable to metabolize protein. The resulting toxins can cause severe mental retardation. A special diet can prevent this from occurring.

Protective factors.   Circumstances and interactions that frame and support healthy development.

Psychoanalytic theorists.   Emphasize the systematic variation in psychological and social variables as a basis for understanding early development.

Punishment.   Any consequence following a behavior that serves to decrease the likelihood that the same behavior will be performed again in the future.

Reinforcement.   Any consequence following a behavior that serves to increase the likelihood that the same behavior will be performed again in the future.

Resilience.   Positive developmental outcomes in the face of adverse life circumstances.

Social learning theory.   Emphasizes learning that occurs through observation and modeling of other people as a basis for understanding early development.

Spina bifida.   A range of conditions caused by openings in the skin or bone that usually cover the spinal cord.

Stages.   Developmental change characterized by the relatively abrupt emergence of new combinations of skills and behaviors.

Synactive theory.   Emphasizes constantly evolving interactions between prenatal and neonatal physiology and the immediate environment to explain the development of premature infants.

Tay-Sachs disease. A progressive neurological disorder caused by the absence of an enzyme, without which nerve cell metabolism results in a toxin accumulating in the brain.

Teratogens. Substances that pass to the fetus through the shared maternal blood supply and act directly to compromise fetal development.

Transactional theory. Emphasizes interactions between the biological status of the child and the quality of the caregiving environment as a basis for understanding early developmental outcomes.

Typical development. The wide range of developmental patterns and sequences exhibited by the majority of young children.

Volitional movement. Voluntary movement; controlled and purposeful motion.

Vulnerability. Increased likelihood of negative developmental outcomes, due to biological or environmental factors or both.

Williams syndrome. A rare genetic disorder presented at birth, caused by missing genetic material on chromosome 17; characterized by heart or blood problems, low birth weight, and hypercalcemia.

INTERNET RESOURCES

Web sites provide much useful information for educators and we list some here that pertain to the topics covered in this chapter. The addresses of Web sites can also change, however, and new ones are continually added. Thus, this list should be considered as a first step in your acquisition of a larger and ever-changing collection.

Center for the Future of Children (Packard Foundation)
   http://www.futureofchildren.org

Children's Defense Fund
   http://www.childrendefense.org/

Children's Institute International
   http://www.childreninsitute.org/

Culturally and Linguistically Appropriate Services (CLAS)
   http://www.clas.uiuc.edu/

Maternal and Child Health National Center for Cultural Competence
   http://www.dml.georgetown.edu/depts/pediatrics/gucdc/index.htm

Zero to Three
   http://www.zerothree.org/

Division of Early Childhood (DEC)
   http://www.dec-sped-org

National Association for Education of Young Children (NAEYC)
http://www.naeyc.org/

Special Education Resources on the Internet (SERI)
http://www.seri.hood.edu/seri/serihome.htm

Child Development Institute
http://www.edipage.com

Early Childhood Care and Development
http://www.ecdgroup.com

Early Childhood.com
http://www.erly.childhood.com

Special Needs Advocate for Parents (SNAP)
http://www.snapinfo.org

The Families and Work Institute
http://www.familiesandwork.org

Reading Resources in Developmental Psychology

Anselmo, S., & Franz, W. *Early childhood development: Prenatal through age eight* (2nd ed.). Columbus, OH: Merrill.
Black, J., & Puckett, M. (1996). *The young child: Development from prebirth through age eight.* Englewood Cliffs, NJ: Prentice-Hall.
Charlesworth, R. (1996). *Understanding child development* (4th ed.). Albany, NY: Delmar.
Krantz, M. (1994). *Child development: Risk and opportunity.* Belmont, CA: Wadsworth.
Trawick-Smith, J. (2000). *Early childhood development: A multicultural perspective* (2nd ed.). Upper Saddle River, NJ: Prentice-Hall.

References

Als, H. (1986). A synactive model of neonatal behavioral organization: Framework for the assessment of neurobehavioral development in the preterm infant and for the support of infants and parents in the neonatal intensive care environment. *Physical and Occupational Therapy in Pediatrics, 6,* 613–653.
Als, H., Hester, B. M., Tronick, E. Z., & Brazelton, T. B. (1982). Assessment of preterm infant behavior (APIB). In H. E. Fitzgerald & M. Yogman (Eds.), *Theory and research in behavioral pediatrics* (Vol. 1, pp. 64–133). New York: Plenum.
Als, H., Lawhon, G., Brown, E., Gibes, R., Duffy, F., McAnulty, G., & Blickman, J. (1994). Individualized developmental care for the very low birthweight preterm infant: Medical and neurofunctional effects. *Journal of the American Medical Association, 272*(11), 853–858.
Bandura, A. (1973). *Aggression: A social learning analysis.* Englewood Cliffs, NJ: Prentice-Hall.
Bandura, A. (1977). *Social learning theory.* Englewood Cliffs, NJ: Prentice-Hall.
Bandura, A. (1986). *Social foundations of thought and action: A social cognitive theory.* Englewood Cliffs, NJ: Prentice-Hall.
Bee, H. (1997). *The developing child.* (8th ed.). New York: HarperCollins.
Benard, B. (1999). From research to practice: The foundations of the resiliency paradigm. In N. Henderson, B. Benard, N. Sharp-Light (Eds.), *Resiliency in action: Practical ideas for overcoming risks and building strengths in youth, families, and communities.* Gorman, ME: Resiliency in Action.

Brofenbrenner, U. (1979). *The ecology of human development.* Cambridge, MA: Harvard University Press.

Burns, T. (1994). *From risk to resilience.* Dallas, TX: The Marco Polo Group.

Cost, Quality and Outcomes Study Team. (1995). *Cost, quality, and child outcomes in child care centers: Public report* (2nd ed.). Denver, CO: Economics Department, University of Colorado.

Diaz Soto, L. D. (1991). Research in review. Understanding bilingual/bicultural young children. *Young Children, 46*(2), 30–36.

Dunst, C. (1981). *Infant learning: A cognitive-linguistic intervention strategy.* Allen, TX: DLM.

Erikson, E. (1963). *Childhood and society* (2nd ed.). New York: Norton.

Freud, S. (1960). *The ego and the id.* New York: Norton. (Original work published 1923)

Gesell, A. (1929). *Infancy and human growth.* New York: Macmillan.

Gesell, A. (1945). *How a baby grows: A story in pictures.* New York: Harper Brothers.

Gesell, A., & Ilg, F. L. (1949). *Child development.* New York: Harper & Row.

Goffin, S. G. (1996). Child development knowledge and early childhood teacher preparation: Assessing the relationship–A special collection. *Early Childhood Research Quarterly, 11,* 117–133.

Gorski, P. A., & VandenBerg, K. A. (1996). Infants born at risk. In M. J. Hanson (Ed.), *Atypical infant development.* Austin, TX: Pro-Ed.

Guralnick, M. J. (1990). Social competence and early intervention. *Journal of Early Intervention, 14*(1), 3–14.

Henderson, N., Benard, B., & Sharp-Light, N. (1999). *Resiliency in action: Practical ideas for overcoming risks' and building strengths in youth, families, and communities.* Gorham, ME: Resiliency in Action.

Horowitz, F. D. (1990). Developmental models of individual differences. In J. Colombo & J. Fagan (Eds.), *Individual differences in infancy: Reliability, stability, prediction* (pp. 3–18). Hillsdale, NJ: Lawrence Erlbaum Associates.

Howes, C. (1987). Quality indicators in infant and toddler child care: The Los Angeles study. In D. A. Phillips (Ed.), *Quality in child care: What does research tell us?* (pp. 81–88). Washington, DC: NAEYC.

Katz, L. (1996). Child development knowledge and teacher preparation: Confronting assumptions. *Early Childhood Research Quarterly, 11,* 135–146.

Knobloch, M., & Pasamanick, B. (1974). *Gesell and Amatruda's developmental diagnosis: The evaluation and management of normal and abnormal neuropsychologic development in infancy and early childhood* (3rd ed.). New York: Harper & Row.

Kopp, C. B., & Parmelee, A. H. (1979). Prenatal and perinatal influences on infant behavior. In J. O. Sofsky (Ed.), *Handbook of infant development* (pp. 29–75). New York: Wiley.

Kunc, N. (1994, November). *Disability and identity.* Keynote presentation. Phi Delta Kappa Leadership Conference, Victoria, British Columbia.

Lewis, M. (1996). Developmental principles and their implications for infants who are at risk and/or disabled. In M. J. Hanson (Ed.), *Atypical infant development.* Austin, TX: Pro-Ed.

Mallory, B. (1992). Is it always appropriate to be developmental? Convergent models for early intervention practice. *Topics in Early Childhood Special Education, 11*(4), 1–12.

McNulty, B., Smith, D. B., & Soper, E. W. (1983). *Effectiveness of early special education for handicapped children.* Colorado Department of Education.

Postman, N. (1984). *The disappearance of childhood.* New York: Delacort.

Sameroff, A., & Chandler, M. J. (1975). Reproductive risk and the continuum of caretaking casualty. In F. D. Horowitz, M. Hetherington, S. Scarr-Salapatek, & G. Siegel (Eds.), *Review of child development research* (Vol. 4, pp. 187–294). Chicago: University of Chicago Press.

Shaffer (1994). *Social and personality development.* Pacific Grove, CA: Brooks/Cole.

Shonkoff, J. P., Hauser-Cram, P., Krauss, M. W., & Upshur, C. C. (1992). Development of infants with disabilities and their families. *Monographs of the Society for Research in Child Development, 57*(Serial No. 230), 1–20.

Skinner, B. F. (1953). *Science and human behavior.* New York: Free Press.

Skinner, B. F. (1983). *A matter of consequences.* New York: Knopf.

Stott, F., & Bowman, B. (1996). Child development knowledge: A slippery base for practice. *Early Childhood Research Quarterly, 11,* 169–183.

Tjossem, T. D. (Ed.). (1976). *Intervention strategies for high-risk infants and young children.* Baltimore, MD: University Park Press.

Watson, J. B. (1928). *Psychological care of the infant and child.* New York: Norton.

Werner, E. (1990). Protective factors and individual resilience. In S. Meisels & J. Shonkoff (Eds.), *Handbook of early childhood intervention* (pp. 97–116). New York: Cambridge University Press.

Werner, E., & Smith, R. (1982). *Vulnerable but invincible: A longitudinal study of resilient children and youth.* New York: McGraw-Hill.

Western Regional Center for Drug-Free Schools and Communities. (1991). *Fostering resilience in kids: Protective factors in the family, school, and community.* Portland, OR: Northwest Regional Educational Laboratory.

York, S. (1991). *Roots and wings: Affirming culture in early childhood programs.* St. Paul, MN: Redleaf Press.

2

INFANCY: FROM CRADLE TO PLAY GROUP

The magician is seated in his high chair and looks upon the world with favor. He is at the height of his powers. If he closes his eyes, he causes the world to disappear. If he opens his eyes, he causes the world to come back. If there is harmony within him, the world is harmonious. If rage shatters his inner harmony, the unity of the world is shattered. If desire arises within him, he utters the magic syllables that cause the desired object to appear. His wishes, his thoughts, his gestures, his noises command the universe.

Selma Fraiberg

▼ Chapter Objectives

After reading this chapter, you should be able to:

- ▼ Identify the influence of family and cultural contexts on infant development.
- ▼ Describe infant sensory capabilities and physical growth.
- ▼ Explain the role of parent–infant interaction in early motor, cognitive, and social development.
- ▼ Summarize principles and sequences of infant skill acquisition across motor, cognitive, and social domains.
- ▼ Recognize variations in infant growth and behavior across motor, cognitive, and social domains and draw conclusions about the impact on development.

As you think about and apply chapter content on your own, you should be able to:

- ▼ Observe principles of development, and estimate the approximate ages of infants you encounter.
- ▼ Formulate your own opinions about the relative contributions of maturation and individual differences to the development of babies you observe.
- ▼ Begin to think about ways to support the developmental needs of infants across a wide range of abilities.

Vignette 2.1: ***What's Wrong with Cara?***

Cara is almost 8 months old and crying loudly and insistently. It is almost midnight, and her parents, Jamie and Marie, are trying to sleep in the next room.

"She can't be hungry," mumbles Marie, "she just finished her nighttime feeding about 20 minutes ago. I changed her entire outfit, so she can't be wet, either. What can be wrong?"

"She has been sleeping through the night for months now; maybe it's just a relapse, or maybe she's teething," suggests Jamie tentatively.

Marie isn't convinced. "She started up so suddenly. Maybe she had a bad dream. But she sounds more mad than scared, doesn't she?"

Both parents get up and go into Cara's room. Jamie speaks softly without turning on the light, and Cara quiets briefly but begins to holler as soon as they turn around to leave. Marie rubs Cara's back, and she almost stops crying, only to resume full blast when left alone. After debating the pros and cons of various solutions, Marie and Jamie decide to take the baby into bed with them, in the hope of getting some rest. Cara again stops crying for a time but squirms and fusses, clearly not about to fall asleep. Soon she resumes crying in earnest, kicking her legs and flailing her arms. Thinking that Cara might be ill or have an ear infection, the parents get up again and take her temperature. There is no fever and the baby is crying nonstop.

By now it is after 1 o'clock in the morning, and as Cara's crying escalates, her parents revert to approaches that worked when she was a newborn. Marie tries unsuccessfully to nurse her. Jamie walks the baby around the house and even tries taking her for a ride in the car, an activity guaranteed to induce sleep in the first weeks of life. Cara is inconsolable, and as she continues to thrash about and scream, her parents become increasingly frantic.

"I think we should call the doctor!" asserts Marie desperately.

"Let's give her a bath first," Jamie advises in a momentary flash of creativity. "She is always so calm and relaxed after her bath." Jamie fills the sink with warm water while Marie begins undressing Cara.

Abruptly the crying stops and in the silence, Marie exclaims, "Oh, no. You poor baby! My poor Cara; I'm so sorry." Jamie runs into the baby's room expecting the worst and finds both mother and infant smiling broadly. "Look, Jamie. The last time I changed Cara, her little toe somehow got wrapped up in a loose piece of elastic from the footie of her outfit. As soon as I took her foot out, she stopped crying! That was the whole problem."

Indeed, within seconds Cara lay completely exhausted in her mother's arms and began to drift off to sleep. It will be some time, however, before her parents calm down enough to go back to bed themselves. Over hot chocolate Jamie says wistfully, "If only she could have just told us what was wrong 2 hours ago!"

The story of Cara's midnight adventure illustrates a number of the themes central to the study of infancy. These themes form the framework for the content presented in this chapter:

- The development of infants during the first year of life is inextricably grounded in both physical development and relationships with caregivers.
- Earliest abilities of infants allow them to be active participants in social interactions, which in turn provide a meaningful context and incentive for development of cognitive, motor, and communication skills.

*This chapter is divided into two sections, and should be assigned in two parts. The first section includes pages 40 to 63 and the second section includes pages 63 to 85.

- Babies are full of wonderful surprises and never cease to amaze the adults who know and care for them.

The birth of a child is a meaningful event in every culture in the world and most often an occasion associated with customs and rituals shared by family and friends. In Western cultures, birth is associated with marriage, medical care, childbirth education, baby showers, birth announcements, photographs, gifts, and a period of recovery for both newborn and mother. For new parents, the first child requires a dramatic change in roles as adults assume new responsibilities and engage in new activities. Without really thinking about it, most parents expect that the infant will recognize and smile at them within a few weeks, conform to the family's daily schedule for eating and sleeping within a few months, begin to walk and use language within the first year. Infancy is considered for this chapter to extend from birth until babies begin to walk, which on average covers approximately the first year of life. Infancy is a distinctly intimate period of development, during which caregiving adults become acquainted with tiny new people as individuals, and babies become active social participants, all within a context of mutual affection.

FAMILY CONTEXT

Cultural background and family structure dictate the exact routines and activities that are played out during the first year of a baby's life. Some newborns are taken out in public and held by any number of people; others stay at home with one caregiver. In some cultures and some families, it is taken for granted that mothers' caregiving responsibilities take priority over employment, education, or other personal pursuits. Other parents share caregiving tasks or find reliable childcare resources so that mother and father can both continue to work or go to school. Newborns may live with only one parent and may be cared for by extended family members, especially in cultures where aunts, uncles, or grandparents have prescribed responsibilities for new babies. Same-gender couples may adopt infants, as do single mothers and fathers. Babies may sleep in beds with adults until they are preschoolers or be expected to sleep in their own cribs from birth. In some families, everyone talks to babies from the day they are born; in others, babies are not considered to be conversational partners until they themselves start to use words. There are parents who start investigating preschools before their babies are born; in other families, children stay at home until it is time for kindergarten; other parents choose to school their sons and daughters at home.

There is extreme variability in the home and family contexts into which babies are born, and no one environment is best. As long as infants receive adequate nourishment in a safe and responsive environment, with at least one adult who makes it his or her business to provide consistent and affectionate care, developmental progress in the first year is likely to conform to family and cultural expectations. Sometimes, however, babies are born with biomedical or identified risk conditions that require specialized care. This chapter summarizes common patterns of development in physical, cognitive, and social-affective domains and discusses individual differences due to physical disabilities, sensory impairments, and disruptions in social-affective interactions during the first 18 months of life.

THE NEWBORN

The hard work of labor and the excitement of birth signify an emotional passage from pregnancy to parenthood, with long-awaited introductions between parents and newborn as the culminating event. The initial appearance of *neonates* contrasts sharply with the chubby, alert faces and cuddly bodies of older babies framed in media images and family photographs. Newborns greet the world with scrunched up faces, squinty eyes, tightly fisted hands, flexed limbs, and sometimes pointy shaped heads or damp, pasty skin. At birth, infants most often weigh between 5½ and 10 pounds and measure from 18 to 22 inches in length, with an average weight of about 7½ pounds and length of 20 inches from head to foot (Black & Puckett, 1996). The head accounts for about one third the body length, so newborns appear top heavy, especially when lying with their arms curled together on their chests and knees pulled up toward their abdomens. Babies will grow on the average 10 to 12 inches in the first year and triple their body weight, the most rapid period of physical growth until adolescence. The upright postures and controlled movements of 1-year-old babies make changes in height and weight appear all the more impressive.

The way newborns look is a clear reflection of the dramatic differences between floating in the warm, dim, close, quiet uterine environment and spreading out in the cold, bright, open, loud world outside the mother's body. Getting used to life outside the uterus takes time and is supported by close physical contact between infants and adults (Hofer, 1981). Although unable to survive independently at birth, human newborns are exceedingly well equipped to captivate adults responsible for their care. The majority of new mothers and fathers find their own babies to be beautiful, although initially a newborn's appearance can be startling. Their relatively big heads, large eyes, tiny features, and helpless postures most often elicit a powerful desire from caregivers to protect and nurture (Bowlby, 1969). Newborns usually sleep for only 1½ or 2 hours at a time, although they may be napping and dozing for up to a total of 20 hours a day. Babies at birth nurse an average of 10 times a day and use about 10 diapers, also. The tendency of adults to pay close attention and provide constant care for newborn infants is a fortunate circumstance; there is a lot to do!

Infants may be extremely limited in physical prowess at birth but are quite capable of using their senses to take in events in their surroundings. The physical structures for vision, hearing, touch, smell, and taste are fully developed at birth. The senses constitute a particularly sophisticated apparatus for making connections with and learning about the world and enable babies to be especially receptive to the people who care for them. There is a large body of research literature from the 1980s in the area of basic infant sensory function, with new research methods and technology adding to the knowledge base all the time. Although scholarly explanations for the origin and purpose of early sensory skills vary, it is clear that babies are born ready to interact and learn.

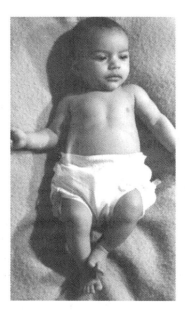

Young infants appear quite helpless, but have surprising abilities for survival, social interaction, and learning.

Consider the following consistent results from research on infant sensory capabilities. Newborns can hear human voices almost as well as adults can (Werner & Gillenwater, 1990) and can discriminate their own mothers' voices from the voices of other women (DeCasper & Fifer, 1980). They can focus their vision well on objects within 8 inches of their eyes and look longest at objects that have dark and light contrasts and motion (Flavell, Miller, & Miller, 1993; Haith, 1980). A few days following birth, breast-fed babies are able to recognize the odor of their own mothers' milk (Cernoch & Porter, 1985; Porter, Makin, Davis, & Christensen, 1992) and seem to develop a preference for looking at their own mothers within the first few days of life (Walton, Bower, & Bower, 1992). Rates of breathing and heartbeat tend to become more regular and body temperatures more stable when newborns are held close to an adult's body (Hofer, 1981).

Now imagine the relative positions of a parent, most often the mother, and a newborn during nursing or bottle-feeding. The mother's face is most likely just about 8 inches from the baby's eyes, with hairline, eyebrows, eyes, and mouth contrasting with skin, and eyes and mouth moving as she talks to the baby and changes facial expressions. The infant is close to the mother's body and exposed to that unique scent during each feeding, with skin-to-skin contact for nursing babies. During feeding, a newborn is snuggled cozily against the warmth of a larger body, with one little ear close to a beating heart. There could not possibly be a better match between an infant's sensory abilities and the naturally occurring routines of caregiving in the early months! From the very beginning of life, the infant's inborn sensory abilities support participation in social interaction and promote development of an emotional bond with caregivers. As the baby grows, sensory abilities and social relationships in combination will furnish a strong foundation for learning.

PHYSICAL GROWTH AND MOTOR DEVELOPMENT DURING INFANCY: REFLEXIVE AND RUDIMENTARY MOVEMENT

At first glance, newborn infants appear to have a long way to go in terms of physical development. Tiny and vulnerable beings with little purposeful movement and even less mobility, they are limited to lying or being held. Neonates can open their lips to nurse or cry but are unable to bring their hands to their mouths. They can turn their faces from side to side but cannot hold heads upright and steady. Less obvious at birth is the incredible repertoire of abilities that provide a foundation for rapid motor development during the first 12 months of life. With surprising ease, most infants will become upright, mobile, and intentional in their social and physical interactions.

Newborn babies exhibit many different movement patterns but have little voluntary control over their actions. After all, their physical experiences before birth were contained by the secure environment of the womb, supported by *amniotic fluid*, and limited during the final weeks of pregnancy by being upside down with the head snugly within the mother's *pelvic girdle*. For the first few weeks of life, babies can be observed to move in much the same manner as they did *in utero*. They lie with arms, legs, and neck curled toward the middle of the body, stretch their limbs with little jerks or in long languorous arches, and burrow their heads into the corners of cradles and cribs. Infants acquire control over their bodies as their central nervous systems mature and in synchrony with the responses they elicit from the people and objects in their immediate environments.

Reflexive Movement and Brain Development

Babies can be observed to exhibit many different patterns of motor activity before they develop control over their movements. Observers of newborns see many actions that seem random and uncontrolled, and now and again tiny babies seem to frighten themselves with the movements of their own bodies. For the most part, earliest motions are *reflexive* rather than voluntary, with specific actions of the arms, legs, and body elicited by sights, sounds, touches, or the position of the infant's head. Reflexes equip the newborn with automatic movements that sustain survival and provide an important foundation for later motor development. Reflexive movement originates in the lower and midbrain, the sections of the brain most developed at birth (see Fig. 2.1). Let's take a closer look at some of the reflexes that supply infants with opportunities to move before they can control bodies in a purposeful manner.

Survival Reflexes

Two reflexes of obvious significance to survival are breathing and sucking. Infants are not required to breathe in utero but begin to do so reflexively as soon as their bodies contact air at birth. Requirements for nourishment are likewise supplied through the bloodstream during pregnancy, but as soon as babies are born reflexes cause them to position their heads and suck from a nipple. The *rooting reflex* is an automatic response of turning toward a touch or stroke on the cheek, resulting in a high likelihood of con-

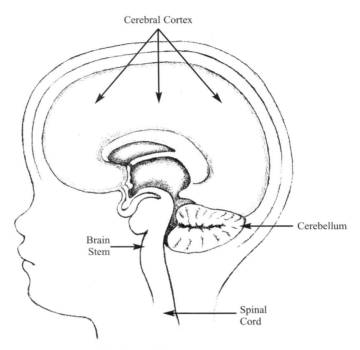

FIG. 2.1.   Side view of the brain.

tact between the baby's mouth and a source of food. The *sucking reflex* is then activated, permitting the infant to perform the complex sequence of closing the lips, sucking, and swallowing in coordination with breathing. Reflexive movements allow newborns to be active participants in their own survival from the first moments of life.

Primitive Reflexes

Some reflexive actions of newborns are primitive counterparts of complex voluntary skills such as walking and grasping that develop within the first year of life. Long before babies can intentionally grasp and hold objects, pressure on the side of the palm near the little finger will stimulate the fingers and thumb to close in a *reflexive grasp*. Newborn infants also exhibit a *stepping reflex*, moving their legs up and down in a stepping motion when held upright with their feet contacting a surface. Grasping and stepping are movements that clearly foreshadow more sophisticated, critical early motor skills. The purpose and origin of other *primitive reflexes* (Table 2.1) are less clear but are probably genetic holdovers from behaviors that helped ensure survival in the long-distant biological past of the human species.

Primitive reflexes usually become stronger and more evident in the movements of infants for 2 months or so and then disappear by about 6 months of age. Movement patterns that continue to be dominated by primitive reflexes inhibit acquisition of rolling, sitting, crawling, and walking and can serve as early warning signs for concerns about a child's central nervous system. *Atypical infant reflexes* can be exagger-

TABLE 2.1

Primitive Reflexes

Moro reflex	When there is a rapid change in head position or a sudden loud noise, the head falls back, arms and fingers extend and go out and up from trunk (birth to 4 months).
Grasp reflex	Hand stays in fisted position; when hand is touched near little finger, a strong grasp results (until 3 to 4 months).
Asymmetrical tonic neck reflex	When infant's head is turned to side, arm on face side extends, and arm on skull side flexes; a "fencing posture" most easily seen in supine lying (0 to 4 months).
Symmetrical tonic neck reflex	When head is extended, arms extend, and hips and legs flex; when head is flexed, arms flexes, and hips and legs extend (2 to 4 months).
Tonic labyrinthine reflex	When baby lies supine, limbs and trunk are predominately extended; when baby lies prone, limbs and trunk are predominately flexed (0 to 4 months).

ated versions of primitive reflexes that interfere with voluntary movement and often indicate brain injury sustained during the prenatal or perinatal periods. For example, a *bite reflex* might cause an automatic, uncontrollable clamping together of the jaw whenever the inside of the mouth is stimulated. This reflex compromises smooth coordination of sucking, swallowing, and breathing and later impedes chewing and brushing teeth. Another atypical pattern is an *extensor thrust*, when tipping the head back causes a generalized extension of muscles from head to toes: The tongue sticks out, shoulders pull back as hips thrust forward, legs stretch out and may cross, and toes point. This reflex quite obviously interferes with infants looking upward toward caregivers or tipping their heads back to drink from cups. Sustained primitive reflexes or atypical reflex patterns are sometimes mistaken for intentional misbehavior in toddlers and preschoolers but are automatic movements over which children have no control whatsoever. A child who consistently exhibits unusual patterns of motor behavior should be referred for neurological examination and evaluation for physical therapy services.

Brain Development

Investigations of brain structure and function using modern imaging technology suggest strongly that the basic framework of cells in each person's brain is developed and arranged before birth, determined by heredity (Shatz, 1997). In the first few months of life, however, rapid brain growth is centered in the cortex, where more complex and voluntary motor activity is controlled. The brain actually triples in weight in the first year or 2 of life, the dramatic increase accounted for by growth of trillions of precise connections among brain cells (Huttenlocher, 1994). During the first 3 years of life, the brain itself creates an overlapping tangle of pathways among brain cells many times the actual connections needed for efficient thought and action. A child's early experiences provide the input that organizes, strengthens, and refines some connections, and eventually eliminating those which are redundant (Shatz, 1997; Chugani, 1998). The "selective pruning" of neural connections is completed during adolescence, culminating the evolution of the generalized motor activity of infancy to the sophisticated voluntary skills that incorporate meaningful information from the environment into mobility and social interactions (Brodal, 1992; Chugani, 1998).

Gross Motor Development: Moving Against Gravity

By what process does the infant progress from random and reflexive movements in a lying position to walking upright in the first year? *Gross motor development* refers to progressive voluntary command over the large muscles of the body. Muscles that control the neck, torso, arms, and legs allow infants to move against gravity by holding their heads up, sitting, crawling, and walking. Gross motor development involves a continual interplay between the static forces of maintaining postures and the dynamic forces of movement.

During the first year of life, a process known as *myelination* results in nerve pathways being coated with myelin, a waxy substance that efficiently directs nerve impulses from the brain and spinal cord to specific muscles. As nerve pathways are myelinated, the infant is able to gain voluntary control over muscles along the route. Formation of the myelin sheath progresses from the baby's head downward along the spinal column and from the middle of the body outward toward the extremities (see Fig. 2.2).

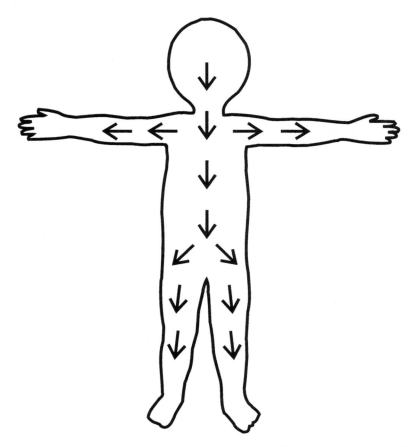

FIG. 2.2.   Voluntary control of movement develops from head to feet (cephalo-caudal) and from the middle of the body toward the (proximal-distal) extremities.

This head-to-toe sequence of motor control is known as *cephalocaudal development*, meaning literally head to tail, and is reflected in the postures infants can maintain in sitting positions and in lying both *prone* (on their stomachs) and *supine* (on their backs). The cephalocaudal sequence of development determines that infants are able to hold up their heads before they can control their torsos for sitting, can sit before they can manage their legs for crawling, and can crawl before they can walk.

People who have little experience with infants tend to think that babies "just lie around" until they are about a year old and then learn to walk. In reality, there are a number of *rudimentary movement* skills that develop in a coherent sequence during infancy. A sequence of major gross motor milestones and associated age ranges is contained in Table 2.2. It is important to remember that each baby develops on an individual timetable, and that some youngsters begin to walk without ever crawling or cruising, so the ages given are only approximations.

Head Control

An earlier reference was made to the large size of an infant's head relative to the rest of the body. Compared to adult bodies, an infant's head accounts for a much greater proportion of body length and weight. At birth, it is impossible for tiny neck muscles to hold up such relatively heavy heads. One of the first thing caregivers learn is to support the newborn's head, to keep it from awkwardly flopping down to the chest, over to the shoulders, or worse yet backwards into space! The baby's first major physical task is to develop control of the head and neck. Head control is especially important, because it is a prerequisite for most other gross motor skills.

Gravity exerts a powerful influence on the tiny bodies of newborns. The entire length of their bodies is supported as they lie in cribs or are held in someone's arms. Younger infants spend a lot of their time lying on their stomachs and on their backs. Many prefer lying on their backs because it is easier to turn their heads from side to side. One of the earliest indications of developing head control is when a baby momentarily holds her head up while lying on her stomach, or pulls her head out and away from the caregiver's chest when being held upright. These early attempts require obvious effort, and often result in only a momentary look around before the tiny head collapses forward. Over time, neck muscles become stronger, and central nervous system maturation

TABLE 2.2

Gross Motor Development Milestones

Rolling	3 to 4 months
Supports self on forearms in prone position	2 to 4 months
Sitting	5 to 7 months
Crawling/creeping	8 to 10 months
Pull to stand	7 to 9 months
Cruising	10 to 12 months
Standing	10 to 12 months
Walking	10 to 14 months

allows babies to gain control of their heads. Two- to 3-month-old infants can hold up their heads without the constant support of a caregiver's hand, whether held at an adult's shoulder or in a sitting position. When lying on the floor, 3- to 4-month-old babies can lift up their heads and turn them from side to side, in prone as well as supine positions. During the first few months, the head still appears heavy and wobbly when the infant is tired or concentrating his attention elsewhere. By 4 months, most babies have good control of their heads and can smoothly turn from side to side in all positions to look around at interesting events in the environment.

Prone Lying

Being able to purposefully extend muscles along the spinal cord allows babies to defy the pull of gravity and take advantage of a number of more sophisticated body positions than simply lying on their stomachs and backs. One of the first new postures combines control of the shoulders with head control, as infants begin to hold their heads up while supporting themselves on their forearms while lying prone. Starting at about 2 months, babies lying on their stomachs will pick their heads up to look around; as they begin to lift their shoulders as well, it becomes possible to bear weight with their forearms on a firm surface. By 4 months of age, typically developing children can lift their heads and upper chests up when lying prone and by 6 months can support themselves on their hands, with arms fully extended, holding the head upright and raising the entire chest (Fig. 2.3). In this position, only the hands support the top half of the body, and babies can look to either side, ahead, and upward to explore interesting sights and sounds in the immediate environment.

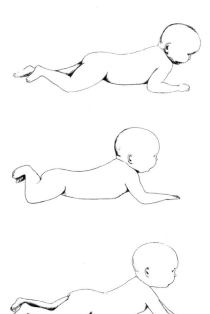

FIG. 2.3. Prone lying. When lying on their stomachs, babies first hold their heads upright, then can raise their shoulders, and finally straighten their arms to raise their chests.

Sitting

The ability to control the shoulders and torso is also evident when babies are held in sitting positions. Newborns held in sitting positions will curl forward with totally rounded backs and their chins falling to their chests, an awkward posture that explains the natural tendency of caregivers to hold new babies in a reclining position. Two- to 4-month-old infants can hold their heads erect when propped in a sitting position or supported around the torso by an adult's hands. Most babies learn to sit independently between 5 and 7 months, with straight backs and flawless head control by 8 or 9 months. At first, sitting is a proud but tentative posture to maintain, with a turn of the head to one side being enough to cause the baby to fall over in that same direction. Eventually, infants learn to automatically put their hands down to prevent losing their balance when they lean or fall forward, to either side, and later backwards. Figure 2.4 illustrates the progression of independent sitting skills.

First Controlled Maneuvers

Once babies can successfully bear weight and maintain prone, supine, or sitting postures, the next task is to be able to transfer weight from side to side and rotate their trunks to allow movement. In the prone position this maneuver involves shifting weight from one arm to another, holding the chest up with one hand while freeing up the other hand for reaching and grasping. Typically developing infants are able to support themselves on their stomachs with one arm and reach with the other arm to the side, front, or even across the body to retrieve toys by about 7 months. Once the new position is steady, babies use it to eagerly explore toys and can entertain themselves for extended periods of time on a blanket on the floor.

Shifting and rotating weight also gives infants the ability to reach to the front, side, and across the *midline* of the body without losing balance in sitting positions. By 1 year of age, babies can generally get themselves easily from lying on the floor to a sitting position and back down again and maintain balance while reaching upward, to both sides and the front. Assuming and maintaining a variety of different postures while lying and sitting becomes automatic and no longer requires focused attention or effort.

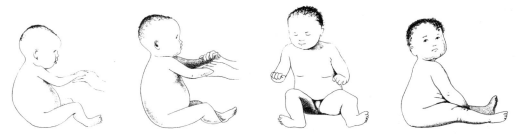

FIG. 2.4.   Independent sitting. Infants develop the ability to sit independently by first holding their heads upright and steady, then gaining extensor control downward along the spinal cord.

> *Movement in all positions*
> *has a foundation in a similar progression:*
>
> Bear weight → Shift weight → Rotate

The groundwork for independent mobility is laid as infants become able to and interested in changing the positions of their own bodies in space. It is from the prone position that many 4- to 6-month-old babies begin to roll over from stomach to back, perhaps reaching for something with one hand and failing to maintain balance on the opposite arm. They quickly learn to control their descent from prone lying and to roll intentionally from back to front. At the same age (6 to 8 months) little ones can also be observed to pivot around in a circle on their stomachs to get toys that are out of reach and to lift their feet straight up in the air and even into their mouths when lying on their backs. Figure 2.5 illustrates a few of the first controlled maneuvers.

All of these skills illustrate that infants who are developing typically have achieved initial voluntary control over the length of their spinal cords from head to toe, during the third quarter of the first year of life. Observing babies of this age reveals the absolute delight they take in movement as well as the satisfaction and confidence in physical activity that develops along with voluntary control of large muscles.

Moving on All Fours

Once infants can assume and maintain postures on their stomachs and backs and in sitting positions, they usually exhibit great enthusiasm for becoming mobile. Some babies decide that rolling over (and over and over) is a good way to get around and use their newfound skill to move from place to place on the floor. Others begin to *crawl* around with their tummies on the floor or to pull their knees up under their bottoms when lying prone and push up on extended arms, rocking back and forth in preparation for moving about on all fours. By 10 to 12 months of age, most infants will be getting about on their hands and knees with stomachs off the floor in a *creeping* position (Fig. 2.6). Creeping foreshadows all the basic elements of walking, including head control in all positions as the baby creeps and looks around simultaneously, full extension of the entire back, and a synchronized and reciprocal movement pattern with alternate movement of one arm and the opposite leg. Hands and knees form only four small points of contact with the ground. The progression of

FIG. 2.5.   First controlled maneuvers. Rolling, pivoting, and raising the legs and feet in supine lying demonstrate the infant's early abilities in controlling complex movements.

The intense concentration and diligent effort necessary to master new motor skills is evident as this baby tries to get into position for crawling.

FIG. 2.6.   Creeping and crawling. Babies first use their arms and legs to creep with their stomachs on the floor, then raise to their hands and knees and rock, in preparation for crawling on all fours.

movement against gravity has come a long way, and once babies are mobile they move quickly and seem tireless!

Walking

As infants roll, crawl, or creep close to furniture, large toys, and the legs of bigger people, they begin to use their arms to pull themselves to upright kneeling positions and soon place one foot flat on the floor to stand (Fig. 2.7). At first babies lean their chests against couches, chairs, and low tables for support, and from a kneeling or standing position the hands are free to manipulate and explore. Soon the sight of a

FIG. 2.7.   Standing and walking. Before their first birthdays, babies begin to balance in kneeling positions, pull themselves to stand, "cruise" along furniture, and eventually walk independently.

toy or person out of reach encourages sideways movement and the baby takes first tentative steps to one side and then the other. For most babies, it is only a matter of weeks before they are standing with only their hands for support and letting go occasionally to stand alone momentarily. Cruising confidently around furniture, they plop backward onto the floor to get down or if they lose their balance. Parents and other caregivers usually help out by holding the baby upright in a standing position and encourage walking by gradually reducing assistance, first providing substantial support around the torso, then fading to the arms, two hands, and then one hand as the baby's balance improves. Within a couple months after their first birthdays, typically developing infants are walking around with the easily recognizable high guard position of the newly upright and mobile: legs stiff and locked at the knees, hands held up and away from the body at shoulder level.

New walkers move first with feet wide apart, by shifting weight from one foot to the other, with almost as much movement from side to side as forward, and dropping to all fours to creeping if speed is a priority. As balance improves, the torso rotates against the hips, and the arms come down to swing forward in synchrony with opposite legs in a smooth reciprocal movement. Now only two tiny feet in contact with the floor support the child's body, balancing to stand and moving to walk. Creeping is abandoned for upright postures, and speed is achieved by stiff early attempts at running.

Fine Motor Development: Reaching and Grasping

The advantages of being upright usually become obvious once youngsters experience the freedom of independently changing positions from lying prone and supine to sitting to creeping. The many interesting objects, people, and events babies see in their environments motivate them to move from place to place to grab things and to remain close to caregivers. By the time infants are walking, they have good control of their arms and hands for chewing, poking, turning, banging, and dumping toys, although as newborns they were unable even to bring their hands up to their mouths. This section provides a closer look at how babies develop the ability to reach and grasp in the first year of life.

Reaching

Earliest movements of the hands and arms are reflexive, seen when newborns make jerky outward movements of their arms in response to loud noises or automatically grasp a finger inserted between their own. Voluntary control of the arms, hands, and fingers advances from the midline of the body outward to the extremities, as progressive myelination promotes the development of purposeful actions from haphazard movements. Initially, infants can be observed to wave their arms in random, wobbly movements when lying on their backs. Their fingers are closed, tightly at first, gradually loosening during the first months; movement of the hands tends to increase when babies see something interesting. By the age of 3 months, the majority of babies are holding their hands open, opening and closing their fingers as if warming up for finger play.

In sitting positions or lying on their backs, these same infants will bat and swipe in the general direction of mobiles, faces, and other items of visual interest, often making contact with the side or back of the hand. At this point, the infant has most control of the shoulders and upper arms, so the arms appear to flail around in a rather uncoordinated fashion. It is not unusual for 3-month-old babies to bonk themselves in the foreheads when trying to bring their hands or rattles to their mouths.

Repetitious activity such as waving the arms and kicking the legs usually includes both limbs simultaneously and provides babies with feedback about the consequences of their actions. Over the next few months, reaching becomes much more coordinated, and by 5 months of age, most infants are reaching in a directed fashion toward objects. The more sophisticated reaching behaviors demonstrated in the last half of the first year are called *visually directed reaching*, because most often reaching is motivated when the baby wants to touch or hold something she sees (Fig. 2.8).

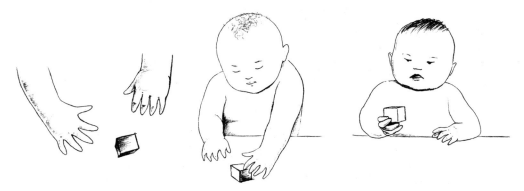

FIG. 2.8. Visually directed reaching. Reaching begins when infants reach with both hands for whatever they see. Soon smaller objects are approached with just one hand, and the hand shape begins to mirror the size and shape of the object before contact.

Visually directed reaching most often begins as a *bilateral reach*, as both arms stretch forward in response to interesting sights. Gradually the infant learns to use each arm separately and will demonstrate a *unilateral reach*, using only the one arm that is free or closest to the object. Close attention to the development of reaching behaviors shows that early in the sequence, babies will contact an object with their hands before opening the fingers. As infants gain experience with reaching and grasping, the hands assume the size and shape of the object as they reach for it, *before* contact, presumably based on a combination of the visual characteristics of the object and baby's experience with manipulating objects (Bower, 1977a). Voluntary control of reaching and grasping indicates that myelination has progressed from the spinal cord along the arms to the palms of the hands and along to the tips of the fingers. Being in command of reaching and grasping means that a 1-year-old baby has direct access to the physical environment for self-directed exploration and learning.

Using the Hands

By the time infants are 1 year old, they are quite adept at grasping, holding, releasing, manipulating, and transferring large and small objects. Let's explore the process by which the fisted, passive hands of the newborn develop in 1 year to become capable of such precise and mature maneuvers. As with gross motor abilities, the development of grasping skills typically proceeds according to a predictable sequence. Control of the hand and fingers develops from the outside, or *ulnar side*, of the hand toward the thumb and forefinger, or *radial side*, and from the palm to the tips of the fingers, or *palmar to digital control*, as shown in Fig. 2.9.

For the first few months of life, infants watch their hands move in and out of their visual field as they would any other object. They will move their eyes to follow the movement of their own hands by about 3 months of age and will hold rattles or small blocks placed in their palms for a short period of time. Babies can be enchanted by their own fingers during the next month or 2, engaging for extended periods of time in finger play and beginning to shake and bang as they hold onto objects for longer times. By 4 to 6 months of age, babies have figured out that hands and fingers can be used as tools to retrieve and manipulate items. They can be observed to gaze at and actively grasp toys placed within their reach, bring objects to their mouths, hold two little things at once, bang them together at the midline, and transfer things from one hand to the other and back again. Table 2.3 lists some of the major accomplishments in the fine motor domain during the first year of life.

Early Grasping

Hand-sized items such as blocks and small toys are first picked up by using the outside fingers to scrape the item into the palm (Fig. 2.10), whereas tiny items such as cereal and raisins are approached with the same fingers in a raking and scratching motion (Fig. 2.11). As control of the fingers advances toward the thumb and forefinger, the middle fingers become the most active in both raking smaller items and picking up hand-sized toys. By the age of 7 months, most typically developing infants will approach and hold a small block or rattle with the thumb and forefinger against

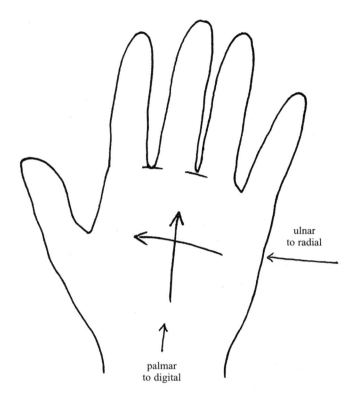

FIG. 2.9. Using the hands. A child's control over grasping develops from the palm of the hand outward to the fingers (palmar-digital) and from the little finger toward the thumb (ulnar-radial).

TABLE 2.3

Fine Motor Development Milestones

Keeps hands open when awake	2 to 3 months
Bats and swipes at objects	2 to 4 months
Reaches for objects	3 to 6 months
Grasps hand-sized objects	3 to 6 months
Transfers objects from hand to hand	5 to 6 months
Reaches across midline	5 to 6 months
Grasps tiny objects with thumb and forefinger	8 to 12 months

the palm. More mature command of the fingers is demonstrated by 8 months, as infants begin to point and begin trying to pick up tiny items with their thumbs and forefingers.

By their first birthdays, most babies are becoming adept at picking up small objects of all sorts between the tips of their first fingers and thumbs in a *pincer grasp* (Fig. 2.11), with the hand resting on the adjacent surface. The smooth motion of thumb and forefinger toward bits of food on the high-chair tray or little remnants on

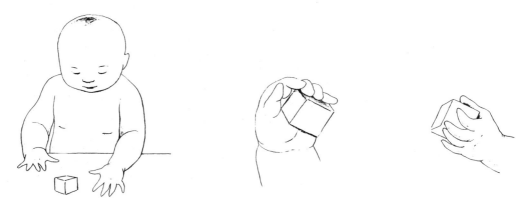

FIG. 2.10.   Grasping hand-sized objects. Babies first capture objects by "sweeping" their hand along a surface to grasp the object between their palm and the outer fingers, and later develop a more mature grasp between the thumb and first two fingers.

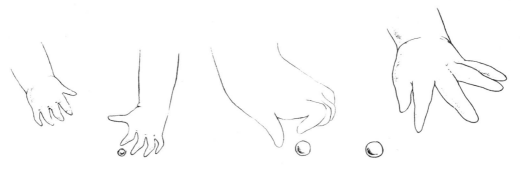

FIG. 2.11.   Pincer grasp. Infants initially approach tiny objects by scratching at them, then learn to use their thumb and the side of their forefinger. A mature pincer grasp involves use of the thumb and the tip of the forefinger.

the floor marks the culmination of radial-digital control in the hands. This developmental milestone can also cause anxiety for caregivers if babies use their precise pincer grasps to put all sorts of little objects indiscriminately into their mouths.

Variations in Motor Development

Observers in Western cultures expect to see 1-year-old infants engaged in the types of activities represented in timeless media images and countless family photographs. Older infants move smoothly and with confidence from one position to another and are equally comfortable in sustaining lying, sitting, and upright postures. One minute finds them engrossed with putting small plastic items into containers and dumping them out over and over; the next minute they are moving quickly around the room in search of new adventures. A typically developing 1-year-old child is already in possession of an array of gross and fine motor skills believed to form a solid foundation for problem solving, play, self-care, and academic endeavors of toddlerhood and preschool.

Babies have a new perspective on the world when they begin to stand upright and move about on their own. The age at which children begin to walk independently varies greatly.

The immense variability in development of early motor skills is obvious to even the most casual observers of infants and reflected in the age ranges for successful performance of specific items on developmental tests. For example, early independent walking skills fall between 12 and 18 months across a number of tests (Cohen, Gross, & Haring, 1976) depending on exact criteria and the groups of children with whom the tests were developed. Most people who work with babies know some tiny ones who have begun walking by 8 months of age and others who are well past their first birthdays before taking independent steps. The 8-month-olds are not necessarily gifted; more likely they are motivated and encouraged to be upright and mobile and are easily successful at gross motor skills. Similarly, the 14-month-olds are probably not exhibiting developmental delays; in all likelihood their interests and experiences have provided them with early success in language, social, and fine motor skills. Similar typical variations in the acquisition of early motor skills can be observed in development of head control, sitting, rolling, standing, cruising, visually directed reaching, and use of the hands for grasping. By the time children are 2 years old, it is impossible to tell whether they walked at 8 or 15 months or began to use a fine pincer grasp at 10 or 14 months.

An additional aspect of variability in infant motor development emerges from the meanings that caregivers attach to increased competence in movement. Walking, for instance, is presented in this chapter as the logical next step in a biologically based process of myelination from head to feet. What it means for a child to begin walking, however, varies among cultural and family contexts. Walking may be perceived as a positive milestone that reflects cultural values of independence and individuality or as a mere matter of convenience in families with new babies who also need to be carried. Walking might also increase risk of injury and mean extra supervision to protect from dangers in the immediate environment as illustrated in Vignette 2.2. In some cultures, tradition dictates that the movements of infants should be restricted in order to promote social bonding and attention to spiritual over physical events (Lake, 1990). In other cultures, walking is taken as an important passage from infancy to childhood and is associated with expectations that the child will also be more able to learn and communicate. Each child's caregiving environment, therefore, shapes both opportunities and expectations for early motor behaviors within the general parameters defined by biology and heredity.

Vignette 2.2: *Motor Development in an Alaskan Village*

I had the wonderful opportunity a few years ago to observe developmental screening assessments in a Native Alaskan village on an island in the Bering Sea between Alaska and Russia. During the late June week of my visit, the sun shone almost 24 hours a day, close to a foot of snow covered the ground, and everyone was anticipating the break up of the sea ice that had completely surrounded the island since early winter.

After seeing a number of infants who came to the clinic with their mothers and grandmothers, the assessors became concerned that youngsters in this village did not seem to be pushing up on their arms in prone lying, rolling over, sitting independently, crawling, or walking at the expected ages. The measured "delays" in motor development were not at all congruent with the alert, lively, and proficient performance of the babies on fine motor, social, and cognitive items. Caregivers were consistently unconcerned and portrayed the infants as "still practicing" the movements in question.

An explanation for this seemingly peculiar pattern in the attainment of movement skills surfaced quickly when one mother was asked if her 6-month-old had the opportunity to spend much time on the floor on her stomach. The incredulous, horrified reactions of all the native women present were clear signs that the Anglo test administrators were abundantly uninformed about the life ways of the village! Further description of the baby's home environment revealed that the floors of houses built on blocks above the permafrost were frigid and fraught with sharp knives and other dangers of indoor preparation of meat during the long winter months.

Before they could walk, all babies were held, carried on adults' backs inside parkas or snuggled in beds. Only the most negligent of caregivers would even consider placing infants on the floor! And so it was that most infants in the village developed gross motor skills during the short summer months, and we learned that developmental assessments, at least in the motor domain, were best conducted in the fall. (Kris Slentz)

More extreme variations in infant motor development are associated with specific conditions that cause delays or divergence from patterns and sequences of movement. As indicated earlier in this chapter, the movement patterns of younger babies are relatively limited in both number and quality, so early identification of motor disorders usually indicates extensive and pervasive disruptions in the development of rudimentary motor skills. Problems in the course of early motor development may originate in the *musculoskeletal system* of muscles, bones, joints, ligaments, and tendons or the *neuromotor system* that connects the brain and nerves to control movement.

Malformations of the musculoskeletal system are often identified at birth or shortly after. About 1 in 1,000 babies is born with one or both feet twisted inward and upward, a condition with the scientific name *talipes equinovarus*, commonly known as *clubfoot*. These infants are placed in leg casts from the very first days of life to gradually reposition the feet and sometimes require corrective surgery between 4 and 6 months of age. *Achondroplasia*, or *short-limbed dwarfism*, is diagnosed when children are born with disproportionately short upper arm and thighbones and unusually large heads and trunks relative to the rest of the body. Dwarfism occurs relatively rarely (1 in 10,000 births), and although surgical and hormonal treatments are available, they are rarely effective in increasing growth of the short bones (Dormans & Batshaw, 1997). Motor development is delayed for infants who must wear heavy casts, and the discomfort following surgery interferes with rolling, sitting, and standing. Disproportionately larger heads are even more difficult to control, and shortened limbs present difficulties for weight bearing and balance. Because clubfoot and dwarfism are disorders of the muscles and bones only, infants with these conditions generally have intact central nervous systems and typical cognitive development.

The most common early diagnosis involving the neuromuscular system is *cerebral palsy*. Cerebral palsy includes a range of movement disorders that result from lesions or abnormalities in the part of the brain that controls motor functions. The brain injuries that cause cerebral palsy most often occur before birth but may also result from head injuries or illnesses in young children. It seems that a wide variety of sources can cause damage to the motor cortex, including all of the causes of disability covered in chapter 1. Cerebral palsy is nonprogressive, meaning that the brain injury itself does not get worse over time. However, as the central nervous system matures, the impact of cerebral palsy on voluntary movement becomes more and more obvious. Premature infants who weigh less than 1500 grams are at especially high risk for cerebral palsy and are usually monitored closely. Other possible indications are tightly fisted hands after 3 months of age, the persistence of primitive reflexes past 1 year of age, asymmetrical movement patterns, delayed walking, and a marked preference for use of one hand before 18 months (Pelligrino, 1997).

The diagnosis of cerebral palsy describes a wide range of movement and posture problems affecting different parts of the body, and two infants with cerebral palsy can manifest very different motor abilities. Special terms are used as shorthand to describe both the types of movement patterns and the limbs involved. *Spasticity* is a type of cerebral palsy characterized by tight or rigid muscle tone (*hypertonia*), resulting in taut flexion or contraction of the body parts affected. Babies with spastic cerebral palsy hold their hands, arms, legs, or trunks or any combination of these folded tightly together or stiffly straight and rigid. Their tiny muscles are incapable of the smooth, finely graded sequences of extension and flexion necessary for typical patterns of reaching, grasping, sitting, and standing. Shifting weight is also problematic and prevents development of balance and the usual protective mechanisms of extending the arms to protect against falling from sitting, standing, and walking positions.

If only the legs are affected, the child is said to have spastic *diplegia*, whereas dysfunction of the arm and leg on one side of the body is called *hemiplegia*. Involvement of all four limbs, trunk, and often lips and tongue is termed spastic *quadriplegia* and may compromise speech as well as movement. Figure 2.12 illustrates the more common patterns of limb involvement in cerebral palsy. More severe forms of cerebral palsy are often diagnosed in infancy, with provision of physical, occupational, and speech therapy, singularly or in combination, from the first months of life. Individualized programs of positioning and handling allow caregivers to facilitate typical movement patterns, improve range of motion, and maximize interaction with both social and physical environments.

Other types of cerebral palsy include extremely low (*hypotonia*) muscle tone and involuntary movements involving the entire body. The random actions of newborns appear to persist when babies with *athetoid cerebral palsy* begin trying to use their arms and legs for purposeful activity. Fluctuating muscle tone dominates little arms and legs, causing unintentional movement that vacillates between rapid jerking and slow writhing.

Infants who experience cerebral palsy exhibit a wide range of functional abilities. Some babies learn to reach, grasp, sit, stand, and walk with characteristic jerky and

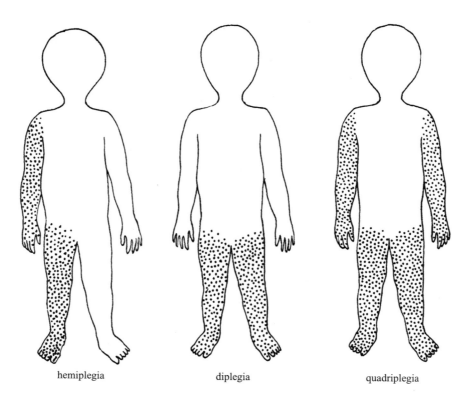

hemiplegia   diplegia   quadriplegia

FIG. 2.12.   Cerebral palsy. Patterns of limb involvement and associated labels of cerebral palsy.

awkward movements; other little ones need specialized equipment to facilitate sitting, standing, and walking and may be unable to master voluntary reaching and grasping. Because malformations in one area of the brain are associated with irregularities elsewhere in the brain, cerebral palsy often co-occurs with mental retardation, sensory impairments, and seizure disorders.

Early childhood educators are likely to encounter infants with a variety of motor disabilities or movement disorders. Early diagnosis is critical for the identification of special service options and coordination of therapeutic treatments for motor disabilities in infancy. Early intervention services usually focus on the characteristics of the child and on beneficial accommodations and alterations in caregiving practices. Infants who have difficulties controlling their bodies, moving around, and manipulating objects are at increased risk for delayed development in cognition and social interactions because of the underlying physical components of early cognitive and social skills. As you read the following sections, notice the many ways in which specific motor skills support the development of infant cognition and social-affective growth.

INFANT COGNITIVE DEVELOPMENT: LEARNING ABOUT THE WORLD

The relatively sophisticated manipulation and mobility skills of a typically developing 1-year-old are inextricably linked with the process of learning about people, objects, and events. Reaching and grasping, for instance, are of little intrinsic value in isolation; it is the exploration of interesting objects and the pleasant interplay with familiar people that provide early learning opportunities. By the age of 1 year, babies use their motor skills to interact with familiar caregivers, to investigate toys, and to make interesting things happen in their immediate environments. They recognize familiar people, associate specific activities with daily routines, imitate new actions, find partially hidden objects, and are beginning to use word symbols to communicate.

The Nature of Infant Intelligence

It is fairly obvious that infants do not comprehend the world in the same way that adults do, nor do they appear to understand their surroundings as preschoolers do. Because adults do not remember their own infancies, theories of infant intelligence are based on observation and interpretation of infant behavior. The most thorough and detailed description of the growth of infant cognition is contained in the theories of Jean Piaget (1896–1980).

Piaget described the type of intellect operating between birth and 18 months of age as *sensorimotor cognition*. The term connotes that infants learn about their surroundings through an interactive combination of sensory information and motor activity. From this perspective, infant cognition is considered to be an action-oriented endeavor rather than the abstract thought processes that comprise intelligence in older children and adults. Piaget's theory explains *assimilation* as the incorporation of new information through simple early action *schema*, such as looking, touching, holding, and sucking. New sights, sounds, tastes, smells, and textures challenge the baby's existing behavioral repertoire, creating an atmosphere of *disequilibrium* because of the discrepancy between prior knowledge and new information. The baby resolves these discrepancies through a process of *accommodation*, experimenting with more sophisticated and diverse motor actions in response to new sensory experiences. Learning occurs as infants develop more effective movement patterns, which in turn generate successively more diverse, independent, and efficient sensory and motor experiences.

A quick review of visually directed reaching illustrates Piaget's theory nicely. A baby activates a simple batting and swiping scheme in response to toys or mobiles within the field of vision, and random contact causes the object to move. Additional sensory input is furnished by the hands, and more sophisticated visual tracking is required as the toy moves. The infant assimilates increasingly complex tactile and visual information and accommodates by gradually refining accuracy of his reach. Once he can reliably control reaching with each hand, the shapes and sizes of the objects continue to provide new visual and tactile cues that prompt accommodation of hand position and placement to match what he sees.

Infant Sensory Capabilities

An earlier section of this chapter summarized the sensory capabilities of newborns as providing an excellent foundation for learning and for social interaction. As babies grow, their visual and auditory skills develop in synchrony with motor and social abilities. Vision and hearing are especially critical for early cognitive development and have been studied extensively in laboratory settings by infant researchers. Documented changes over time in infant visual and auditory responses correspond fairly well with the sequence of cognitive development proposed by Piaget.

Vision

Research on visual preferences of infants is based on the supposition that babies look longest at things they prefer most (Flavell et al., 1993). The features of the human face seem to capture the attention of babies more often than just about any other form, probably because the patterns of contour, contrast, and movement in facial features come into the limited visual range of babies more often than other objects. From an early age, babies also seem to recognize the faces of familiar caregivers. For the first 2 months of life, infants tend to direct their attention to the outer edges of objects, scanning in a somewhat random fashion around the boundaries of contrast and contour, focusing for only a couple seconds at a time on any given point (Haith, 1980). Babies this young will also track objects moving horizontally and vertically by following with their eyes as the person or toy moves. This type of visual attention is commonly observed during caregiving activities like feeding, bathing, and changing, when the adults and infants are oriented and interacting face to face. Alert little eyes are clearly focused on the adult's face but appear to glance quickly around the perimeter, looking most at the hairline and chin.

At about 2 months of age, a significant change occurs in the scanning patterns of most infants. They begin to focus their attention for longer periods of time and on the inner features of an object, looking more closely, for example, at a caregiver's eyes and mouth (Haith, 1980). By 3 months of age, typically developing babies are combining head control with visual tracking, turning their heads smoothly to follow objects moving in all directions. They also begin to shift attention from one object to another, for instance, from an adult's face to a toy and back again. As a consequence of more sophisticated focusing, scanning, and tracking skills, 3- to 6-month-old infants are able to use vision as a tool for exploring and learning about their surroundings. Visual acuity gradually increases with voluntary control of facial muscles, but a child's visual acuity continues to develop until 3 or 4 years of age (Boothe, Dobson, & Teller, 1985). The seemingly effortless hand–eye coordination of sighted 1-year-olds using visually directed reaching and pincer grasps reflects elaborate refinement of both sensory and motor skills.

Hearing

Infants seem to enjoy the sound of human voices and will orient their attention toward someone speaking. Initially, a calm voice might result in an overall quieting and gradual turning of the newborn's head toward the sound, and many caregivers instinctively use calm and melodic tones to soothe fussy babies. Infants seem able to discriminate between speech sounds and nonspeech sounds long before they begin to produce the sounds of their native tongues, suggesting to some researchers a preexisting cognitive structure that supports language development (Chomsky, 1988). Very young infants can recognize differences in speech sounds from many languages, including subtle variations in sounds never produced by native speakers in the child's environment.

By 4 or 5 months of age, babies who can hear will turn their heads immediately and accurately to locate the source of a voice or sound, and those who cannot see begin to use sound to locate objects (Bower, 1977b). Noise-making toys hold special appeal for little ones, who can watch and listen simultaneously, using both visual and auditory cues to learn more about their surroundings.

Other Senses

There are fewer studies that address the capabilities of infants to taste and smell, but available research indicates that babies are able to discriminate sour, bitter, salty, and sweet tastes, with a general preference for sweetness (Crook, 1987). Some of the most impressive capabilities of infants have been revealed by experiments that investigate *intermodal transfer*, or the ability of babies to combine and make sense of simultaneous information from sight, sound, and touch (Meltzoff & Kuhl, 1994). Presented with pictures of both parents and a recording of one voice, infants will look consistently toward the picture that matches the voice. Even more impressively, babies as young as 1 month of age have demonstrated visual discriminations based on tactile cues, looking longer at pictures that portray smooth or textured pacifiers they have sucked on previously (Meltzoff & Borton, 1979). Although similar studies

Infants use all their senses to
learn about the world.

with very young infants have not always produced consistent results, there is over-
whelming evidence that by 6 months of age, typically developing infants can consistently transfer and combine information across sight, sound, and touch. Any baby
who picks up a toy, looks at it, shakes it to make a noise, mouths it, and then looks at
it again is demonstrating the integrated use of simultaneous sensory cues.

Becoming Intentional

Infant intelligence has been defined as an iterative process of using sensory input to
direct and refine motor output, resulting in a distinctly immediate, concrete, and
action-oriented means of understanding one's surroundings. What gives rise to higher order mental processes such as memory, logic, and early problem solving that
characterize the thinking of preschoolers? How do babies, by their first birthdays,
recognize specific patterns of sound (words) as representing objects, people, and
events? Piaget's observations of infants led him to hypothesize a series of six substages in the development of cognition between reflexive action and symbolic
thought (Table 2.4), with the first four substages corresponding roughly to the first
12 months of life (Piaget, 1952, 1954). He believed that very young children progressed from reflex and repetition to intention, coordination, and complex combinations of actions and finally to mental representations in all areas of early learning.
Piaget applied his theories of cognitive development across a range of distinct areas
of learning, or *domains* (Table 2.5): knowledge of objects, cause and effect,
means–ends, imitation of gestures and sounds, problem solving, and spatial relations.

   Piaget's perspective on infant intelligence has been criticized as underestimating
the abilities of babies to store, organize, and recall information and also for neglect-

TABLE 2.4

Piaget's Stages of Sensorimotor Development

Piaget's Substage	Age Range	Description
1. Reflexive activity	Birth to 1 month	Automatic, immediate, involuntary responses to sensory events. Example: Babies blink at bright lights, startle at loud noises, and suck on a nipples/fingers.
2. Primary circular reactions	1 to 4 months	Repetitive simple movements or vocalizations that create pleasurable sensations. Example: Babies repeatedly bring their hands to their mouths and suck their fingers.
3. Secondary circular reactions	4 to 8 months	Intentional reproductions of simple actions involving other people or objects, to create interesting or pleasurable effects. Example: Babies kick or bat at crib mobiles to make them move.
4. Coordinated circular reactions	8 to 12 months	Coordinated series of simple actions to produce a desired outcome; the beginnings of cause and effect. Example: Babies bang toys on their cribs and holler to get the attention of their caregivers.
5. Tertiary circular reactions	12 to 18 months	Complex novel actions to solve problems and explore; the beginnings of trial-and-error learning. Example: Toddlers climb on whatever might be handy if they can't reach something they want.
6. Mental combinations	18 to 24 months	Mental images used to solve problems; the beginnings of thinking in addition to action. Example: Older toddlers can tell by looking (or remembering) if something is out of reach and will get something to climb on without trial and error.

ing social components of the environment. Subsequent research has challenged the coherence and invariant nature of the *sensorimotor* stages Piaget described (Fischer, 1980; Aslin, 1998), refined understanding of cognitive sequences (Meltzoff, 1988), and applied tenets of the theory to social interaction (Uzgiris, 1973). Alternate theories of early cognition address the evolution of specific skill sequences and apply an information processing model (Flavell et al., 1993). More recent theoretical perspectives are not necessarily inconsistent with major conclusions of Piaget's theories but can instead be interpreted as refinements in understanding the nature, acquisition, and functional use of particular cognitive skills. Piaget's explanations have held up surprisingly well to empirical scrutiny and are presented here as the most cogent and congruent description of the processes and sequences through which babies acquire knowledge about the world around them.

Reflexive Activity (Birth to 1 Month)

Piaget observed patterns of infant motor activity to be governed by reflexes for the first month of life. Simple schema of looking and sucking, for instance, are activated by visual and tactile stimuli, respectively. Jerky movements of the arms and legs are likewise elicited by rapid changes in the position of the baby's head and by loud

TABLE 2.5

Piaget's Domains of Sensorimotor Development

Sensorimotor Domain	Brief Description
Knowledge of objects	Understanding of the permanence and properties of objects; being able to find hidden objects. Necessary to figure out the functional, socially appropriate uses of objects in the environment.
Cause and effect	Recognition that certain actions produce specific effects; being able to make things happen. Necessary to explore objects and become an active social partner.
Means–ends	Use of objects, or parts of objects, for a specific end; being able to use tools. Necessary for using utensils to eat, crayons to write, little buttons to activate wind-up toys, faucets to turn on water, and doorknobs to open doors.
Spatial relations	Awareness of space, size, and volume; being able to work in both horizontal and vertical planes. Necessary for movement through space, construction, understanding of prepositions.
Imitation of gestures and sounds	Reproduction of the actions and vocalizations of others; being able to copy speech sounds, wave bye-bye when shown how. A powerful skill for efficient learning of language, motor and social skills.
Problem solving	Use of multiple methods to solve problems of learning and living; being able to generate new approaches. Another powerful skill for effective exploration, examination, and negotiation of the social and physical environments.

noises. The relationship of sensory input and motor output at this earliest juncture is immediate and automatic and entirely consistent with what was presented in the section on reflex activity earlier in the chapter.

In Piaget's (1954) view, inborn reflexive responses provide the foundation for simple patterns of movement that are modified from the beginning of life by sensory experiences. Babies seem not to pay much attention during the first few weeks of life to the actual sights, sounds, and textures of their environments or to the consequences of their own actions. It is as if each action is separate from the next in space and time, directed by internal cues rather than the particular events that provide sensory information. Soon enough, however, the outcomes of simple schema capture babies' attention.

Primary Circular Reactions (1 to 4 Months)

During the first few months of life, babies experience a number of pleasurable results from reflexive activity. Scanning the edges of faces and objects provides engaging visual events, especially from the facial expressions of attentive caregivers. Contact between infants' own hands and cheeks often produces the opportunities for sucking thumbs or fingers. Holding objects placed in tiny palms can occasion interesting sights and sounds. Although the objects themselves seem to hold little interest at this point, infants begin to organize movement to produce and prolong specific sensory experiences.

Repetition of simple actions is the hallmark of motor activity by the age of 4 months: bringing hands to mouth for the sake of oral stimulation; waving, banging, and shaking rattles for the sake of the action; kicking for the sake of kicking. Voluntary control of movement allows production of more complex movement schema. For example, reaching and grasping provides multiple opportunities for infants to initiate motor activity that results in exciting sensory experiences. Sucking comes to serve a self-soothing function to be continued purposefully, and babies quickly learn to kick or wave to produce movement from a mobile, sound from a noise-making toy, or social interaction from a caregiver.

Secondary Circular Reactions (4 to 8 Months)

After months of engaging in a wide variety of repetitious motor activities, the focus of infants' attention seems to shift front their own actions to the objects, events, and people in their surroundings. Babies begin to integrate visual, tactile, and auditory information, and movement becomes increasingly intentional as specific actions become associated with certain outcomes. Fussing, smiling, and vocalizing, for instance, might result in a nice interaction with an adult but are not likely to activate a toy. Conversely, waving and banging a toy will get visual and auditory results from the toy, but these are probably not as pleasurable as smiling and reaching when interacting with a caregiver.

The most important cognitive transition around the middle of the first year seems to be that infants begin to make connections between their own actions and happenings in the environment. They begin to use their hands as tools for finger feeding and become interested in toys such as busy boxes that require a variety of different actions to produce consistently different visual, auditory, and tactile outcomes. Eight-month-old babies will use their voices to capture adult attention, hold up their arms to be picked up, and snatch a cloth repeatedly from a caregiver's face during peekaboo but employ a totally different series of actions in play with toys. Babies of this age are also beginning to match particular actions with specific objects after some trial and error, such as hugging stuffed animals, banging drums, and mouthing teething rings, rather than using the same series of schema indiscriminately on all objects.

Coordinated Circular Reactions (8 to 12 Months)

In the last quarter of the first year, infants typically become adept at combining actions in coordinated efforts to achieve particular ends. A pincer grasp formerly used primarily to pick up finger food from the tray of the high chair is pressed into service to activate a crib toy or to pick blocks from a container. Simple and separate schema for looking and touching are combined into more complex routines for examination of toys by grasping, turning, poking, and simultaneous visual exploration of separate features. Close attention to and multiple experiences with objects and people promote formation of the very first mental images, or internal representations, of toys, pets, and caregivers. Piaget labeled this phenomenon *object permanence* and emphasized the importance of these first mental pictures or thoughts as critical first steps toward symbolic thought and memory, enabling infants to comprehend the existence of objects and people separate from their own immediate sensory and motor experiences.

Babies in this period are actively engaged in exploring both the social and physical realms, applying their growing knowledge of objects and people to produce complex initiations and responses and to imitate new sounds and gestures. The baby who bangs toys against the crib or floor while hollering to attract the attention of an adult in the other room or who pulls at an adult's arm while pointing to a toy that is out of reach is demonstrating relatively sophisticated cognitive processes. This little one is confirming, by his or her actions, the existence of a mental image of the caregiver, as well as knowledge that both people and toys can be used as tools to achieve separate ends. In addition, the infant is demonstrating the ability to discriminate between the properties of objects and people and communicating a clear intent to cause a specific effect in the immediate environment.

By the time infants are 1 year of age, they have clearly differentiated strategies for intentional initiation, exploration, and responding within the immediate environment. Sensory perception is fully integrated with voluntary movement, positioning babies for the cognitive transition from action to thought that occurs between 12 and 18 months. Babies approaching their first birthdays are no longer content to be passive recipients of social and perceptual events. Instead, they have developed expectations for activities based on frequent associations, for example, the baby who expects to go for a ride in the car whenever he sees a parent holding car keys and putting on a coat. And whereas the 4-month-old infant did not seem to mind being picked up and moved around in tandem with the caregiver's timetable, the 1-year-old is not always tolerant of having activities interrupted, toys removed, or expectations violated. Parents and other adults who provide infant care echo Piaget's explanation of early cognitive development in the phrase, "All of a sudden this baby has a mind of her own."

Variations in Infant Cognitive Development

Impairments in movement, vision, and hearing can clearly have a negative impact on the development of voluntary movement schema. Infants with *congenital* vision and hearing disorders may be unable to make use of visual or auditory cues, and infants with motor disabilities are often compromised to some extent in the development of voluntary movement. Early intervention and therapy services are designed to evaluate in detail each baby's level of functional abilities, provide typical movement experiences, and maximize alternative sources of sensory input. For example, parents and teachers of blind infants learn to watch the baby's hands instead of facial expressions and to provide tactile and auditory cues when presenting toys and interacting (Fraiberg, 1977).

Infants who spend the first few weeks or months of life in the intensive care nursery, especially if they have immature central nervous systems, may be bombarded with more visual, auditory, and tactile stimulation than they can assimilate (Goldberg & DeVitto, 1982). These infants sometimes appear to cope by falling asleep or shutting down and blocking out all sensory input. Caregivers may need to alter their practices to recognize atypical infant cues and provide responses that make use of each baby's sensory and motor strengths.

Babies with motor and sensory disabilities often need continued intervention to encourage the development of intentional activity within their immediate environments. The best results are obtained for infants whose surroundings are responsive to their early attempts to have an impact on people and events and continue to ensure rich sensory input and feedback that is useful to the child. Some disabilities such as Down syndrome result in atypical brain structure and function and compromise infants' abilities to pay attention to, remember, or make associations between their actions and the results on toys and people. Again, specialized early instruction for babies with cognitive delays can provide more frequent opportunities within daily caregiving routines to focus attention and develop intention in motor activity.

Babies who have sensory impairments must assimilate information from their environments without the availability of visual or auditory input or both, a distinct disadvantage for the development of sensorimotor skills. Exploring the properties of objects and developing object permanence are especially likely to be delayed in the absence of visual cues, as well as visual tracking and visually directed reaching. Early identification and intervention of motor and sensory disabilities provides resources for adaptations and modifications in caregiving practices, toys, and equipment that offer alternative avenues for sensory input and movement. Specialized care practices, informed by careful assessment of neurological status, support gradual introduction of appropriate amounts of stimulation as the baby matures.

INFANT SOCIAL-AFFECTIVE DEVELOPMENT: BECOMING A SOCIAL PARTNER

Although limited in the number and types of behaviors they exhibit, babies are uniquely equipped from birth to engage in social interactions and garner the affection of adults responsible for their care. Observations of mothers with their newborns show uniform patterns of interaction across cultures and across first and subsequent births. In the first moments of new life, mothers tend to touch their babies gently and talk in quiet, excited tones about how the infant looks and acts (MacFarlane, 1977). The birth of a child is also the birth of new social relationships between infants and parents, siblings, grandparents, other extended family members, and friends, all within the cultural context of the family. Each family's routine of daily caregiving activities forms the backdrop against which infants develop relationships, with earliest interactions centering around biologically based schedules for eating and sleeping.

Sleep–Wake States

Parents in our culture expect that usual adult sleeping schedules will be disrupted when there is a new baby in the house. New mothers and fathers often experience sleep deprivation despite the fact that the average newborn sleeps an average of 16 to 18 hours out of 24. Caregivers' sleep patterns are disturbed because at birth infants sleep for only 3 to 4 hours at a stretch and because these short periods of sleep are dispersed indiscriminately throughout daytime and nighttime hours (Minde, 1998).

In most families, caregiving practices encourage infants to sleep more often during the night and less during the daytime, beginning in the first few months of life. On the average, 6-month-olds sleep for 6 hours at a time, waking for shorter periods

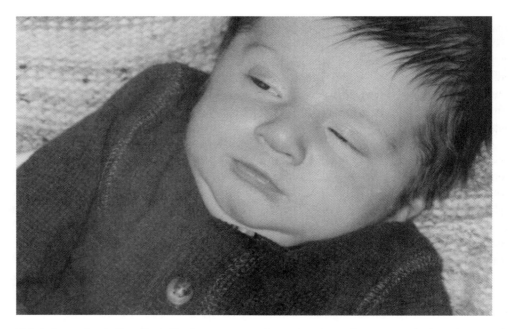

This infant, who is literally half asleep, was awake and active only moments before the picture was taken, and quietly sleeping seconds later.

in the night, with longer waking periods and frequent but brief naps during the day. Twelve-month-olds still sleep almost as many hours of the day as newborns, but their sleep patterns reflect daily schedules of families and rhythms of light and dark. They are most often awake during daytime hours, except for morning and afternoon naps, and asleep for the duration of the night (Anders, Goodlin-Jones, & Zelenko, 1998).

It is easy to determine if older children are asleep, awake, getting sleepy, or just waking up, but things are not so clear with newborns who shift quickly and abruptly from one *sleep–wake state* to another. Table 2.6 describes each state and the associated patterns of activity, breathing, responsiveness, and facial movement first described

TABLE 2.6

Infant Sleep–Wake States

Sleep–Wake State	Description
Quiet sleep	Eyes closed, little or no movement, regular and slow breathing; quiet and restful.
Active sleep (REM sleep)	Eyes closed, twitchy movements of face, eyes, and limbs; may whimper, grimace, fuss; increased brain activity.
Drowsiness	Still and quiet but eyes periodically open and close; easily aroused by movement and stimulation.
Awake and alert	Eyes open, breathing even, little movement; quiet and attentive.
Awake and active	Eyes open, moderate movement of limbs and face, breathing faster; less attentive.
Fussing/crying	Eyes often squinted or shut, breathing rapid and uneven, limbs move rapidly and jerkily; loud and distressed.

by Wolff in 1966 and since modified by numerous researchers. At birth, the entire cycle of quiet sleep to active sleep to quiet wakefulness, alert wakefulness, and fussing or crying occurs every 1½ to 2 hours. One moment new babies will be awake, nursing vigorously and looking intently at the caregiver's face; the next they are in a deep sleep and no amount of gentle jiggling and touching can arouse them. And then without warning, and often just as the exhausted parent is climbing into bed, the same baby is awake and crying loudly.

After 1 month to 6 weeks, babies begin to exhibit predictable transitions across sleep–wake states, cycling more smoothly and gradually. Studies of infant sleep show that babies experience both active and quiet sleep in alternating periods throughout the night, with the relative amount of active sleep decreasing during the first year of life (Anders et al., 1998). About 70% of parents report that their babies sleep through the night by 3 months and 75% to 90% of families have uninterrupted sleep by the time their infants are 9 months old (Minde, 1998). In actuality, all babies appear to wake up for brief periods a few times each night and either fall back to sleep on their own or cry out for a caregiver. In the majority of families, routines for night awakenings become less interactive and more perfunctory over time, resulting in shorter periods of wakefulness in the night and a shift from crying to self-soothing as babies get older (Anders et al., 1998).

Babies who sleep more at night are awake more during the day, providing increased time for play and interaction. Crying occurs often in the evening at first and gradually comes to signal that the infant is hungry or uncomfortable. Before the middle of the first year, parents of typically developing infants can identify different-sounding cries of their own babies for hunger, anger, boredom, and fear (Wiesfield, Malatesta, & DeLoach, 1981). Periods of quiet alertness increase in length as infants mature, allowing sustained attention to toys and increasing opportunities for parents to get to know their newest family members.

The interaction between individual differences and caregiving practices is particularly evident in the observation of state-related behaviors. Some infants exhibit intense, predictable, and for caregivers, seemingly interminable periods of crying every evening and during the night. Other wee ones are allowing the household 10 hours of uninterrupted sleep by 2 months of age. Many babies like to catnap during the day; others take long naps morning and evening. Although central nervous system maturation seems to control to a great degree the ability of infants to sleep longer periods, bedtime and middle-of-the-night routines are also clearly important factors in shaping sleep habits. Infants who learn to expect a play session after each night-waking, for instance, are more likely to signal for a parent's attention. Babies born prematurely are more likely to have disorganized sleep–wake cycles or cries that caregivers describe as unpleasantly high pitched or both. In families who have reasonably consistent daily routines and stable caregiving interactions, most babies will begin to develop predictable schedules for eating and sleeping by the age of 3 months. Infant cycles of sleep and wakefulness often determine the household schedule, as illustrated by Vignette 2.3, contributed by Dana Brown, who was a graduate assistant at the same time she was a new mother.

Vignette 2.3: *Newborn Sleep–Wake States*

If I have learned anything over the past 2 months of being a new mom it is that sleep is an essential and valuable commodity that I have until now taken for granted. More important, it is an activity that determines the outcome of my entire day, along with that of my baby. Before entering the field of education, I thought that the term sleep–wake states simply referred to the periods of time when a baby slept or was awake. However, after reading about child development, I quickly learned that the definition of sleep–wake states *involves alternating periods of quiet and activity, degrees of sleep and wakefulness, with occasional fussing and crying thrown in for good measure. All of this terminology really confused me until I had a baby and was able to associate each period with what I was capable of doing. You see:*

Quiet sleep *actually means the period in which I can vacuum or take a shower. White noise is okay, and there is some time.*

Active sleep *actually means the period in which I can sit quietly but* not *walk around. Any little thing will wake him up.*

Drowsiness *actually means the period in which I can do laundry or homework. I'm quiet if I want him to sleep and can make noise if I want him to be awake.*

Quiet wakefulness *actually means those precious moments when all his attention is focused on me. He's just happy.*

Alert wakefulness *actually means the period in which we get a 10-minute warning with periodic grunts and lots of restless movement before fussy and crying.*

Fussing/crying *actually means DROP EVERYTHING AND ATTEND TO THE BABY!*

Caregiver–Infant Interactions

Because milestones such as smiling and waving have little meaning outside the context of relationships, any discussion of infant development in the social domain must include caregivers. Mothers and fathers are usually the primary caregivers for newborns, but very young infants are increasingly being cared for by relatives or in childcare centers. Your future role as an early childhood professional might well include providing care for very young infants, so the term *caregiver* can apply to you and your colleagues as well as to parents.

At the moment of birth, the nature of an infant's relationship to other people changes from a biological to a social connection. The vast majority of babies do not have to learn to be social, because the sensory capabilities described earlier in the chapter predispose them to be responsive to the voices, faces, and touches of their parents. Conversely, most parents seem to be equally well prepared, without specific training, to appreciate and accommodate the unique qualities of their infants. Babies who are fed when they are hungry, changed or bathed or both when wet or soiled, and clothed for the weather learn that their basic needs will be taken care of consistently. Infants also become aware that their own behaviors have an impact on people and events in their surroundings.

Erik Erikson (1902–1994) believed that developing a sense of trust in the first year of life was a critical first stage in the psychosocial development of children. From his perspective, infants need to acquire a basis of trust in the world as a predictable place and in their own abilities as an active social participant by age 1. Erikson (1963) describes the eventual development of a sense of trust or mistrust as being determined primarily by the consistency and quality of early caregiving practices. Irregular, unkind, or unreliable caregiving practices teach babies to expect confusion and harshness in their surroundings. The resultant foundation of mistrust of self and others, in Erikson's view, can hinder development of autonomy and initiative during the toddler and preschool years.

Other explanations of early infant social development have emphasized biological and interactive processes. Sander (1969) described early infancy as a time of biological regulation to the routines, schedules, and interactions of the family. Most professionals agree that both maturation and experiences shape the interactions that develop between infants and their caregivers. The word *interact* connotes that the baby and adult are acting on each other in a mutual and reciprocal fashion, so the characteristics of both contribute to the quality of the interaction.

Each infant initially contributes his or her unique disposition, temperament, physical status, patterns of sleep, and the clarity of their cues and signals for adult attention and care. Parent contributions to the interaction at the outset include temperament; physical status, knowledge, and attitudes about children and parenting; expectations for the baby; and their own history as children and parents. Responsive parents are also quite skilled at initiating and structuring caregiving and early play interactions until babies develop more sophisticated skills.

The anticipated result of countless interactions over the first few months of life is a warm and trusting relationship between adult and child, often referred to by the term *attachment*. Almost all books on early childhood development address the topic of attachment, and it makes intuitive sense that it is important for babies to develop special emotional bonds with their parents and other close caregivers, and vice versa. It is also fairly self-evident that the quality of any particular infant–caregiver relationship reflects a complex combination of constitutional, experiential, and situational variables for both adult and baby. Some babies are born into cultures that value independence and discourage close physical relationships; others grow up expecting affection to be expressed by hugging, holding, and kissing. Pregnancies may be planned or unplanned, joyous or stressful. Some parents have happy personalities, good health, and adequate financial resources to ease the changes that accompany a new family member. Others may have diagnoses of depression or chronic illnesses or live in poverty. And although most babies are healthy and spend their first weeks at home with their families, some have chronic illnesses or disabilities that require prolonged or repeated hospitalizations or both. The majority of infants, with and without disabilities, experience loving interactions with adults who provide care for them by the time they are 6 to 8 months old. A number of family circumstances, as well as characteristics of adults and babies can potentially disrupt the development of affectionate relationships.

There is a large and interesting body of literature on attachment, including a variety of theoretical perspectives and research results. Research studies on attachment often employ a series of structured laboratory episodes called the "strange-situation" to evaluate infants' patterns of toy exploration, reactions to strangers, separations from and reunions with caregivers (Ainsworth, Blehar, Waters, & Wall, 1978). Researchers observed very young children and their mothers in a room with interesting toys. Children's reactions were noted carefully as they played, when parents left and returned, and when strangers entered the room. Three patterns of attachment were originally identified through research (Table 2.7): secure attachments, resistant attachments, and avoidant attachments. Numerous subsequent studies have investigated the relationship between the quality of early attachment and developmental outcomes in areas such as academic achievement, social competence, and self-esteem.

A thorough reading of the literature on attachment reveals a number of divergent views on the subject. Although the term in popular literature indicates an emotional bond, other theoretical perspectives stress an evolutionary explanation for the close relationships between infants and caregivers; those infants who stayed close to their caregivers physically were most likely to survive (Bowlby, 1969). Another viewpoint explains attachment as a pattern of behaviors learned in response to the reinforcing aspects of feeding and comfort that caregivers provide; the caregiver becomes associated with positive feelings, and the baby wants to continue reinforcement (Sears, 1963). Another theory emphasizes advances in cognitive and perceptual capabilities that allow infants to form, discriminate, and manipulate mental representations of caregivers (Shaffer, 1999). This concept of *people permanence* in turn provides an organizing structure for infants to learn new information through close association with an adult who points out and explains the important aspects of babies' environments.

The strange-situation research paradigm has been criticized for placing undue stress on infant subjects, for focusing on mothers, for being culturally biased, and of being of limited utility after about 2 years of age (Shaffer, 1999). One author was skeptical about conclusions drawn from "the science of the strange behavior of children in strange situations with strange adults for the briefest possible periods of time" (Bronfenbrenner, 1977, p. 522). Rather than attempting to explore all sides of attachment theory or research in any detail, we instead highlight a sequence of specific social behaviors that are demonstrated by infants as participants in unique relationships with their caregivers.

TABLE 2.7

Categories of Attachment

Attachment Category	Description
Secure attachments	Children play comfortably when their parents are present, checking visually every so often and showing interesting toys. They appear distressed when left alone and seek to be close when parents return and when a stranger enters the room.
Resistant attachments	Children play without engaging parents or checking very often. They may be distressed to be left alone but do not seek to be close when parents return or when a stranger enters.
Avoidant attachments	Children avoid proximity with parents and seem relieved to be left alone. They appear tense when the parent returns and may approach the stranger rather than the parent.

Infant Social Skills

Although newborns may not seem to be very active social partners, by about 6 weeks of age, they begin to indicate a preference for social interaction over play with toys or other objects (Schaffer & Emerson, 1964). Interactions between babies and care-givers provide a necessary framework for acquisition of basic skills in movement, communication, and cognition. More than any other early behaviors, social skills illustrate the arbitrary nature of partitioning development into separate domains. An infant's social smile, for instance, conveys pleasure (communication) at recognition (cognitive) of a familiar person, by coordination of oral-facial muscles (motor) into an identifiable social signal. Waving bye-bye demonstrates the same combination of more complex behaviors across motor, communication, and cognitive domains. The critical social importance of the early smile and the more sophisticated wave derives from the tendency of other people to smile and wave in return. The specific social skills addressed in this chapter are part and parcel of a process that binds person to person in distinctly human interactions.

Social Smile

Within the first 4 to 6 weeks of life, and often just as parents' stamina for provid-ing 24-hour care is wearing thin, babies begin to smile. The type of smile that makes a single interaction worth all the diaper changing, late night feedings, and endless hours of walking a fussy baby is the *social smile* that is clearly elicited by a familiar person. Adults irresistibly interpret every infant's social smile as an indication of comfort and pleasure: "I'm happy to see you! You're grand!"

Variations of the social smile include laughing, chortling, and gurgling; there is rarely a question about the infant's meaning. This is not the vague, fleeting, ephemer-al smile that the newborn produces when asleep or resting. The social smile is direct-ed at a specific person, and recipients usually learn quickly how to elicit a repeat per-formance. The social smile may be employed rather indiscriminately for a couple months but usually appears more often in the presence of familiar people (Schaffer & Emerson, 1964). Infants rapidly become adept at using the smile as a strategy for initiating social interactions.

Stranger Anxiety

Infants in some families seem to be passed constantly from one person to the other at social gatherings; everyone wants to hold the baby. A 3-month-old may show unmistakable delight in the attention, only to frown, bury his face and clutch dra-matically at his father when the family reunites 3 months later. If the well-intentioned relatives persist in trying to hold the infant, he might just cry tragically and reach inconsolably for one of his parents (or a sibling if the parents are absent). This baby is showing *stranger anxiety* at people who are unfamiliar to him, and the fact that they are related and remember him perfectly does nothing to put him at ease. He is demonstrating that he knows the difference between familiar and unfamiliar people and also that he has developed a level of trust and comfort with his caregivers that

Earliest interactions between babies and familiar caregivers are the context for development of increasingly more sophisticated social, motor, communication, and cognitive skills.

these other people have yet to earn. The relatives who are willing to put in some time interacting with the infant while he sits on one of his parent's laps will soon be rewarded. Not all babies react intensely and obviously, but an astute observer can almost always notice subtle differences in behavior (smiling, eye contact, body orientation, movement) when infants are with familiar and unfamiliar people.

Proximity Seeking and Separation Anxiety

The infant described in the previous paragraph was too young to have independent mobility skills; he couldn't crawl or walk away, so he was reduced to clinging and crying. Once babies begin to crawl and walk, they can demonstrate their desire to be near familiar people by moving themselves closer. By the time they are 1 year old, most typically developing babies will also use their voices and call out to bring a caregiver into closer proximity. The negative counterpart of *proximity seeking* is a feeling of anxious fearfulness that results when babies are separated from their primary caregivers. *Separation anxiety* has a strong cognitive component rooted in object permanence. Infants who have constructed mental representations of their caregivers are threatened by the absence of the person who matches their mental image. After a number of such disappointments, the baby begins to anticipate the distress and becomes anxious in anticipation of separations. Separation anxiety is most often evident at times of predictable separation, such as daily arrivals at childcare, and is likely to reoccur or intensify when the youngster is coping with other threats and stresses. Illness, schedule changes, lack of sleep, and moving are examples of the many circumstances that increase infants' reliance on the physical and emotional presence of caregivers.

Social Referencing

Infants are constantly encountering new objects, people, and circumstances, and by the time they are about 1 year old, trust that familiar adults will keep them safe and comfortable. When a 14-month-old encounters a horse for the first time, she has limited experience to help her determine if the huge hairy beast is more likely to be fun and exciting or scary and dangerous. So she looks to her mother, literally, to interpret the situation. If the mother loves horses and is smiling, calm, and talking to the animal in pleasing tones, the baby will probably approach the horse. If the mother is tense and frightened herself, however, it takes only one look for the infant to understand that this is a situation that requires caution. Looking to familiar adults to interpret ambiguous or confusing situations is known as *social referencing* and reflects a set of complex social skills that require babies to discriminate facial expressions and body language, make associations with feeling states, and alter their own behaviors accordingly. Social referencing demonstrates quite nicely that interactions with caring adults provide exceedingly effective and, in this case, efficient opportunities for infants to exercise their most sophisticated social, motor, and cognitive abilities. It is a subtle but powerful form of communication through which the baby asks, "Is this a good idea for me? Is it safe?" and receives an answer without the need for words.

Prelinguistic Communication

We often think of communication beginning at the point that babies begin using simple words, or the emergence of symbolic communication in the form of language at about 1 year of age. However, if communication is defined as the ability to "express oneself in such a way that one is readily and clearly understood" (American Heritage Dictionary, 1982), anyone who knows infants knows that they communicate quite effectively from the first days of life. Babies furrow their brows, tense their limbs, frown, and cry; they wave their arms, smile, and coo; they scrunch up their faces, kick, and scream on occasion; they sit very still, open their eyes wide, and laugh out loud; and they point, generate a string of sounds, and bounce up and down excitedly. The truth is that most infants are sophisticated at social communication long before they produce a single word. In this section we examine the development of communication from an infant's first cry through the transition to language.

Crying

Infants first communicate by crying, often interpreted by adults as a signal that the newborn is cold, wet, hungry, or otherwise uncomfortable and distressed. Parents and other caregivers who respond to crying newborns by picking them up and talking quietly are pleased and somewhat fascinated that they can so easily quiet and comfort their babies. Responsive caregivers can tell by the sound of a 2- to 3-month-old infant's cry if they are hungry, frightened, bored, or just fussy.

Early Vocalizations

For the first couple months of life, babies make many sounds that seem to have little relationship to communication. They gurgle, bubble (sometimes literally), and make throaty sounds when they are comfortable and during feedings. They sputter, shriek, howl, and grunt when they are uncomfortable, hungry, or overstimulated. Nasal vowel sounds that emerge at approximately 3 months of age often provide additional cues that allow caregivers to attach different meanings to different types of cries. Once infants begin to make cooing sounds, they begin to vocalize when they are alone and during face-to-face interactions. For about the first 4 months of life, babies' vocalizations are dominated by vowel sounds ("ooh," "uh," "eh," "aaah"). Vocal play with nonspeech sounds (grunts, growls, squeals, shrieks) follows quickly. With this relatively small repertoire of sounds, infants are able to initiate, respond to, and maintain distinctly social interactions with caregivers.

Once babies begin to use sounds to interact, they quickly become enthusiastic and competent social communication partners. They use eye contact, smiles, and sounds to engage and respond to adult attention, as well as directing their gazes and orienting their heads and bodies to control the intensity and pace of interactions. The vocal interplay that occurs many times daily between caregivers and young infants quickly becomes coordinated and synchronous interaction routines, with elegant and extended patterns of turn taking. Infant specialists have compared these early interactions to communicative "dances," with a rhythm similar to that of conversations and an emotional melody (Stern, 1977; Tronick, 1989). Enjoyable face-to-face interactions are believed to promote positive mutual attachments (Isabella & Belsky, 1991) and to provide a foundation for becoming a conversational partner once language develops (Stern, 1977).

Babbling

Typically developing 6-month-olds who are beginning to imitate become delighted players of reciprocal vocal games, using both nonspeech and speech sounds. They have been practicing with a variety of sounds for about 2 months and now begin *babbling* using a combination of vowel and consonant sounds. At first infants produce isolated single consonant–vowel syllables: "da," "ka," "la." The variety of different sounds produced quickly increases, and babies begin to expand sound combinations and string single syllables together: "lal," "kak," "di-di," "ma-ma," "ga-ga," "beb-beb." By the time most babies reach their first birthdays, they are jabbering away, using a wide variety of sounds in endless combinations.

Also between 6 and 9 months, youngsters seem to begin using vocalizations with intent, for example, to call out for caregivers or to protest a toy's being removed. They learn to recognize their own names and the names of familiar people and objects. These striking elaborations of basic communication skills coincide with the development of object permanence, intent, and early means–ends skills in the cognitive domain and allow babies to understand that sounds can refer to concrete items and that their voices can be used as tools for making things happen.

Transition to Symbolic Communication

By their first birthdays, most infants are poised to make a great leap from concrete to symbolic forms of communication. They exhibit clear communicative intent by pressing motor and vocal behaviors into use for gaining and directing the attention of adults, expressing needs, and sharing information. They associate specific gestures to signal specific messages, such as pointing and vocalizing to say, "I want that," or "Look over there." One-year-old babies also use sophisticated *protoforms*, or mutually recognized signals, such as banging an object and calling out to get a caregiver's attention or tugging on an adult's pants and pointing to share information or express a need.

Babies move from using signals to using symbols when they begin putting specific, consistent combinations of sounds together to represent familiar objects, people, and events. These early word approximations may or may not resemble real words but are recognizable uses of sounds to communicate. An infant may holler "ma-ma" or "da-da" when she wants to be taken out of her crib, clearly referring to her parents. A child may use an idiosyncratic combination of sounds such as "ake" to refer to the family dog, Jake, and all other dogs as well.

Early word approximations are refined through imitation into the word symbols understood by speakers of the native language. Many year-old infants are thought to be speaking a language of their own when they combine word approximations with melodic patterns of pitch, inflections, and intonations that are recognized by adults as questions, statements, demands, greetings, and stories. One-year-olds are superb tellers of tales, rewarding the interested listener with long strings of seemingly cogent (if technically meaningless) comments. The next task for a new language learner is to master the meanings of words and the rules of grammar, accomplishments that are covered in the next chapter.

Most of the existing research on prelinguistic communication and attachment addresses mothers and infants, because the majority of adults worldwide who provide care for infants are women. There is no doubt, however, that babies use interactions with any person who regularly provides care as a venue for development of social communication skills and attachment relationships. Most babies who live with both parents show clear evidence of positive interactions with their fathers (Lamb, 1981) despite the fact that fathers typically spend less time with their infants than do mothers (Parke, 1981). Fathers who provide primary care are likely to be as good or even better than mothers in comforting and caring for babies, whereas others take on the role of preferred playmate by engaging in physical and prelinguistic interactions (Lamb, 1981). Teachers and caregivers in high-quality childcare settings also promote secure attachments (Kagan, Kearsley, & Zelazo, 1978). In some cultures, older siblings or grandparents routinely take on primary caregiving roles.

The important issue seems to be that infants have opportunities to engage in consistent, predictable, and responsive interactions with caring people over a period of time early in life. Once babies establish a warm, mutually satisfying, and trustful attachment to one person, they seem quite able to quickly form similar relationships, and equally satisfying interactions, with many people (Schaffer & Emerson, 1964).

Variations in Infant Social-Affective Development

Newborns who are ill, born prematurely, endure prolonged hospitalizations, or experience any combination of these may experience painful, invasive surgeries and other medical procedures. It is easy to understand why these babies might not associate adult caregivers with comfort and pleasure. They may cry excessively, are sometimes unusually irritable, and may be unable to respond to social interactions until their central nervous systems mature and their physical status becomes more robust. For months, some premature babies seem to spend most of their time either sleeping or crying, with very little tolerance for stimulation of any kind (Field, 1987). The cries of many infants born prematurely are described by caregivers as being weak, high pitched, and shrill (Zeskind, 1980), injecting an element of irritation and tension into parents' responses to crying and further delaying the early reciprocal interactions associated with comfort and calming.

Conversely, infants with Down syndrome are often described by parents as being placid and easy going, not crying as much as expected. These babies may be less effective at signaling distress and engaging a response from caregivers, also decreasing the frequency of social interactions during the early months. Cognitive delays can impede acquisition of object permanence, imitation, and means–ends abilities, posing problems for the acquisition of symbolic communication. In fact, the failure of infants to acquire language is often the first indication of cognitive delay.

Cerebral palsy can affect the muscles of the face and mouth, making production of consonants difficult and causing delays in the development of babbling. Infants who cannot hear do not listen to their own early vocalizations and soon stop babbling. They also miss hearing the speech of others, making vocal imitation virtually impossible and limiting access to the intonations and inflections of the spoken language. Excellent resources are available in most communities for infants with all types of special needs, with most current approaches focusing on the context and content of early relationships between babies and their caregivers. Parents and siblings, extended family members, and sitters are supported to learn effective, individualized strategies for modifying social interactions to accommodate babies' special needs.

Nonorganic failure to thrive is one of the most extreme variations in infant social development (Heffer & Kelley, 1994). Babies who fail to thrive appear physically sound but do not gain weight, have delayed motor development, and are generally unresponsive to social interactions. The pattern of depressed, apathetic, noncommunicative behaviors has also been observed in infants reared in institutions where physical care and nutrition were adequate but devoid of social interaction. The long-term effects of failure to thrive syndrome include permanent social, cognitive, and movement delays (Lozoff, 1989).

One prevailing hypothesis is that infants exhibit the failure to thrive syndrome when they are deprived of affectionate, responsive caregiving (Shaffer, 1999). Babies who fail to thrive often live in homes where chronic poverty, marital discord, mental illness, and other problems drain the emotional resources of adults and limit their capacities for social interactions with young infants. Difficulties in establishing satisfying feeding routines may contribute to deficiencies in physical growth, and the production of growth hormones is apparently impeded by the lack of social and emotional interactions (Tanner, 1990). Hospitalization often results in rapid weight gain and increased social responsiveness in babies who have previously failed to thrive. The multiple problems of families that precipitate failure to thrive syndrome, however, require intensive services that address environmental factors such as living conditions, parenting skills, financial resources, mental and physical health.

IMPLICATIONS FOR CAREGIVERS OF INFANTS

Recommendations for best practice in infant care have evolved and changed dramatically over the years in industrialized countries, at least somewhat as a function of the prevailing theories of development described in chapter 1. There is no need to go to the literature on childrearing, however, to discover how rapidly caregiving practices for infants have transformed. The next time you attend a baby shower, simply ask grandparents, parents of middle school children, and new parents about feeding schedules, bathing and diapering tactics, sleeping arrangements, and the requisite equipment. Differences of opinion about natural childbirth, bottle versus breast-feeding, daily schedules, and optimal ways of interacting will be obvious among generations and different families. Forces driving revisions in parenting practices over time include the results of increasingly sophisticated infancy research; an expanded knowledge base on early development; advances in medicine and social services; and the influences of marketing on the use of infant clothing, toys, and equipment.

Let's review a few of the major points from this chapter to guide the discussion of infant caregiving. First, infants change rapidly in the first year of life, so you should expect caring for newborns to be much different than caring for 1-year-olds. Second, keep in mind that physical maturation provides an important framework for learning in the first year of life, so adequate appreciation of infant caregiving demands relies on a thorough understanding of early motor development. And finally, infant intelli-

Caregivers of infants take pleasure in the rapid changes in development they witness and promote during the first year of life.

gence is an action-oriented type of cognition that is inseparable from movement and social interaction. Providing high-quality care for babies means balancing knowledge of infant physiology with developmental knowledge and sensitivity to family care-giving practices.

Eating and Sleeping

Infants eat and sleep a lot, and the younger they are, the more often they eat and sleep. Caregivers can expect to spend a large proportion of time feeding, changing, and bathing young infants, just as parents do when babies are at home. Safety is an important consideration, and leaving infants alone is hardly ever a good idea. Babies choke easily, which has implications for both eating and sleeping. Many infants thrive on milk or formula only for the first 6 months of life; others begin eating solid food as early as 2 months of age. Infant caregivers must always take care to communicate with families about the details of formula, breast milk, and schedules for feeding and sleeping. To the extent possible, home schedules should be followed in the childcare setting. Current thinking is that young babies should sleep on their sides to prevent choking and sudden infant death syndrome (SIDS).

Crying

Parents, grandparents, pediatricians, and psychologists disagree to this day about how quickly to respond to infant crying. There seems to be a consensus that consistent responses to cries of genuine distress (hunger, fear, discomfort) have the result of reducing crying over time, but disagreement still exists about whether or not fussiness should require the same level of intervention (Bee, 1997).

Child Care

The mothers of more than half the infants in the United States, Canada, and Northern Europe work outside the home. Perhaps some of the readers of this book plan to become infant-care specialists in childcare settings. Affordable, high-quality infant care is particularly difficult to find in the United States (Howes, 1990; Howes, Phillips & Whitebrook, 1992). Many parents and child-care professionals alike wonder about the impact of early out-of-home care on the social and emotional development of babies. A review of available information on alternate care for infants provides cause for both optimism and concern.

First the good news: Daily childcare in a high-quality setting is unlikely to harm the cognitive or emotional development of infants from two-parent families. Infants who receive full-time childcare are apt to receive especially sensitive and responsive care when they are with their parents and form secure attachment relationships with their parents as well as their child-care providers (Hoffman, 1989). There is also convincing evidence that excellent programs of infant child care can promote cognitive, social, and emotional development into the primary and middle school years (Carolina Abecedarian Project, 2000).

Now the bad news: High-quality infant care is hard to find and often not affordable for families whose lives are already constrained by unemployment, chronic illness, substance abuse, and poor education. Research on families in which the working mother is a single parent suggests much poorer social and cognitive outcomes for infants enrolled in group care. The inferior outcomes are assumed to reflect a combination of factors from stressful homes and child-care arrangements that are of poor quality (Howes, 1990; Shaffer, 1999). Inadequately trained caregivers responsible for large groups of infants can exacerbate the impact of overburdened family lives. Fortunately, well-trained providers working in high-quality settings, with appropriate ratios of adults to children and a minimum of staff turnover, can provide a level of care that compensates for difficulties at home and actually improves developmental outcomes for infants at risk because of environmental factors (Belsky, Steinberg, & Walker, 1982).

CONCLUDING REMARKS

The overriding theme of this chapter is that relationships and interactions with adults provide a necessary foundation for healthy development in infancy. Caring adults ensure the safety and survival of newborns and promote positive developmental outcomes by providing appropriate social, cognitive, and motor experiences for their babies. Responsive caregivers read babies' cues and respond accordingly, communicate in ways that match their infants' levels of comprehension, and provide access to new activities. This is not to say that the developmental patterns or caregiving practices with which we are most familiar are the only standards. The child development literature that provides the knowledge base for this chapter includes only a small percentage of studies from non-Western cultures, so the view presented here is by no means universally representative (New, 1994).

In Western cultures, however, the quality of interactions between caregivers and infants predicts the degree of competence preschoolers demonstrate socially with peers and in language development (Bornstein & Tamis-LeMonda, 1989), attesting to the importance of positive early relationships. Good parenting and good teaching share similar characteristics for infants (Mahoney, Robinson, & Powell, 1992), indicating that the roles of adults in creating supportive environments and facilitating the development of new skills are parallel at home and in alternate-care settings. This is a powerful statement for students in early childhood education, as it speaks directly to the significance of your potential role with the youngest of children.

EXTENDING YOUR LEARNING

1. Select two infants who seem to be developing on roughly the same timetable. Interview their parents to identify similarities and differences in extended family involvement; traditions surrounding pregnancy and birth; daily schedules; caregivers; and their specific practices for feeding, changing, bathing, and play.

2. Take any opportunity that presents itself to observe newborn babies. Accept invitations to be present at the birth of nieces, nephews, friends, or to visit as soon as possible. Make notes about the appearance of the neonate.

3. Arrange a visit to a newborn nursery to observe. Check with your instructor and the hospital to ensure that you have the appropriate permission and that your visit is timed for the convenience of the staff.

4. Observe a 2-month-old baby during waking and sleeping hours to watch for signs of primitive reflexes. List the reflexes you see and the conditions that elicited them.

5. Read more about early brain development or watch the ABC News video: *From the Beginning*, Prime Time Live with Diane Sawyer (July 19, 1995, Segment 3), or both. Try to separate science from media hype.

6. Document the progression of skills in gross motor development by observing infants at 2 months, 6 months, 9 months, and 14 months. List the positions (lying, sitting, standing, crawling, etc.) each baby takes, the skills they demonstrate in mobility, and the components of earlier movements that you see in each progressive age range.

7. Spend time with a family whose cultural background differs from your own. Try to identify similarities and differences in traditions, expectations, parenting practices, and the meanings attached to infant behaviors.

8. Document the progression of skills in reaching and grasping by observing infants at 2 months, 6 months, 9 months, and 14 months. List the skills demonstrated in reaching and grasping and the components of earlier movements that you see in each progressive age range.

9. Document the progression of skills in social communication development by observing infants at 2 months, 6 months, 9 months, and 14 months. List the sounds each baby makes, the uses of communication, and the responses of caregivers.

10. Observe parents and other infant caregivers feeding, diapering, bathing, and playing with the infant. List opportunities for acquisition and practice of social, cognitive, and motor skills.

11. Visit an inclusive child-care program that serves infants across a range of ability levels. Document the simplest and most complex abilities you observe in social, cognitive, and motor skills by listing them in each domain. Can you identify infants with specific disabilities? List similarities and differences you observe in the development of the babies with and without disabilities.

VOCABULARY

Accommodation. The development of more sophisticated and diverse motor actions in response to new sensory experiences.

Achondroplasia (short limbed dwarfism). The condition in which a person is born with a disproportionately short upper arm and thigh bone and an unusually large head and trunk.

Amniotic fluid. Liquid surrounding the baby inside the uterus.

Assimilation. The incorporation of new information through simple early-action schema such as looking, touching, sucking, and holding.

Athetoid cerebral palsy. Fluctuating muscle tone that dominates arms and legs causing unintentional movement that vacillates between rapid jerking and slow writhing.

Attachment. The warm and trusting relationship that develops between infants and their primary caregivers.

Atypical infant reflexes. Involuntary movement patterns that persist past the first few months of life and interfere with voluntary movement.

Babbling. Vocal play using combinations of consonants and vowels.

Bilateral reach. Reaching with both arms stretched forward.

Bite reflex. Automatic, uncontrollable clamping together of jaw when the inside of the mouth is stimulated.

Cephalocaudal development. The head-to-toe sequence in which motor development occurs.

Cerebral palsy. A neuromotor disorder expressed as a range of movement disorders; caused by lesions or abnormalities in the part of the brain that controls motor function.

Congenital. Hereditary; present at birth; determined by genetics.

Crawl. Prone movement across a surface, using hands/arms and knees/legs, with stomach resting on the surface.

Creeping. Movement across a surface using hands and knees only ("on-all-fours"), with stomach lifted off the surface.

Diplegia. Spasticity in legs only.

Disequilibrium. A discomforting discrepancy between existing knowledge and the demands of newly assimilated information; results in accommodation.

Extensor thrust. Generalized extension of muscles from head to toes when head is tipped back.

Gross motor development. Progressive voluntary command over the large muscles in the body.

Hypertonia. Tight or rigid muscle tone.

Hypotonia. Extremely low muscle tone.

In utero.   Inside the uterus.

Intermodal transfer.   Ability to combine and make sense of information from sight, sound, or touch simultaneously.

Midline.   The middle of the body along a vertical line from head to feet; midline divides the body into two symmetrical halves.

Musculoskeletal system.   Includes muscles, bones, joints, ligaments, and tendons.

Myelination.   The process of nerve pathways being coated with a waxy substance to direct nerve impulses from the brain and spinal cord to specific muscles.

Neonate.   Newborn infant.

Neuromotor system.   Connects the brain and nerves to muscles for control of movement.

Nonorganic failure to thrive.   Condition characterized by undernourishment, apathy, and depression, without medical or biological explanation.

Object permanence.   The ability to comprehend the existence of objects and people separate from one's own immediate sensory and motor experiences; knowledge that objects and people exist even if not immediately available through sight, sound, touch.

Palmar to digital control.   Control of hand and fingers that develops from the palm outward to the finger tips.

Pelvic girdle.   Bone structure that includes the hips and pelvis.

Pincer grasp.   Using the tips of first fingers and thumb.

Primitive reflexes.   Involuntary movement patterns of typically developing infants during the first few months of life; early reflexes that are replaced by voluntary actions like sitting, crawling, and walking.

Prone.   Position of lying on one's stomach.

Protoforms.   Communicative signals using voice, objects, and gestures to convey meaning prior to use of language.

Proximity seeking.   Infant attempts to stay close to caregivers.

Quadriplegia.   Spasticity in all four limbs, trunk, and often the lips and tongue.

Radial side.   Inside of the hand (thumb and forefinger).

Reflexive.   Involuntary, unlearned, or instinctive movement.

Reflexive grasp.   Result of fingers and thumb closing together when the palm is stimulated with pressure.

Rooting reflex.   Automatic response of turning toward a touch or a stroke on the cheek, resulting in the high likelihood of contact between the baby's mouth and a source of food.

Rudimentary movements.   Primary movement skills; moving against gravity, maintaining posture, and independent mobility.

Schema.   The simple action sequences of infants; repetitious action sequences that support early knowledge of the world.

Sensorimotor cognition.   Infant (0 to 18 months) intelligence; an action-oriented construction of knowledge through an interactive combination of sensory information and motor activity.

Separation anxiety.   Distress at being separated from a primary caregiver, often in anticipation of the separation.

Sleep–wake state.   Predictable changes in infants' state of arousal and consciousness, from deep sleep to active alertness.

Social referencing.   Making sense of ambiguous situations by interpreting the social cues of primary caregivers.

Social smile.   Infant smiles in response to other people.

Spasticity.   A type of cerebral palsy characterized by hypertonia, resulting in tight flexion or contraction of the body parts affected.

Stepping reflex.   Movement of legs up and down in a stepping motion when held upright with feet contacting a surface.

Stranger anxiety.   Discomfort and distress when faced with strangers.

Sucking reflex.   A complex sequence of closing the lips, sucking, and swallowing in coordination with breathing.

Talipes equinovarus (club foot).   A condition in which a child is born with one or both feet twisted inward and upward.

Ulnar side.   Outside of hand, along the little finger.

Unilateral reach.   Reaching with one arm stretched forward.

Visually directed reaching.   Reaching motivated by desire to touch or hold something within one's visual field.

INTERNET RESOURCES

Web sites provide much useful information for educators and we list some here that pertain to the topics covered in this chapter. The addresses of Web sites can also change, however, and new ones are continually added. Thus, this list should be considered as a first step in your acquisition of a larger and ever-changing collection.

American Academy for Cerebral Palsy and Developmental Medicine
http://www.aacpdm.org

Classroom Connect
http://www.classroom.net/home.asp

Early Childhood Educators' and Family Web Corner
http://users.sgi.net/~cokids/

The ECEOL-I Website
http://www/ume.maine.edu/~cofed/eceol/website.html

The Families and Work Institute
http://www.familiesandwork.org

I Am Your Child
http://www.Iamyourchild.org

International Society of Infant Studies
http://www.isisweb.org

National Network for Child Care
http://www.nccc.org/homepage.html

Special Needs Advocates for Parents (SNAP)
http://snapinfo.org

United Cerebral Palsy of New York City
http://www.ucnyc.org/about/about.com

WORLD Association for Infant Mental Health
http://pilot.msu.edu/user/waimh/

Zero to Three
http://www.zerotothree.org/

References

Ainsworth, M. D., Blehar, M. C., Waters, E., & Wall, S. (1978). *Patterns of attachment: A psychological study of the strange situation.* Hillsdale, NJ: Lawrence Erlbaum Associates.

American Heritage Dictionary: 2nd College Edition. (1982). Boston: Houghton-Mifflin.

Anders, T. F., Goodlin-Jones, B. L., & Zelenko, M. (1998). Infant regulation and sleep–wake state development. *Zero to Three, 19*, 5–8.

Aslin, R. N. (1998). The developing brain comes of age. *Early Development and Parenting, 7*(3), 125–128.

Bee, H. (1997). *The developing child* (8th ed.). New York: HarperCollins.

Belsky, J., Steinberg, L. D., & Walker, A. (1982). The ecology of daycare. In M. E. Lamb (Ed.), *Nontraditional families: Parenting and child development.* Hillsdale, NJ: Lawrence Erlbaum Associates.

Black, J., & Puckett, M. (1996). *The young child: Development from prebirth through age eight* (2nd ed.). Englewood Cliffs, NJ: Merrill-Prentice-Hall.

Boothe, R. G., Dobson, V., & Teller, D. V. (1985). Postnatal development of vision in human and non-human primates. *Annual Review of Neuroscience.*

Bornstein, M. H., & Tamis-LeMonda, C. S. (1989). Maternal responsiveness and cognitive development. In M. Bornstein (Ed.), *Maternal responsiveness: Characteristics and consequences* (pp. 49–62). San Francisco: Jossey-Bass.

Bower, T. G. R. (1977a). *The perceptual world of the child.* Cambridge, MA: Harvard University Press.

Bower, T. G. R. (1977b). Blind babies see with their ears. *New Scientist, 73,* 256–257.

Bowlby, J. (1969). *Attachment and loss. Vol. 1: Attachment.* London: Hogarth Press.

Brodal, P. (1992). *The central nervous system: Structure and function.* New York: Oxford University Press.

Bronfenbrenner, U. (1977). Toward an experimental ecology of human development. *American Psychologist, 32,* 513–531.

Carolina Abecedarian Project. (2000). *Early learning, later success: The Abecedarian study.* Chapel Hill, NC: Frank Porter Graham Child Development Center.

Cernoch, J. M., & Porter, R. H. (1985). Recognition of maternal auxiliary odors by infants. *Child Development, 56,* 1593–1598.

Chomsky, N. (1988). *Language and problems of knowledge.* Cambridge, MA: MIT Press.

Chugani, H. T. (1998, April). *Adaptability of the developing human brain.* Presentation at the Developing Child Brain and Behavior Conference. Early Childhood Initiative Project: University of Chicago.

Cohen, M. A., Gross, P. J., & Haring, N. G. (1976). Developmental pinpoints. In N. G. Haring & L. J. Brown (Eds.), *Teaching the severely handicapped* (Vol. 1). New York: Grune & Stratton.

Crook, C. (1987). Taste and olfaction. In P. Salapatek & L. Cohen (Eds.), *Handbook of infant perception, vol. I: From sensation to perception* (pp. 237–264). Orlando, FL: Academic Press.

DeCasper, A. J., & Fifer, W. P. (1980). Of human bonding: Newborns prefer their mother's voices. *Science, 208,* 1174–1176.

Dormans, J. P., & Batshaw, M. L. (1997). Muscles, bones and nerves: The body's framework. In M. L. Batshaw (Ed.), *Children with disabilities* (4th ed., pp. 315–333). Baltimore, MD: Paul Brookes.

Erikson, E. (1963). *Childhood and society* (2nd ed.). New York: Norton.

Field, T. M. (1987). Affective and interactive disturbances in infants. In J. D. Osofsky (Ed.), *Handbook of infant development* (2nd ed.). New York: Wiley.

Fischer, K. W. (1980). A theory of cognitive development: The control and construction of hierarchies of skills. *Psychological Review, 87,* 477–531.

Flavell, J. H., Miller, P. H., & Miller, S. A. (1993). *Cognitive development* (3rd ed.). Englewood Cliffs, NJ: Prentice-Hall.

Fraiberg, S. (1977). *Insights from the blind.* New York: New American Library.

Goldberg, S., & DiVitto, B. A. (1983). *Born too soon: Preterm birth and early development.* New York: W. H. Freeman.

Haith, M. M. (1980). *Rules that babies look by.* Hillsdale, NJ: Lawrence Erlbaum Associates.

Heffer, R. W., & Kelley, M. L. (1994). Nonorganic failure to thrive: Developmental outcomes, psychological assessment and intervention issues. *Research in Developmental Disabilities, 4,* 247–268.

Hofer, M. A. (1981). *The roots of human behavior: An introduction to the psychobiology of early development.* San Francisco: Freeman.

Hoffman, L. W. (1989). Effects of maternal employment in the two-parent family. *American Psychologist, 44,* 283–292.

Howes, C. (1990). Can the age of entry into child care and the quality of child care predict adjustment in kindergarten? *Developmental Psychology, 26,* 292–303.

Howes, C., Phillips, D. A., & Whitebrook, M. (1992). Thresholds of quality: implications for the social development of children in center-based care. *Child Development, 63,* 449–460.

Huttenlocher, P. R. (1994). Synaptogenesis, synapse elimination, and neural plasticity in human cerebral cortex. In C. Nelson (Ed.), *Threats to optimal development: Integrating biological, physiological, and social risk factors* (Vol. 27, pp. 35–54). The Minnesota symposium in child psychology.

Isabella, R. A., & Belsky, J. (1991). Interactional synchrony and the origins of infant–mother attachment. *Child Development, 62*, 373–384.

Kagan, J., Kearsley, R. B., & Zelazo, P. R. (1978). *Infancy: Its place in human development.* Cambridge, MA: Harvard University Press.

Lake, R. (Medicine Grizzlybear). (1990). An Indian father's plea. *The Education Digest, 56*(3), 20–23.

Lamb, M. E. (1981). The development of father-infant relationships. In M. E. Lamb (Ed.), *The role of the father in child development.* New York: Wiley.

Lozoff, B. (1989). Nutrition and behavior. *American Psychologist, 44*, 231–236.

MacFarlane, A. (1977). *The psychology of childbirth.* Cambridge, MA: Harvard University Press.

Mahoney, G., Robinson, C., & Powell, A. (1992). Focusing parent–child interaction: The bridge to developmentally appropriate practices. *Topics in Early Childhood Special Education, 12*(1), 105–120.

Meltzoff, A. N. (1988). Infant imitation and memory: Nine month olds in immediate and deferred tasks. *Child Development, 59*, 217–225.

Meltzoff, A. N., & Borton, R. W. (1979). Inter-modal matching by human neonates. *Nature, 282*, 403–404.

Meltzoff, A. N., & Kuhl, P. K. (1994). Faces and speech: Intermodal processing of biologically relevant signals in infants and adults. In D. Lewkowicz & R. Lickliter (Eds.), *The development of intersensory perception: Comparative perspectives* (pp. 335–369). Hillsdale, NJ: Lawrence Erlbaum Associates.

Minde, K. (1998). The sleep of infants and why parents matter. *Zero to Three, 19*, 9–14.

New, R. S. (1994). Culture, child development and developmentally appropriate practices: Teachers as collaborative researchers. In B. L. Mallory & R. S. New (Eds.), *Diversity and developmentally appropriate practices: Challenges for early childhood education.* New York: Teachers College Press.

Parke, R. D. (1981). *Fathers.* Cambridge, MA: Harvard University Press.

Pelligrino, L. (1997). Cerebral palsy. In M. L. Batshaw (Ed.), *Children with disabilities* (pp. 499–528). Baltimore, MD: Paul Brookes.

Piaget, J. (1952). *The origins of intelligence in children.* New York: Macmillan.

Piaget, J. (1954). *The construction of reality in the child.* New York: Basic Books.

Porter, R. H., Makin, J. W., Davis, L. B., & Christensen, K. M. (1992). Breast-fed infants respond to olfactory cues from their own mother and unfamiliar lactating females. *Infant Behavior and Development, 15*(1), 85–93.

Sander, L. W. (1969). The longitudinal course of early mother–child interaction. Cross case comparison in a sample of mother–child pairs. In B. M. Foss (Ed.), *Determinants of infant behavior IV* (pp. 189–228). London: Methuen.

Schaffer, H. R., & Emerson, P. E. (1964). The development of social attachments in infancy. *Monographs of the Society for Research in Child Development, 29*(3, Serial No. 94).

Sears, R. R. (1963). Dependency motivation. In M. Jones (Ed.), *Nebraska Symposium on Motivation* (Vol. 11). Lincoln: University of Nebraska Press.

Shaffer, D. R. (1999). *Social and personality development* (4th ed.). Pacific Grove, CA: Brooks/Cole.

Shatz, C. J. (1997). The developing brain. In *Mind and brain: Readings from the Scientific American* (pp. 15–26). New York: Freeman.

Stern, D. (1977). *The first relationship: Infant and mother.* Cambridge, MA: Harvard University Press.

Tanner, J. M. (1990). *Fetus into man: Physical growth from conception to maturity* (2nd ed.). Cambridge, MA: Harvard University Press.

Tronick, E. Z. (1989). Emotions and emotional communications in infants. *American Psychologist, 44*, 112–119.

Uzgiris, I. C. (1973). Patterns of cognitive development in infancy. *Merrill Palmer Quarterly, 19*, 21–40.

Walton, G. E., Bower, N. J., & Bower, T. G. (1992). Recognition of familiar faces by newborns. *Infant Behavior and Development, 15*, 265–269.

Werner, L. A., & Gillenwater, J. M. (1990). Pure-tone sensitivity of 2- to 5-week old infants. *Infant Behavior and Development, 13*, 355–375.

Wiesfeld, A. R., Malatesta, C. Z., & DeLoach, L. L. (1981). Differential parental response to familiar and unfamiliar infant distress signals. *Infant Behavior and Development, 4*, 281–296.

Zeskind, P. S. (1980). Adult responses to the cries of low and high risk infants. *Infant Behavior and Development, 3*, 167–177.

CHAPTER

3

TODDLERHOOD: FROM PLAYGROUP TO PLAYGROUND

Children . . . are the last candid audience left. They don't care what the critics say and they let you know immediately what delights and what bores them.

Gian Carlo Menotti

▼ Chapter Objectives

After reading this chapter, you should be able to:

- ▼ Identify significant influences of family and cultural contexts on toddler development.
- ▼ Describe the impact of temperament on development of cognitive, social, and motor skills during the toddler years.
- ▼ Summarize principles and sequences of toddler skill acquisition across motor, cognitive, and social domains.
- ▼ Recognize variations in toddler growth and behavior across motor, cognitive, and social domains, and draw conclusions about the impact on development.

As you think about and apply chapter content on your own, you should be able to:

- ▼ Observe principles of development and estimate the approximate ages of toddlers you encounter.
- ▼ Formulate your own opinions about the relative contributions of gender, parenting, experience, and maturation on the development of toddlers you observe.

Vignette 3.1: *Excerpts From a Toddler's Diary (Written by His Mother)*

July 12   *Here we are at Keystone for a family reunion. Dustin is nearing the 2 year mark and clearly is in his element here with the woods, river, horses, swimming pool, and best of all, the SHUTTLE BUS! He loves the walks outdoors and the "big kids," his cousins. He is the baby of the bunch but truly a boy and not a baby anymore. An indication of that change is that he has of late become quite fascinated with babies. He always notices babies, takes care of his animal and doll babies, and takes great pleasure in playing baby himself. "Me baby" means he wants to be held horizontally and talked to like an infant. He looks at photos of last year with great interest but hasn't quite grasped that he is the baby in the pictures. It's like he is on the edge of understanding something wondrous . . . Looks at books and yells out words for things he recognizes but skips quickly over the pictures he doesn't have the words for.*

Dustin loves to run these days, in particular up and down the hall, in the grass, and on the driveway. He climbs on EVERYTHING. He feeds himself with spoon and fork without too much mess, although if anything spills, he's sure to smear it around. Dustin still often wants a "bot" (bottle) and "dees" (his yellow blanket) at bedtime, or if he is hurt, threatened, or insecure. He asked for them quite a few times on waking and naptime the first couple days we were here; he seemed so disoriented. He doesn't seem to understand the notion of a trip or visit—that it has a planned beginning and end—but now he does remember specific people from earlier in the summer.

He has favorite books and manipulative toys and is a big talker these days. Puts his little thoughts into words and will persist if we don't understand, then finally give up with a sigh, "No Mama." His longest intelligible sentence to date: "Mama pees opa babox." (Mama, please open sandbox.) A couple of mysteries: "bof" (drive), "yah-yah" (outside).

December 19   *Two years plus is the absolute peak of cuteness. Dustin talks in these clipped little sentences: "Me go outside see Jake." Very earnest and repeats, repeats, repeats to get it right. Uses loud, soft, sweet, and naughty tones of voices, although not always at the right times. Relates past events and is starting to understand time and distance: "Far, far, far away"; "Couple minutes." Remembers things that are shocking to us: Someone mentioned Alaska the other day and he said "My daddy was Alaska" (in October). Uses the past tense, possessives, and subject–object nouns in very creative ways: "Ours go home"; "Him havin' breakfast"; "Me done nap." He doesn't use "t," "g," "ch," or "k" in an initial position, so "tookie" is cookie, "det" is get. "Me det it Tissmas?" is a classic (Will I get it for Christmas?). Dustin wants "Tookies, yites (lights) on tree, and yinkle bells (jingle bells) on door," so he should get everything he asks for. . . .*

Potty training has been up and down. He does well for a while and then relapses if sick, tired, traveling, or out. When riding in the car, he notices every little thing outside and maintains a running commentary: "Booboo car. Call towtuck" (Wrecked car needs a towtuck); "Cows poopin' over there." "My 'moketacks 'n towers" (Seattle skyline); "Me yike yakes" (I like lakes). He gets so excited about people coming to visit or going away himself. He'll sort of bounce or jump up and down on his toes, clap and make an "ooh, ooh" noise. Nice to see him anticipating things.

August 22   *And now our boy is almost 3! Such a grown up boy; even when he plays he has to be "big" bear, or have adult roles like ranger, fireman, doctor, plumber. He has a whole wall of costumes, and we never know from day to day who he'll want to be. . . .*

He's a good eater but still uses his fingers sometimes to push food on the utensils. He stuffs BIG bites of food a lot but can pour and serve a little. Still loves baths and showers but does NOT like being wiped up after meals. He can undress all the way and is starting to dress himself. I don't push the dressing thing, because I guess I like the physical contact twice a day. I think he does, too, because he asks to be tickled or have his back rubbed before going to sleep.

He is pretty agile but quite cautious about heights since falling off the top of a big slide and face-first into the dirt from a spinning playground merry-go-round. I guess he has good reason. He hiked for miles on the last camping trip, as long as it was flat. Manipulative and imaginative play are great favorites at home, and since camping he puts fires "dead out" and "steals" food for his meals like a bear. Amazing language—long complex sentences with conjunctions, prepositions, clauses, idioms. My favorites among his hundreds of vocabulary words are: "bloculars" (binoculars) and "ambalumps" (ambulance). He still calls his special little blankies "dees" and "dat," but if someone doesn't understand, he'll say "My blanket!"

He has given up the bottle entirely after losing the last one but still maintains verbally that he has one "at home," and he's out of diapers, which is fine by me. He has lots of little friends at child care but still misses his old sitter, Terry. He has started to use questions to find out what he needs to know about our schedules: "We stay here another night?"; "Where we going now?" I can tell he has a good memory of home, because when we are away he talks (sometimes sadly) about his bed, the sandbox, neighbor friends, the dog.

The diary entries you have just read provide but a brief record of the rapid growth and development that takes place during the toddler years and outline nicely the themes of this chapter:

- Physically, toddlers begin to apply basic motor skills of reaching and grasping to functional play with manipulative toys and become increasingly coordinated at activities like scribbling. They refine rudimentary gross motor skills and apply them to playground equipment, riding toys, and so on.

- During the second year of life, children make a great mental leap with development of mental representations and related cognitive abilities. Symbolic language develops quickly between ages 2 and 3.

- Socially, toddlers begin to develop a sense of self in relationship to their caregivers, environments, and other children. Their newfound motor and cognitive skills support a tendency toward independent behaviors, individualized interests, and unique personalities.

The word *toddler* brings to mind images of very small children walking about a bit unsteadily to experience and explore the world, eagerly curious and wonderfully cute. Although the passage from infant to toddler is technically achieved with mastery of unassisted walking, there is considerable variability in the exact age at which babies begin to move about in an upright position. As described in chapter 2, a majority of infants begin walking sometime between 10 and 15 months of age, but some set out as early as 8 months. Youngsters who begin walking before 1 year of age usually continue to be referred to by parents and professionals alike as babies until sometime between their first and second birthdays, perhaps because specific language, self-care, and social milestones also signal an end to infancy. In early childhood programs, the toddler room often houses 2-year-olds. For purposes of this chapter, toddlerhood is considered to extend from approximately 1 year to 3 years of age, an admittedly arbitrary time frame, but one that corresponds nicely with major transitions in cognition, communication, self-care, and fine motor development.

FAMILY CONTEXT

Toddlers are definitely active participants in family life and are engaged in different types of relationships with parents and other caregivers than in infancy. Almost all babies who experience predictable caregiving routines have become regulated by age 1 so that their own schedules for eating, sleeping, and playing correspond to the unique rhythms of their families' days. In some families, this means an early awakening, dressing, breakfast, and playtime before a drive to child care while parents work. A baby with this schedule might nap only once during the day, come home to have another nap while the family eats dinner, and play with parents and siblings before a later evening feeding and bedtime.

Another baby may get up later, nurse, bathe, and dress with a parent who stays home or with an in-home caregiver. This child would perhaps have a very different schedule, staying in one setting, taking two daytime naps, and going on outings to do errands and shopping. Bedtime for this little one might occur earlier, following some early-evening play and feeding before the family dinner. Family members will have altered and modified their lifestyles to accommodate the changing needs of the newest family member. Whatever a family's customary habits, the child's physical needs and social expectations are shaped by daily routines during the first year of life, in synchrony with caregiving practices.

Socially, toddlers are increasingly adept at combining motor, cognitive, and communication skills to express their individual personalities. They develop definite preferences for food, toys, and people and can be persistent at making their wants and needs known, especially when vocabulary fails them. Longer waking periods during the day allow for extended periods of interaction and more independent play. One-

Toddlers are generally energetic, enthusiastic, and active as they make the developmental transitions from infancy to the preschool years.

and 2-year-olds move quickly from action to thought in cognitive processes, learn many concepts, and are able to communicate their ideas. The toddler's increased independence in mobility and cognition is a powerful combination, often perceived by caregivers as "a mind of his own" or "her strong will." A closer examination of developmental processes across all domains can inspire a positive and constructive interpretation of that hallmark of toddlerhood: the constellation of behaviors commonly labeled "the terrible twos."

PHYSICAL GROWTH AND MOTOR DEVELOPMENT DURING TODDLERHOOD: LATE RUDIMENTARY–EARLY FUNDAMENTAL PHASE

Toddlers are up and moving, using every one of the rudimentary postures and movement skills developed during the first year of life. Even a brief observation reveals quick changes of body position from lying on the floor, to sitting, all fours, standing, squatting, upright again, and back to the floor (sometimes abruptly!). Rolling, creeping, and walking are all used for mobility, along with some quite interesting individual versions of scooting on bottoms, "commando crawling," and "bear walking" on hands and feet with backsides in the air. The primary developmental accomplishments of 1- and 2-year-olds in the motor domains include refinement of such rudimentary skills as walking and grasping skills and application of motor skills to functional activities. For the first year, physical activity of all types is often enjoyed for the sake of action, but toddlers increasingly use movement as a foundation for independent performance in social interactions, self-care, and play. *Fundamental movements* and manipulation skills provide an essential foundation for increased autonomy at home, in the classroom, and on the playground.

Physical Growth

The rate of growth slows dramatically following the first year of rapid increases in height, weight, and brain development. Most toddlers will grow about 2 inches in height and gain 5 to 6 pounds each year, becoming leaner with relatively longer arms and legs, appearing less round in shape by their third birthdays. The middle of the body (armpits to knees) becomes progressively heavier relative to the head, although at age 2, the head still comprises one quarter of the total body length. Toddlers' heads, arms, and torsos continue to weigh more than the bottom halves of their bodies, resulting in a high *center of gravity* (Lowrey, 1986). In combination with relatively short legs and tentative balance, babies exhibit the appearance of "toddling" for quite some time after they master independent locomotion.

Toddlers sleep fewer hours than do infants, with more sleep occurring during nighttime hours and naps typically morning and afternoon. During the day, 1- and 2-year-olds are awake for longer periods, up and moving for the sake of getting things done. A higher proportion of their sleep is deep, quiet sleep, and in general they fall asleep easily and are able to go back to sleep during the night without help from an adult (Anders, Goodlin-Jones, & Zelenko, 1998). Even babies who share beds with parents may forgo nighttime feedings. In most families in which the youngest child is over a year old, everyone is sleeping through the night.

By the time they are a year old, most babies have a number of teeth and have been eating some solid foods for at least a few months. The first teeth to come in are most often in the front of the mouth, first the lower and then the four upper incisors. By 30 months, babies usually have in the neighborhood of 20 teeth, including the first sets of molars. They can eat almost anything that adults eat and begin to develop individual preferences for certain foods.

Recent research summaries provide evidence for the common wisdom that girls mature physically somewhat faster than boys during infancy and the early childhood years, although the magnitude of gender differences is not very great (Bee, 1997). Girls on the average mature somewhat more quickly and at a more even pace than do boys, as measured by developmental milestones such as walking, hopping, and copying lines and shapes (Ames, Gillespie, & Haines, 1978). There is, however, almost as much variation within groups of young boys and girls as between the two groups, so expectations that any particular child will mature quickly or slowly based solely on gender are unwarranted. Although most researchers and theorists emphasize the important influence of social interactions and role expectations for male and female children, there is increasing evidence for biologically based differences in the effects of similar experience on boys and girls (Rutter, 1987; Werner, 1990).

Gross Motor Development: Refining Basic Skills

In the previous chapter, the section on gross motor development ended with babies standing upright and perhaps taking first tentative steps. Remember, though, that many little ones start walking sometime after their first birthdays. As with all early motor skills, the timing of independent walking depends on the interaction between each infant's unique biological timetable and the characteristics of the settings in which they live and grow. Babies who are adept at crawling and cruising may have less reason to step out on their own. Those who spend time with older toddlers and preschoolers, or whose families have closely spaced younger siblings, might be more motivated to develop mobility skills. In some families or communities, for example, in very cold climates, babies are kept up off floors during the long, frigid winter months; in some cultures babies are swaddled and carried for the first year. By 18 months of age, the vast majority of children who have the opportunity to do so are walking easily and enthusiastically. Evaluation by a pediatrician or physical therapist is indicated for babies who are 1½ years old and not yet walking, unless there is a ready cultural or familial explanation. (Revisit Vignette 2.2 in the previous chapter for just such an explanation.)

Walking

At first, independent walking is very much the business of falling forward and catching oneself, step by step. Babies at this point are generally more skilled at bearing weight in a standing posture than at shifting weight smoothly for walking. Turning to look or change directions can easily precipitate a fall. The lurching initial forward movements relax within a few weeks as balance improves so that the arms are lowered and knees bend when stepping (Fig. 3.1). By 18 months of age, youngsters are generally walking with a more narrow stance and a smooth gait, shifting weight from side to side without losing their balance and able to rotate their trunks while moving. These babies can stop and start forward motion, make turns, look around while moving, and proudly carry toys while walking, all without falling. Many 2-year-olds seem to prefer running to walking, and zip around with increasing stability and grace.

Babies often revert periodically to creeping for a few months after they learn to walk, especially when they are tired or speed is important. Initial attempts at running can add an element of haste that jeopardizes stability and results in a temporary return to the stiff legs and *high guard* of early walking. Being upright provides a new perspective on the world, and toddlers can be observed experimenting with the outlook from a variety of positions. They will bend over backward while being held on someone's lap or put their heads to the ground to look through their legs, alternating the positions repeatedly as if comparing the views. Most babies enjoy being held up in the air and bounced on bigger knees, swinging in baby swings, and riding in moving vehicles of any size. Those toddlers who prefer slow, steady movement to fast changes of position communicate their preferences with easily readable facial expressions (pleasure vs. fear), vocalizations (laughing vs. crying), and body orientations that indicate a desire either to continue or to escape.

One- and 2-year-olds can commonly be seen playing in a stable squatting position, with feet wide apart and diapers not quite touching the floor, although at first they need to hold onto something while standing up again. Between 18 months and 2 years, most babies learn to *stoop and recover*, bending down to pick something up off the ground and standing again without support, and most 2-year-olds can bend

FIG. 3.1. Walking and running. Infants begin walking with stiff, tentative steps, but soon progress to a smooth reciprocal gait, and running.

from the waist and stand again quite easily. By their second birthdays, most babies can move from sitting to standing in one fluid motion.

Climbing

Toddlers often seem intrigued with climbing and fearlessly begin trying to get up and down on the furniture, stairs, and bigger people in their immediate environments. One- and 2-year-olds seem to approach stairs four and five times taller than they are without any apparent consideration of the effort that will be involved in getting to the top, or the possibility of becoming stranded in the middle, or an understanding about how to get down again. Imagine how huge a set of 16 stairs must look to a little person perched on hands and knees at the bottom! Nonetheless, the desire to climb, perhaps combined with curiosity about what is at the top, propels toddlers upward.

One-year-olds typically approach stairs first by climbing upward on all fours, and later by *marking time* with both feet, stepping carefully on each stair while holding an adult's hand or a railing. Even though most babies begin climbing up onto stairs and furniture before trying to come down again, sudden changes of attention or shifts of weight can easily result in an unanticipated fall. Intentional climbing down almost always follows climbing up, and more cautious toddlers persist in going down the stairs feet first on their stomachs or backsides long after they learn to walk up.

Fortunately, perception of depth and distance also improve from the time babies begin to walk, and by the time they are 2 years old, a majority of youngsters can plan fairly complex sequences of movements by coordinating perceptual, motor, and cognitive skills. For example, a 20-month-old on the sofa might respond to a reminder to turn around by looking over her shoulder and judging the distance to the floor. Able to hold a mental image of what is behind her, she can turn her head back to a stable forward position while pushing off the seat cushions and extending her legs down to the floor.

Play Skills

It appears that toddlers begin to build mental images of their own bodies through gross motor experience, so that the process of moving about and changing body positions also contributes to the toddler's sense of *body image*. A child who repeatedly climbs into and out of an adult- and then a child-sized chair is likely learning about the relative size of his own body (Gallahue, 1989). It is not uncommon to see toddlers squeezing themselves into tight spaces under tables or in toy boxes or crawling under tables and standing up only to bump their heads. One toddler we know has spent hours taking all the toys from his toy box, piling them carefully on the floor, and climbing into the toy box himself. He will then lie over the pile of toys, put some of the toys back, and climb in again. His next move is to methodically take the toys into another room and make a pile there, lie down on it, roll over, and go back to climbing in and out of the toy box. This toddler is using his quite impressive gross motor abilities to learn about how much space he takes up relative to his toys and in turn is applying increased awareness of his own body to movement activities.

Motor planning can also be observed as toddlers coordinate knowledge about their bodies with more complex sequences of motor activity, for example, getting themselves into and out of child-sized chairs and walking with pull toys. Rudimentary skills of walking, reaching, and grasping are by this time solid components of the child's motor repertoire and no longer require concerted practice or concentration for successful performance. The toddler's attention is, therefore, available for the more functional pursuits of play, interaction, and exploration. Toy manufacturers have capitalized on the fact that the play of 1- and 2-year-olds often mimics the activities of adults. Toddler-sized wheelbarrows, kitchen appliances, lawnmowers, and riding toys provide perfect opportunities for toddlers to exercise their best gross motor, social, and cognitive skills all at once.

Riding toys without pedals may seem quite simplistic compared to tricycles and bicycles but require coordination of sitting balance, visual attention, steering with the hands, and pushing with the feet at the same time. Most young children learn first to balance in a sitting position with their feet raised on the vehicle while an adult pushes. Caregivers tend to tire of bending and pushing about the time that toddlers find their balance and lower their feet to the ground. First attempts at using feet to push oneself on a riding toy often result in a reverse motion, but eventually youngsters figure out how to plant their feet at the front of the vehicle and pull themselves forward. Steering follows, as youngsters develop the ability to propel with the feet and at the same time use their arms to alter direction based on visual information.

Fine Motor Development: Using the Hands

Toddlers are fairly adept at using their hands as tools to accomplish goals such as finger feeding, pushing, pulling, poking, pointing at, and examining interesting objects in the environment. Important developmental tasks for 1- and 2-year-olds involve using fine motor skills to solve problems that emerge during play and to advance independence in play and self-care activities.

In play, 1-year-olds seem intrigued with putting small objects into big containers and dumping them out again. Their hands form the approximate shape and size of each small object before touching it, and they release blocks into buckets with an accurate and coordinated action. Most children between the ages of 1 and 2 figure out that they can grasp very small objects two at a time in one hand and may gleefully hold out two hands with multiple objects in each for adult inspection. If they are holding a small toy in each hand and want to pick up a third, one object will be transferred into the other hand to solve the problem of grasping yet another. Two-year-olds will repeatedly stack a few objects, or put things in a line. Caregivers often remark about the enthusiasm toddlers have for putting away toys, although the youngsters often want to dump everything out again immediately and do it all over!

Two-year-olds quickly learn to use *pincer grasps* to pull toys on strings or dangle and swing them in the air and use *wrist rotation* to purposefully turn a plastic container over to empty out the smaller items inside. The same wrist action is sometimes used to dump the contents of drinking cups, much to the delight of babies and the consternation of caregivers. Increased ease and control of wrist rotation allows toddlers to begin using a spoon to scoop food for eating and to enjoy toys with knobs to twist. Pincer grasp and wrist rotation also provide powerful tools for undressing, and

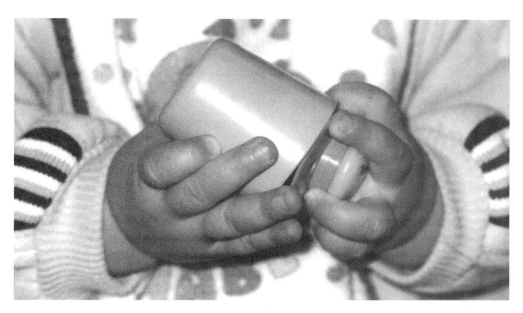

Toddlers are quite adept at using their hands to grasp, manipulate, and explore more than one object at a time.

many toddlers seem compelled to take off their shoes, socks, hats, and mittens repeatedly. Two-year-olds who are encouraged also become adept at removing shirts, pants, and coats. Modesty is not much of an issue with toddlers, and many parents find it hard to keep their toddlers dressed, especially when the weather is warm.

Toddlers become quite masterful at using their hands. It is important to note that refinement of reaching and grasping is highly dependent on opportunity and experience. The ages at which toddlers acquire fine motor skills vary in large part according to family expectations for self-care activities like dressing, tooth brushing, and eating with utensils, as well as the availability of blocks, toys, or other manipulative objects in their environments. The cognitive components of tool use and spatial relations are discussed in a later section on cognitive skills, but the development of scribbling provides a nice example for the sequence of fine motor development in tool use. Similar sequences could be applied to use of a spoon.

A 12-month-old baby might hold a large crayon or marker in his or her hand, turn it over for inspection, and maybe bang it against the table or other toys. Chances are the crayon is initially held in a *cylindrical grasp*, with fingers curled around and thumb on the top and a 50–50 chance of the marking end pointing downward. Even if the banging hand were directed toward a large piece of paper and marks were made, the baby would be unlikely to notice or try to reproduce them. From the baby's point of view, banging is the activity in progress, and replacing the crayon with a rattle or a small block would not probably change the action.

With experience, most toddlers gradually take notice of the results of their arm movements, especially if adults are encouraging and prompt the use of large colorful markers. Once a child's attention shifts from the motion to the resulting marks on the paper,

FIG. 3.2.   Scribbling. Earliest scribbles are random and often horizontal. Soon distinct lines and shape emerge, and are later combined to represent people and objects.

the whole arm usually begins to move horizontally rather than up and down. The *random scribbling* produced at this point is still very action oriented, without any apparent attempt to represent anything in the child's environment (Brittain, 1979). Over time, the relative focus of scribbling is transferred to the product, however, and 2-year-olds often quite are proud of their drawings. By the age of 3 years, typically developing children are often experimenting with a variety of lines and circles, curves and dots known as *controlled scribbling* and holding the crayon in a grip that more closely approximates an adult *pencil grasp* (Brittain, 1979). At this point, fine motor skills are well developed and used increasingly in the context of cognitive, social, and independent self-care activities.

Variations in Toddler Motor Development

Although many babies with special needs are healthy and within the norms for physical development, the growth of 1- and 2-year-olds with disabilities may vary due directly or indirectly to characteristics of their conditions. Babies born prematurely, who spend the first few months of their lives in the intensive care nursery, often lag behind others their age in height and weight for the first 2 or 3 years of life (Goldberg, 1982). Toddlers with Down syndrome tend to be shorter, have lower muscle tone, and are often less active than their peers. Very high or low muscle tone throughout the body associated with cerebral palsy sometimes results in problems in eating, digestion, and elimination that can slow the pace of physical growth. Conditions like cleft lip and palate that affect the mouth can disrupt chewing, swallowing, and the emergence and location of teeth. *Congenital* heart problems occur frequently in combination with other disabilities, with an adverse effect on both growth and physical activity. Infants and toddlers with disabilities are also more likely than other babies to become ill and be hospitalized, compromising nutritional intake and diverting the energy required for physical growth and development to the more basic functions of survival, healing, and health maintenance.

Perhaps because so many people in Western cultures wear glasses or contacts to correct less-than-perfect vision, most of us take our sight for granted and don't often stop to consider what life would be like if we couldn't see. Use of the hands, as you read in previous sections, is quite dependent on visual information, so toddlers with visual impairments are especially at risk for delays in fine motor development. The sight of people, objects, and events in the immediate environment provides significant incentives for babies to move, reach, and grasp, so poor vision poses problems in motivation as well as in skill development. If visual input is confusing or lacking altogether, youngsters are dependent on auditory and tactile information to inspire interest and interaction. It is not surprising that toddlers with visual impairments may be delayed in the development of independent mobility and visually directed reaching and grasping skills.

Toddlers with very poor but functional vision often begin wearing corrective lenses by their first birthdays, and for these youngsters putting on and taking off glasses becomes a part of their dressing routines. Making sure that toddlers with poor vision are always close enough to see what their peers can see from farther away is a good overall approach, as is providing more obvious visual cues through the use of high-contrast and larger objects. Increasing the amount of useful visual information is essential for toddlers with poor vision but obviously beside the point for those who don't see at all.

Youngsters who are blind or have significant visual impairments need an assessment of the environment to ensure safety as they move around and plenty of experience handling objects, playing with manipulative toys, and learning self-care skills. It is important to remember that toddlers who can't see are likely to rely more heavily on hearing and touch to obtain information about their surroundings, with tactile prompts being especially important for youngsters who are just learning language. Selecting toys for their tactile properties can enhance a blind child's understanding of objects, and manipulative toys that also produce noise when activated provide additional information. Keep in mind that young children are very adaptable and learn inventive strategies for negotiating the early childhood years; toddlers with visual impairments are no exception. Parents and vision specialists will be your best resources in providing care to toddlers who don't see well, and many professionals find their own creativity expanded as they come to understand development from a different perspective.

Youngsters with Down syndrome are likely to attain motor skills more slowly than their peers, especially evident for activities such as scribbling that also have strong cognitive components. The low *muscle tone* often associated with Down syndrome can make it difficult for toddlers to maintain steady postures and move through the environment. Many toddlers with Down syndrome are still mastering independent walking, so they may rely on creeping longer and need to be carried more often than other toddlers. The information in this chapter should help you in telling the differences between motor difficulties and cognitive delays for these children, and your observations can provide invaluable input for the early interventionists with whom you work.

TODDLER COGNITIVE DEVELOPMENT:
BECOMING A SYMBOLIC THINKER

A quick review of the previous section reveals that the motor behavior of typically developing toddlers is determined to some extent by maturation and physical growth but also is governed by increasingly sophisticated cognitive processes. Body image, spatial relations, perspective taking, depth perception, problem solving, visual information, and tool use are all terms that refer to both cognitive and motor development between ages

1 and 3. An important cognitive passage marks the toddler years according to the Piaget-ian framework introduced in chapter 2: At about 2 years of age children move from sen-sorimotor interactions to *preoperational thought*. Rapid advancement in fine motor, social, and language development during the second year of life can be explained in large part by a move from an action-oriented to a thought-based understanding of the world. Review Table 3.1 for an overview of Piaget's description of the progression of sensorimotor development; in this chapter, we focus on substages 5 and 6.

Tertiary Circular Reactions (12 to 18 Months)

Piaget described the first half of the second year of life as a period of transition from action to mental processes such as prediction and memory. The behavior of 1-year-old babies indicates that they understand the permanence of objects and people, interact with intent, imitate some familiar sounds and gestures, use their hands as tools, and are beginning to anticipate the effects of their own behavior. Between 12 and 18 months, babies apply these skills with vigor, assimilating more sophisticated information and making mental as well as physical accommodations in subsequent behavior.

During the early months of toddlerhood, children move from action on concrete objects to simple manipulations of mental images, recognizing for instance a favorite

TABLE 3.1

Piaget's Stages of Sensorimotor Development

Piaget's Substage	Age Range	Description
1. Reflexive activity	Birth to 1 month	Automatic, immediate, involuntary responses to sensory events. *Example*: Babies blink at bright lights, startle at loud noises, and suck on a nipples/fingers.
2. Primary circular reactions	1 to 4 months	Repetitive simple movements or vocalizations that create pleasurable sensations. *Example*: Babies repeatedly bring their hands to their mouths and suck their fingers.
3. Secondary circular reactions	4 to 8 months	Intentional reproductions of simple actions involving other people or objects, to create interesting or pleasurable effects. *Example*: Babies kick or bat at crib mobiles to make them move.
4. Coordinated circular reactions	8 to 12 months	Coordinated series of simple actions to produce a desired outcome; the beginnings of cause and effect. *Example*: Babies bang toys on their cribs and holler to get the attention of their caregivers.
5. Tertiary circular reactions	12 to 18 months	Complex novel actions to solve problems and explore; the beginnings of trial and error learning. *Example*: Toddlers climb on whatever might be handy if they can't reach something they want.
6. Mental combinations	18 to 24 months	Mental images used to solve problems; the beginnings of thinking in addition to action. *Example*: Older toddlers can tell by looking (or remembering) if something is out of reach and will get something to climb on without trial and error.

toy that is partially covered up by a blanket. Recognition of a partially visible object requires a clear mental representation of the object and the ability to rotate the mental image to match the portion visible. Toddlers also begin active exploration of spatial relations in play, begin to imitate unfamiliar sounds and gestures, and reflect accurately the functions of various objects in their play.

Internal Representations (18 to 24 months)

Piaget's observations led him to believe that around the age of 2 years, most children are capable of simple mental processes based on symbolic functions of thought and language (Piaget, 1954). During the second year of life, toddlers become quite sophisticated at finding solutions to new problems without reverting to trial and error, using words as symbols to label concepts, understanding cause and effect, and imitating complex behaviors from memory. Although not all early childhood professionals agree that Piaget's stages are discreet and exclusive from one another (Fischer, 1980), much of the current research in developmental psychology supports the basic sequences of specific skill development he described or provides additional explanation and refinement of the major tenets of the theory. A more careful examination of a few of the specific cognitive processes within subdomains or branches of sensorimotor development as they develop during the second year of life reveals the types of sequences that Piaget observed.

Imitation

During the first year of life, most babies demonstrate the ability to imitate vocalizations and gestures, a skill that is typically acquired in a predictable sequence based on two general principles. First, imitation of the familiar is easier than imitation of something unfamiliar. Second, babies learn to imitate actions that are visible to them as they are reproduced before they will imitate something they can't see. For example, gestures are easier to imitate than sounds, and gestures using the hands or feet are easier than facial expressions (unless using a mirror).

Imitation is a skill that most children acquire early in life, and there is in fact some evidence that even very young infants can imitate in an imprecise fashion (Melzoff & Moore, 1983). How do babies master a skill as complex as observing the behavior of another, remembering what they have seen, and producing a matching behavior? The first obvious imitations usually occur around 5 or 6 months of age when the baby is engaged in motor activity such as clapping or banging. If a caregiver imitates the infant, chances are the baby will continue reproducing the action. Of course, in this scenario, it is quite likely that the child would continue clapping or banging anyway, but the interaction quickly becomes a turn-taking game.

Before too long the parent or teacher can initiate the imitation game, as long as the action is familiar to the baby. Peekaboo and patty-cake games and waving good-bye. often begin in this way. Once the rules of the game are established with gestures, babies will begin imitating sounds they already make. Babies are quite entertaining when experimenting with blowing bubbles and "raspberries," shrieking, growling, and babbling, and many caregivers are compelled to imitate the noises, setting off a round of the imitation game. By the time babies are a year old, most of them can imitate gestures such as clapping, covering the eyes, and raising arms and will repeat sounds and words that they already use.

Between 12 and 18 months of age, babies who have learned the imitation game learn to apply the skill to sounds and gestures that are novel and unfamiliar to them. Toddlers watch the actions of their caregivers and copy them when learning new motor skills such as hopping, using spoons, and scribbling. They imitate new sound combinations to build vocabulary and to play nursery games. Two-year-olds can generally imitate new sounds and gestures of increasing complexity and difficulty. Combinations of sounds are imitated as words, and combinations of words are imitated as short sentences. Imitation of gestures allows 2-year-olds independence in the practice of self-care skills such as hand washing and toileting and promotes imitation of one another in play. The ability to imitate novel sounds and gestures provides toddlers with a powerful learning strategy that provides an efficient and effective method for learning and practicing new behaviors and accounts for the rapid pace of learning in all domains during the second year of life.

Spatial Relationships

Picture a baby between the ages of 1 and 2 years sitting on the floor surrounded by a number of hand-sized toys or blocks and one large container. Chances are you imagine the youngster picking up the smaller toys and putting them into the bucket, and that is exactly the case. Younger toddlers may place just two or three things in the bucket and then move on to banging or throwing the smaller toys or dumping the container. Two-year-olds will methodically place as many as 15 or 20 smaller toys in the container, dump them out, and start all over.

Learning about the properties of objects is serious business for toddlers, and they learn best through hands-on experience. As 1- and 2-year-olds fill and empty containers, they are solidifying their understanding of size and space, figuring out what fits inside something else and how many smaller items will fill up a larger space. Similar to the construction of body image through movement activities, object play provides a concrete, action-based foundation for learning concepts of size, shape, and location. As toddlers begin stacking and lining up two and then up to six little cars or blocks, they are learning about working in two dimensions of space, height, length, and number.

Two-year-olds become increasingly adept at stacking and fitting objects into defined spaces and will work diligently at form boards, pegboards, and simple puzzles of multiple single pieces. They learn that specific words such as the prepositions up, down, in and out describe the position of objects in space and begin using these language symbols to describe objects, themselves, and their actions.

Problem Solving

Toddlers encounter any number of simple problems in their daily lives, from how to get out of the crib, to how to reach that cracker on the table, to how to carry four toys at once. Before a year of age, babies work out solutions to similar but simpler problems through trial and error and learn to recognize solutions apparent in their immediate surroundings. Perhaps they have learned that calling for an adult works better for getting out of the crib than climbing and falling, and they know to crawl purposefully to the table in order to reach for a cracker. Toddlers persist in using trial and error but also try new solutions to old problems. A basket, for example, will hold all six toys the youngster wants to transport but might be too big or heavy to carry once it is full. As toddlers approach their second birthdays, they begin to solve problems without needing to try each solution.

One-year-olds also begin to see the relationship between objects and their functions, and their play becomes more specialized. Whereas younger babies will look at, bang, chew, and throw any object in their grasp, toddlers are much more discriminating. Without benefit of trial and error experimentation, they will hug their "stuffies," roll balls, put hats on their heads, and scribble with crayons, knowing from memory that each object has a specific use. Their play is goal directed, incorporating the socially dictated activities of adults. A typically developing 17-month-old is likely to be a great helper at cleaning up spills, sweeping the floor, washing windows, or doing any other chore that involves a vigorous motor component. It is not uncommon for toddlers to reproduce such activity the next time they encounter a paper towel, broom, or dishcloth, showing that they recall the function of the objects.

Two-year-olds become creative and inventive in solving problems, searching for solutions and trying multiple strategies until they are successful. An experienced toddler who wants to reach a cracker on the table is likely to remember that standing on tiptoes and reaching is not sufficient. She may look around and see the telephone book lying on the floor, look back at the table, and conclude that it also will be an unsuccessful solution. She may cruise into other rooms in search of something that will meet her needs, and after rejecting many possible options on sight, return with the small stool from the bathroom sink. Children this age can pose interesting challenges for caregivers as they become more proficient at solving their own problems!

Means for Obtaining Ends: Tool Use

From spoons to crayons, 1- and 2-year-olds in Western cultures are expected to learn how to use objects as tools for achieving functional ends such as eating or scribbling. Refined control of small muscles in the hand is necessary for competent use of tools, but there is also a cognitive component. Early understanding of means to obtain ends is evident when children point to the knob on a wind-up toy or attempt to wind it themselves. The knob is a means to the end of activating the entire toy. In a more functional manner, doorknobs open entire doors and switches control light across the room. By 18 months of age, toddlers often have learned how to get something that is out of their reach at the table by using a utensil or pulling on a supporting piece of cloth. Toddlers also demonstrate use of means–ends behaviors when they position adult hands to demonstrate or complete a task that is too difficult for them.

Cause and Effect

Understanding of cause and effect goes hand in hand with imitation, using means to obtain ends, and problem solving as toddlers become more competent at independent interactions with adults, peers and objects. Before they are 1 year old, babies often associate one event with another, especially if events occur together regularly in their daily routines. So a baby might associate putting on a coat with going outside or the sound of the running water with bath time. Knowledge of cause and effect requires the additional comprehension that events occur in a particular sequence, in which the first event causes a particular effect, and not vice versa.

We once observed an 11-month-old baby standing at a low table holding a bell, poking at the clapper, and turning it over as he examined it. He was clearly interested in reproducing the bell's noise but hadn't identified the exact cause of the ringing effect. In the course of looking around at the adults in the room, he startled himself by inadvertently ringing the bell, and fell on his fanny, causing the bell to ring quite loudly. He immediately stood up and purposefully plopped down numerous times, watching the bell and listening for the ringing. This little guy was showing the beginnings of cause-and-effect knowledge; he seemed to know that his movement caused the bell to ring but hadn't identified shaking (the clapper against the inside of the bell) as the source of the sound.

Once babies begin to associate events in their environment, the combination of sensory examination and motor activity quickly reveals cause-and-effect relationships. In the previous instance, the child had already associated his actions with the sound of the bell and seemed to understand that his movement was the cause of the sound effects. We could predict that this baby would return to exploring the clapper with his index finger and using wrist rotation to turn the bell over, eventually identifying the action of shaking as the cause of the ringing.

Early Preoperational Thought

Children who demonstrate representational thought and symbolic use of language have made a great leap in cognitive development. Older toddlers are no longer dependent on concrete and immediate actions as a primary means for understanding the world, yet their thought processes are quite different than those of adults. Two-year-olds reason, remember, and draw conclusions but only within the limits of their own viewpoints and experiences. Piaget described the thought process of young children as being *egocentric*, meaning that they can only think about things they experience directly. Toddlers think in very concrete terms, associating one specific idea with another from their personal experience, as illustrated in Vignette 3.2. Some researchers believe that egocentric thoughts assist in the development of memory, by providing a concrete and meaningful context for organization of the child's own experiences into mental representations (Bjorklund & Green, 1992).

Vignette 3.2: *A 2-Year-Old on the Telephone*

Lauren is 32 months old and lives in Washington State. She talks excitedly about a new truck she holds, pointing excitedly to "this one" and "that part," while talking to her Aunt Gail from Alaska on the telephone. It does not occur to Lauren that Gail can't see what she sees, even though it is obvious that Gail is not present in the same room. "It's right here," she says with exasperation, while jabbing more vigorously at the parts in question. From Lauren's perspective, Gail just doesn't seem to be paying attention.

A few months later when Gail calls, Lauren is disappointed that her aunt isn't coming to visit right away, despite the fact that she knows Gail lives far away and is calling from home. Her mother thinks Lauren must have forgotten the airplane ride to Gail's last summer, but the next day when she sees a picture of an airplane in a book Lauren says, "They going to Alaska!"

Two-year-olds demonstrate use of representational thought when they engage in pretend play. Earliest pretend play centers totally on the self, as when 1-year-olds pretend to drink from an empty cup. The pretend play of 2-year-olds includes familiar activities such as eating and sleeping, extended to include adults, dolls, stuffed animals, and even pets. A 23-month-old was once observed offering an empty cup to the family dog and then laughing hysterically at his own joke!

Toddlers combine memory of specific events, knowledge about the functions of objects and social roles, and the ability to imitate during sequenced motor activities. They pretend to drive the family car or a riding toy to a specific destination, cook and eat meals, and dress up to take the roles of fascinating adults they have encountered: doctors, firemen, plumbers, and superheroes. By the time they are 3 years old, many toddlers have begun using boxes for vehicles and blocks for telephones. They understand that little cars represent real cars and are to be driven; plastic dinosaurs repre-

This toddler knows about hats, and is using the basket to represent a hat. If she had a more experience with baskets, she might just as easily turn a hat upside down and use it as a basket.

sent huge monsters and are fearsome; and peg people represent real people, even though they don't have arms or legs. They drive cars by sitting in circular holes made just for them. Representational play requires concrete props such as costumes or miniature versions of real things and allows older toddlers to reproduce their own experiences and observations. As children get older, they require fewer realistic representations in pretend play (Flavell, Miller, & Miller, 1993). Pretending to drive while sitting in a still car advances to using a plastic steering wheel while sitting in a chair, to driving toy cars, and finally to taking trips to far away places in a box that looks nothing like a car and is powered solely by imagination.

It is important to remember that cognitive learning proceeds in concert with motor and social development. Toddlers who are busy playing with toys, interacting with people, and moving about the environment use skills from all developmental domains, and each new behavior learned has application in many different activities. Piaget's sequences seem to provide a relatively neutral framework for evaluating the early cognitive development of infants and toddlers from divergent cultural groups, because the focus is on principles and processes of mental development rather than on culturally specific content (Hale-Benson, 1986). In fact, cross-cultural research validates the existence of similar sequences of development in imitation, problem solving, and functional use of objects across a variety of cultures (Trawick-Smith, 2000).

Pretend play is an important indicator of early cognitive development, especially between the ages of 1 and 3 years. One cognitive psychologist wrote, "It maybe one of those biologically evolved activities that, like language, is spontaneously practiced in all cultures but formally taught in none" (Flavell et al., 1993, p. 82).

Language and Communication

Prelinguistic communication was addressed under social development in the chapter on infancy because of the strong connection to caregiver–infant interactions. Before the age of 1 year, babies communicate with intent, primarily through use of body orientations, facial expressions, gestures, and nonsymbolic vocalizations that mimic the intonations of their native language. At the end of the first year, however, many babies are beginning to use *word approximations*, consistent combinations of sounds as a transition to language, a symbolic system of communication. The cognitive aspects of language learning are based in the representational thought processes described in the previous section. Using toys to represent adult activities and using objects to represent other objects is a more concrete version of using words to represent objects, actions, and concepts.

First Words

Language is a complex and abstract endeavor, wonderfully creative and at the same time governed by a multitude of rules. During the toddler years, language development is focused on *semantics*, or the meanings of words, and on *syntax*, the rules of grammar for the language. Toddlers typically learn noun labels for familiar people and objects in their immediate environments first: mama, daddy, doggie, bottle, bed, cookie, blanket. The exact words will vary, depending on the people and activities of family life. Action verbs often follow quickly, with an emphasis on words that reflect the toddler's daily activities: eat, sleep, go, see. Many early vocabulary words are those that can be interpreted as either nouns or verbs. *Eat*, for example, can mean the action of eating, the food on the table, the feeling of hunger, or the time of day for meals. *Ride* might be used to point out a car, stroller, or riding toy; to request an outing; or to describe the activity of being in a moving vehicle. The acquisition of noun labels and action verbs in early vocabulary is consistent across cultures and reflective of the concrete, immediate nature of early symbolic communication.

An interesting individual difference in early language acquisition was described by Nelson (1973) in an analysis of early vocabulary. Some toddlers seem to focus primarily on words that refer to objects and people, developing strategies such as asking, "Was dat?" (What's that?) to elicit noun labels in response from adults. Nelson considered these children to have a pattern of *referential language*, because so many of their communications either referred to objects or asked for object words. Other youngsters had vocabularies with more words for affect, motion, or location, labeled *expressive language*. Not surprisingly, the pattern of the primary caregiver's language was found to predict whether the toddler would tend to use referential or expressive words.

Each toddler builds vocabulary based on unique experiences, and new words are acquired at an average rate of one word per week until children are 18 months old, at which point there are about 20 to 30 consistent words in regular use. They then begin to acquire new words very quickly through imitation, at the rate of 10 to 30 new words each week, and a 200- to 300-word vocabulary is common by the second birthday (Goldfield & Reznick, 1990). This rapid expansion of vocabulary between 18 and 24 months is consistent with Piaget's contention that toddlers become proficient at representational thought and symbol use during the last half of the second year.

Youngsters who live in bilingual environments seem to learn initial vocabulary without differentiating between languages. Before 18 months of age, they use some words from each language, seeming to prefer whichever form has shorter words with easier sounds (Saunders, 1988). With the usual spurt of vocabulary growth after 18 months, children learning two languages use critical common words from both languages. The total number of words in the vocabularies of bilingual toddlers is roughly equal to the vocabulary of their peers learning only one language. Two-year-olds who are learning more than one language may make up words that are combinations of two words with the same meaning (Arnberg, 1987), for example using *morging* as a combination of the German *morgen* and the English *morning*.

Toddlers' understanding of language also reflects Piaget's hypotheses about cognitive development. At 12 months infants associate words frequently used with people and actions in their immediate environments, including names for family members, favorite toys, places in the house, and simple actions like bye-bye. One-year-olds also respond consistently to combinations of gestures and words that give directions, for example, "come here" with a hand motion or "give me" and an outstretched hand. Two-year-olds will follow one- and two-part directions if they can see the objects and people in question. All the previous examples indicate a process of making associations and using representations as a foundation for symbolic thinking and language learning.

By their third birthdays, children can carry out two- and three-step directions related to retrieving objects and placing or giving them to someone, such as, "Go get your blankie from the crib and put it in the laundry basket." They can also identify pictures of objects, actions, people, and body parts by pointing, even if they can't produce the word labels themselves. Three-year-olds can usually group and match objects by color, size, or shape, although they may not know the words to label the concepts. By the end of the toddler years, the language of typically developing children demonstrates cognitive processes of memory, imitation, categorization, sequencing, and spatial relations.

Beyond Single Words

Once toddlers have a basic vocabulary of approximately 20 single words, the next step is combining two words in rudimentary sentences. The first two-word utterances are combinations that have a single meaning, such as "all gone" or "uh-oh." Two-word utterances using nouns and verbs appear in the language of 18- to 24-month-olds and are constructed based on the meanings of the words used rather than on rules of grammar. Bloom (1973) identified the most common *semantic relationships* of two-word utterances as containing words for agents (those performing an action), actions, and objects. The phrases "Gramma go" and "Kitty eat" are examples of agent–action combinations, whereas "Kitty bed" and "Gramma car" are agent–object utterances. Action-object combinations include "Go car" and "Eat more."

The exact meanings of two-word utterances must be inferred from the context of communications, using additional clues from inflection, intonation, and facial expression. "Mama go" can be interpreted as "Can we go for a ride, Mama" if asked with a questioning inflection by a toddler who is pointing to the car and tugging his mother in that direction with an expectant expression. The same agent–action combination can just as easily mean "Mama, look at that cool car!" for the youngster who was pointing excitedly while exclaiming in a loud voice and looking back and forth between her mother and the passing car. Table 3.2 lists a number of possible semantic relationships in two-word utterances and gives examples from observations of toddlers.

Between the ages of 2 and 3 years, toddlers begin to use longer utterances constructed according to the rules of *syntax* for their native language. The word order of 3-word utterances in English, for example, dictates an agent–action–object sequence. "Mama fall water" is understood to have an entirely different meaning than "Water fall Mama," even without the contextual cues for the missing prepositions. "Mama fall in water" is clearer yet. Typically developing toddlers quickly learn correct word order for their native languages once they begin combining three words into sentences. Mastering syntax requires cognitive skills in sequencing (for correct word order) and categorization (for grouping parts of speech).

Bilingual children may initially learn the rules of syntax for one language and use that grammar across both sets of vocabulary. Longer sentences may contain vocabulary from both languages in a single utterance or repeat a word in both languages. For

TABLE 3.2

Semantic Relationships

Semantic Relationship	Examples
Agent–action	"Me go"; "Papa ride"; "Her eat."
Action–object	"See plane"; "Ride car"; "Sleep blankie."
Agent–object	"Doggy bed"; "Gramma car"; "Me cup."
Action–location	"Get down"; "See there"; "Show out."
Agent–attribute	"Man funny"; "Fire hot"; "Me big."
Possession	"My bites"; "Mama bed"; "Papa cup."
Negation	"No cracker"; "No ball"; "No blankie."
Recurrence	"More eat"; "Go again."

instance, a child learning both English and German might say, "Night-nacht. Me go bed schlafen" when saying goodnight. Sometimes bilingual children will combine the rules of grammar from both languages and use syntax that is incorrect in both languages. A Head Start teacher told us of a child whose mother spoke Spanish at home; the child used the Spanish past tense /o/ ending on English words: "Me pusho" instead of "I pushed."

These children have the advantage of learning two sets of specific vocabulary and rules for word order, verb tense, plurals, past tense but don't yet have the cognitive skills for categorizing the two languages. Although caregivers sometimes worry when young children mix two or more languages, it is an expected phase of bi- or multilingual language acquisition. Over half the children in the world are bilingual (Trawick-Smith, 2000), however, and during the preschool years, they become able to use multiple languages skillfully.

Language and Concepts

Learning language beyond noun labels and action verbs requires a firm grasp of concepts, also. Two-year-old vocabularies include a preponderance of words that address abstract ideas: pronouns, adjectives, adverbs, prepositions and words for color, shape, size, time, number, and size. Adjectives and adverbs include many polar opposites, for instance *hot–cold, big–little, fast–slow, good–bad*. Time, number, and size all include relative concepts such as yesterday, more, and smaller that require abstract comparisons and can take on different meanings, depending on the context and situation. A medium-sized wooden block may be "the little one" during construction with very large cardboard blocks, but "the big one" when playing with legos.

Personal pronouns require at least some understanding of perspective and role, because correct use of words such as I–you, me–you, mine–yours depends on the perspective of the speaker. For instance, when Ben says to Taylor, "I want your toy," *I* refers to Ben and *your* refers to Taylor. For Taylor to understand and paraphrase Ben's idea accurately, he must say, "You want my toy." No wonder toddlers often persist in using *me* when they describe themselves as an agent–subject; "Me going fast" is incorrect syntax, but everyone understands the meaning. Vignette 3.3 describes a particularly interesting error of pronoun use.

Vignette 3.3: Give it to me!

Jessie is 2 years old and attending a family reunion with a number of relatives, adults and children, whom she recently has met for the first time. Twice now she has taken her Aunt Jolene's hairdryer from the bathroom counter. Jessie is fascinated with this particular appliance, understands its function completely, and brandishes it proudly as she walks around putting it to multiple uses. She pretends to dry her own hair, to blow imaginary insects off the deck, and to shoot invisible villains in flagrant violation of her mother's no-weapons rule. The hairdryer is a handy toy for Jessie, because she can quickly switch from shooting to blowing hot air. "Jessie not shoot Mama; Jessie blowing bad bugs." (Great word order, good semantics, inconsistent use of the -ing verb ending, and no personal pronouns.)

Aunt Jolene is more concerned with the continued usefulness of her hairdryer than with the weapons issue. Twice now Jolene has held out her hand and said firmly, "Jessie, give the hairdryer to me. It is not a toy for you to play with."

The next time Jessie sees her Aunt Jolene, she points at her and exclaims righteously, "Me! Jessie not have blow toy now!" She persists in calling Jolene "me," as if it were her name, for days, in clear response to the initial and apparently memorable requests to, "Give the hairdryer to me." Jessie calls herself and others by name and assumes her aunt is doing the same. And despite the hundreds of combined years of language use among the adults present, no one can quite figure out how to correct the error.

By the time children are 3, they are working to master the word order for questions, plurals of nouns, and /ing/ verb endings. Many times toddlers' first attempts at using new syntax rules appear more successful than later modifications, especially in cases of irregular forms. Two-year-olds might learn the plural form *feet* in imitation but later change to saying *foots*. The later error indicates that the child has learned, and overgeneralized, the rule that plurals are generally formed by adding the letter *s*. Irregular plurals must be sorted out one by one, after realization that every rule has its exceptions. By the time children are 3, they are typically good communication partners, understanding the rules of conversation and using language appropriately to represent their experiences, make requests, obtain information, and participate in social interactions with adults and peers.

Variations in Toddler Cognitive Development

The most obvious variations in the rate of cognitive development are associated with conditions like Down syndrome or brain damage that cause serious delays in concept development, representational thought, and use of concepts. Children with mental retardation or serious cognitive delays will by definition learn more slowly than their peers, require more practice to acquire new behaviors, and have more difficulty applying skills in new situations.

Toddlers with cognitive delays may need specialized instruction to become proficient at imitation, problem solving, representational play, and other more sophisticated sensorimotor tasks. Acquiring language is also likely to be a problem for toddlers with cognitive delays because of the underlying cognitive aspects of symbol use and concept formation. Early intervention services can provide resources to evaluate the exact areas of difficulty and design interventions to remediate learning difficulties.

Motor and sensory disabilities can also compromise a toddler's ability to master late sensorimotor skills. Imitation of gestures, for instance, is difficult for youngsters with cerebral palsy, and an understanding of spatial relations can be delayed without the ability to manipulate objects. Imitation and mental representations may develop more slowly in young children who are blind, because they cannot make use of visual cues in the environment. Toddlers who have hearing impairments are often fitted with hearing aids, and those who are deaf will usually be learning a symbolic manual language such as American Sign Language.

Early childhood special educators often prefer to develop programs for toddlers with special needs in the context of child-care centers. Although extra attention may be required for instruction on specific skills, young children with disabilities and delays are usually highly motivated by social interactions with their peers and enjoy the same types of activities all toddlers do. Because so much of the world is still so new to toddlers, and they are so curious, peers with disabilities are almost always accepted without bias or negative expectations. Having the full range of abilities included together in early childhood programs provides at least as many rewards as challenges for children and adults alike.

TODDLER SOCIAL-AFFECTIVE DEVELOPMENT: BECOMING INDEPENDENT WHILE LEARNING THE RULES

The framework described in chapter 2 for social development during infancy was grounded in relationships between babies and their caregivers. The business of getting to know and appreciate each other continues into the toddler years, but at the same time a new social agenda emerges for 1- and 2-year-olds as they strive for independence and autonomy.

Many of the important accomplishments of toddlerhood contribute to a sense of competence and an understanding of the self. One-year-olds generally recognize themselves in a mirror (Lewis & Brookes-Gunn, 1979), and 2-year-olds can identify themselves in pictures. Babies learn to respond to their own names, and toddlers use their names to refer to themselves. Erikson (1963) described the primary social task of children between 18 and 36 months as a struggle for autonomy and independence, achieved in part by separating their concepts of themselves from their concepts of their caregivers.

Once babies learn to walk, they no longer require the close physical contact that comes with being carried. Two-year-olds learn to feed themselves with their own hands or using utensils and to drink from cups instead of, or in addition to, nursing. They begin taking off and putting on their own clothes, tasks previously required of caregivers. Toddlers develop images of their own bodies in space that are separate from the mental representations they have of other people. They learn words to label body parts and words that refer to themselves: me, my, mine. They can build their own creations, play with the toys they like best, and participate (or not!) in sophisti-

A toddler who gives a kiss to his sister is demonstrating his understanding of social conventions for expressing affection. He is likely to reserve such interactions for people with whom he is familiar and comfortable.

cated social interactions. It is no wonder toddlers tend toward increased independence from caregivers at home and in child-care settings; they have the tools and the talent to make their own decisions and do things for themselves.

At the same time, most Western cultures expect toddlers to begin complying with social conventions, following directions, and conforming to common rules of behavior. It takes a lot of practice to learn the rules and to perform new skills without help, and toddlers are often perceived as stretching the boundaries of their own capabilities while testing the limits of caregivers' patience. In Erikson's view, toddlers walk a rather fine line between an individual need to exercise their own competence and group requirements for learning rules and limits of acceptable behavior. He believed that toddlers whose attempts at independent behavior are encouraged in a supportive and safe atmosphere develop the most healthy self-concepts. Erikson worried that overly restrictive environments with an excessive focus on the rules of behavior would result both in toddlers feeling shame about their desires for independence and in doubt about their competence.

A notable criticism of Erikson's theory of social-emotional development is that it is grounded in Western cultural values and child-rearing practices that promote individualism and self-reliance (Trawick-Smith, 2000). In families where toddlers sleep with their parents or siblings, continue to nurse, and are held or carried, there is likely to be much less emphasis on independence and autonomy despite similarities in physical maturation, development of representational thinking, and language learning. In cultures in which collective behavior is valued more than individual accomplishment at all ages, a toddler's sense of competence might well depend more on learning the rules governing group activity than on independence and separation from caregivers.

In addition to cultural variations, individual differences among children determine exactly how toddlers will behave as they master more sophisticated milestones and engage in more complex social interactions. The following discussion of infant temperament provides a good foundation for appraising the influence of individual differences on social development.

Temperament

Adults often discuss children using terms that describe how their offspring act, rather than what they are actually doing: "She has always been an active child"; "He is so good natured"; "She is so impulsive"; "He has always had a quick temper." Parents often remark that they notice differences among their own children from birth. The first baby may be quiet, alert, and awake immediately following delivery, whereas the second child might sleep for hours following a stint of lusty crying. Parents interpret such variations as evidence of each infant's unique personality and adjust their own responses accordingly from the outset. Research in the area of *temperament* offers fascinating insights and raises interesting questions about individual differences in behavioral style as babies interact in the world.

Rothbart (1996) defined infant temperament as "constitutionally based patterns of reacting to stimuli (reactivity) and the baby's capacities for self-regulation" (p. 277), including reactions to novel stimuli, reactions of irritability and frustration, positive mood, activity level, and attention or persistence (Rothbart & Mauro, 1990). These five dimensions of temperament are compared in Table 3.3 to nine dimensions specified by early researchers in the area, Thomas and Chess (1977). Temperament is assessed by direct observations of children in naturalistic and laboratory situations, by caregiver questionnaires, and by behavioral rating scales. The results of temperament assessments have been used to describe in detail the individual behavioral styles of children as a starting point for identifying problems and improving interactions at school and home.

Earlier studies of temperament assessment categorized patterns of ratings into three categories: easy, difficult, and slow to warm up (Thomas & Chess, 1977). The characteristics of children in each category are described briefly in Table 3.4.

TABLE 3.3

Dimensions of Temperament

Rothbart & Mauro (1990)	Thomas & Chess (1977)
Activity level	Activity level
Speed of approach to people and objects	Approach/withdrawal
Fearfulness and distress to novelty	Positive or negative mood
Irritability and distress to frustration	Intensity of reaction
	Threshold of responsiveness
Persistence of attention	Persistence/distractibility

TABLE 3.4

Temperament Categories, as Defined by Thomas & Chess (1977)

"Easy" children: Are regular in their daily schedules for eating, sleeping, and elimination; tend to approach and
  interact in novel situations; are adaptable to change, mild in disposition, and positive in mood.

"Slow-to-warm-up" children: Are not very active; tend to withdraw in novel situations; are not adaptable to
  change; have mild dispositions and negative moods.

"Difficult" children: Are not very regular in their daily schedules for eating, sleeping, and elimination; tend to
  withdraw in novel situations; are not adaptable to change; have intense dispositions and negative moods.

Adapted from Thomas and Chess, 1977.

Although longitudinal research has suggested strongly that "difficult" children are
more likely to pose caregiving challenges and to have academic and behavioral difficulties in school (Chess & Thomas, 1984), the use of temperament categories is problematic for a number of reasons. First, a sizable number of infants exhibit behavioral
styles that do not fall cleanly into any of the three categories. Second, the initial patterns of reactivity and self-regulation seen in infancy change over time as a function of
maturation, are influenced by environment and experience, and are further modified by
the styles of caregivers. During the toddler years, most children learn to control their
own behavior to some extent and to delay gratification, adding an important aspect of
individual differences not readily observable in infants (Rothbart & Ahadi, 1994).

   Additionally, some behavioral characteristics that seem negative at one point in
time may actually be adaptive later on, or vice versa. For instance, infants who tend
to react in a relatively reserved and cautious fashion to new toys are often very successful in initiating social interactions as preschoolers (Kagan, Resnick, & Snidman,
1990). The dimension of persistence–distractibility provides another good example
of how the perceived value of specific behavioral styles can change over time. The
most agreeable way to guide the behavior of curious and active toddlers is to redirect
their attention away from objects and activities that are dangerous or inappropriate by
offering more suitable alternatives. So, being distractible is a good thing for toddlers.
Primary-aged children, on the other hand, are expected to persist at schoolwork, and
being easily distracted by other activity in the classroom becomes problematic. The
last difficulty with using categories of infant temperament is that labeling a child
"difficult" can create a self-fulfilling prophecy by presenting negative expectations
for the child at an early age. Caregivers may be less likely to recognize behaviors
such as crying, disobedience, and interrupting as alterable if they attribute the conduct to children's inherent natures than if they see behavior as the result of interactions within the environment over time.

   Knowledge of the particular dimensions of infant temperament is most useful in
helping caregivers to understand and explain the needs, motivations, and interests of
individual children. The term "tempercept" has been used to convey the notion that
an objective rating of temperamental characteristics is less important than caregivers'
perceptions of the child's behavioral style and the "goodness-of-fit" between a caregiver's and a child's style (Thomas & Chess, 1977). A neutral observer might rate a
toddler's activity level as moderate for her age, for instance, but elderly grandparents

who provide care during the day might portray her as constantly on the move and the parents as less active than her older sister. As a result of different responses to her behavior, the toddler would probably soon learn that active play is encouraged at home and quieter activities appreciated at the grandparents' house. Positive and mutually satisfying interactions seem to depend on a goodness-of-fit between a very young child's temperament and the responses of caregivers more than on any particular patterns of temperament.

A basic knowledge of temperament also provides a useful foundation for understanding and interpreting the distinctive dispositions and developmental progress of youngsters with disabilities and developmental delays. Focusing on the unique personality of each child rather than on disability labels or the acquisition of specific milestones can support caregivers in getting to know children as children first.

Social Games

Toddlers quickly learn to combine motor activity with social interactions for games that require imitation and turn taking. Simple nursery games such as "so big" incorporate imitation and repetition of large gestures that serve to communicate a specific message, for instance, raising up arms to indicate a desire to be picked up. Peekaboo and patty-cake are favorites of 1-year-olds learning how to coordinate their own activity, imitate the behavior of others, and predict responses to their own actions. Typically developing 2-year-olds progress to games with other children that integrate large muscle movements with equipment or rhythm instruments for social games, such as rolling a ball with another person or using sticks to keep beat along with music. Repeated sequences of behavior in which the toddler changes roles, for instance, alternately being chased by another person and then doing the chasing, also combine simple social rules with gross motor activity.

Toddlers learn specific interaction skills long before they understand the general rules and assumptions of social conduct. A 15-month-old in a stroller at the mall may attempt to initiate a verbal interaction with everyone she sees, giving the distinct impression that she believes everyone is there for the express purpose of seeing the baby. Two-year-olds who are close to the ground have been known to identify their caregivers by their shoes, temporarily confusing the familiar objects (shoes) with the social role of providing care. One toddler who mistook another women for his mother while standing in line was quite visibly angry that "Bad lady taked your shoes!" It hadn't occurred to him to look up at the person he was following.

Variations in Toddler Social-Affective Development

Social development during the toddler years is strongly tied to cognitive development and social interactions, so disabilities that cause cognitive delays or disruptions in caregiving interactions can have a negative impact. Toddlers with developmental disabilities like Down syndrome generally attain social skills in a similar sequence but at a slower pace than do their peers. The social smile is likely to be delayed, and toddlers might still be acquiring attachment behaviors such as social referencing.

One developmental disability commonly identified during the toddler years is autism. Autism is caused by abnormalities in the structure and function of the brain, particularly those structures that control social interaction. Autism has been called "a social learning disability" (Mesibov, 1998); current research suggests a prenatal origin. Whereas typically developing infants develop sophisticated strategies for social interaction by their first birthdays, older children with autism often do not make the distinction between people and objects (Klin, 1998). Toddlers with autism often have highly developed schemes of object play but may not have learned the "first language" of reciprocal prelinguistic interactions as young babies. Babies with autism may articulate well in imitation, remember words and phrases, and easily learn complex rules of syntax but often have difficulty using language for a symbolic communicative function (Bristol, 1998). Toddlers with autism are often described as being unable to initiate or respond to social interaction with adults or peers without specialized instruction. As with most developmental disabilities, autism as a diagnosis covers a wide range of functional abilities. Toddlers with autism also tend to be quite skilled at manipulative and visual–spatial tasks. Early diagnosis and treatment of autism addresses caregiver–child interactions as well as cognitive and social goals.

Because the development of social skills is dependent on interactions among people, it is especially important that children at risk for delays in motor, cognitive, and social skills have plenty of opportunities for social interaction. Early interventionists can share many strategies with parents and teachers of toddlers with disabilities to support and enhance development of social skills. Placement in an inclusive setting with peers who are competent social partners is probably one of the best possible approaches for most toddlers with disabilities.

IMPLICATIONS FOR CAREGIVERS OF TODDLERS

Safety

Toddlers often seem driven by curiosity without always having a plan for where to go or any recognition of the hazards in their environments. They can walk around independently and revel in all sorts of motor activity but are still perfecting balance and learning about how their own bodies move around in space. Because of their top-heavy shapes, 1- and 2-year-olds are more likely than older children to fall when they lean over to look at or grasp something. Their strides toward independence and desires to exert control within the immediate environment increase the likelihood that they will engage in activities beyond their abilities or understanding. A 15-month-old who returns again and again to the stairs is not being naughty; she is simply enthusiastic about exploring a new aspect of the house and learning about climbing.

Ensuring the safety of toddlers becomes a primary responsibility for parents and other caregivers, since accidents are the leading cause of death and injury in this age range. Baby proofing of doors, stairs, and windows is necessary to prevent serious injuries from falls. Little fingers need to be protected from exploring electrical outlets, and cupboards need to be cleared of toxic supplies or rigged so curious toddlers can't get at the contents. Toddlers require secure and comfortable places to sleep that contain them when they awake until an adult arrives. Most of all they need supervision during waking hours, with support and assistance for learning how to move around safely in their indoor and outdoor environments. It is often necessary to remind and reposition 1-year-olds to get down from stairs and furniture feet first. Toddlers will learn independent motor skills and the rules for safe play by practicing walking and running on the floors and in the yard as well as by climbing on the stairs and the furniture with direction, guidance, and protection from caregivers.

Mealtimes

Because toddlers are growing more slowly than infants, their appetites usually decrease sometime after their first birthdays (Pipes, 1981). One- and 2-year-olds eat less often and may begin to refuse foods they previously enjoyed, causing caregivers to worry about nutrition. One child may accept only jelly sandwiches, whereas another might ask for toast and yogurt at every meal. Allowing toddlers to make decisions about their own diets is one way to circumvent struggles at mealtime. Sometimes providing a limited number of acceptable menu options addresses the child's desire to exercise choice without compromising nutritional intake, and an acceptable multivitamin can also ease parental anxiety about nutrition. What seems to be important is that toddlers get enough to eat whenever they are hungry and that a variety of healthy foods are offered on a regular mealtime schedule.

Nourishment is an important consideration for toddlers, as an adequate diet is a necessary foundation for cognitive development, and malnutrition has been identified as contributing to both social and academic problems (Stevens & Baxter, 1981). One of the best and easiest ways to support early development in all areas is to ensure that children get enough to eat, especially during the first 2 to 3 years of life. Conversely, hunger among young children is one of life's most tragic circumstances, and we cannot assume that all families have enough food available, even in affluent countries such as the United States and Canada. We once heard a pediatrician compare adequate nutrition in early childhood to a miracle drug that guaranteed increased intelligence, improved physical prowess, and supported more fulfilling social relationships. She was disappointed, however, at the lack of interest among her colleagues and the media in the prevention of hunger.

Many early childhood programs, particularly those designed to meet the needs of infants, toddlers, and preschoolers from families living in chronic poverty, provide snacks and meals to meet minimum daily nutritional requirements for children who attend. Government programs offer surplus food for child-care centers, food stamps to help families afford an adequate diet, and federal programs like Women, Infants and Children (WIC) that subsidize nutrition during pregnancy and the earliest years.

Teething can be a painful process that diminishes appetite and complicates selection of food, with swollen gums and drooling often preceding the actual emergence of new teeth by many days. Sucking on cool, wet cloths or chewing on hard, cold teething toys seems to provide the best relief for many babies and toddlers who are cutting teeth. Patient caregiving practices that calm and distract little ones from the discomfort in their mouths are also recommended: rocking, back rubs, cuddling, stories.

This toddler is putting his fine motor skills to good use to feed himself with a spoon, but keeps the familiar bottle close by for drinking and comfort.

Toileting

Children developing typically are most often toilet trained by the time they are 3 years old (Trawick-Smith, 2000). Most children develop control of the muscles related to toileting between the ages of 2 and 3. Differences among toddlers in the ages at which they are toilet trained probably have more to do with the motivation and practices of caregivers than with physical maturation.

The amount of time and energy devoted to helping children learn independent toileting skills varies greatly from family to family. Some families begin very early and are religious about maintaining a schedule of trips to the bathroom. Toddlers who are used to being dry and clean may become independent in toileting as soon as they are physically mature enough to control the muscles and interpret the cues that indicate a need to use the toilet. Some parents have had good luck waiting until a child has a consistent pattern wetting and then using an intensive method of practice and reinforcement (Azrin & Foxx, 1974).

Other families are more casual about diapering and cleaning up messes and allow toddlers to set their own pace for toileting. Depending on the weather, toddlers may be allowed to go without pants in the summer months to get the feel of being dry during the day. The one certainty about toilet training is that in groups of toddlers there will be those in diapers and those in training pants. Caregivers can expect to be changing some diapers, taking some children to the bathroom on regular schedules, and reminding some children to take themselves. Toilet training is one area in which differences in cultural and family practices will be reflected to a great extent in early childhood programs.

Tantrums

Toddlers often find themselves ready to assert their independence from caregivers before they have the skills to do so with grace and style. Two-year-olds have a reputation for being terrible, but the truth is they are learning to walk a thin line between competence and rules. They need their caregivers much less than they did as infants; they can, after all, feed, dress, and entertain themselves quite nicely. Now, however, they are expected to learn some manners at the table and troublesome concepts like sharing and taking turns with toys. They are constantly being encouraged to use words to express themselves but not if it means interrupting or if they talk too loudly. The finer points of competence come at the expense of freewheeling action, sometimes causing frustration for toddlers.

In the absence of polished negotiation and collaboration abilities, it is not surprising that toddlers are prone to physical expressions of frustration. They yell and flap their arms; they holler and stamp their feet; sometimes they fall to the ground kicking and screaming. Some 2-year-olds have an uncanny ability to sense those situations in which caregivers absolutely cannot ignore a tantrum and quickly learn that the best results occur at the grocery store or when there is a dinner party in progress.

Toddlers tend toward loud, enthusiastic outbursts when they are happy and when they are upset and often seem to be acting out new concepts such as *no* and *mine* just for the sake of practice. Allowing 1- and 2-year-olds to exercise appropriate levels of assertiveness and steering the interaction toward a more positive outcome ("Yes, that is your chair; it's so nice of you to let your friend sit in it.") sometimes prevents escalation of an interaction into conflict. Ignoring negative comments altogether and redirecting the child's attention can also be effective, if circumstances allow.

Sometimes toddlers just cannot make themselves understood and become frustrated with the apparent failures of their caregivers to be sympathetic and responsive. Helping 2-year-olds communicate can go a long way toward preventing tantrums. Especially when little ones are tired, ill, or away from home, they may need to be prompted to point or use other gestures to show what they want. Setting clear limits for acceptable behavior and being consistent in your own responses can help control the length of tantrums ("I want you to sit here on the bottom stair until you stop crying; I'll come talk to you when you can talk quietly."). Toddlers seem to appreciate knowing exactly what is acceptable and unacceptable behavior even though they may choose to act in ways they know are undesirable. They need to be told what to do ("Please sit down and use a quiet voice."), rather than what not to do and left to their own devices to come up with an appropriate alternative themselves ("You can't stand up and yell.").

At times there are no options but to remove youngsters as quickly and quietly as possible from the immediate situation without engaging in all out power battles, a probable explanation for most of the abandoned half-filled shopping carts in stores. The important thing is for caregivers to encourage appropriate verbalizations, actions, and behaviors while respecting toddlers' increasing autonomy and treating mistakes as learning opportunities. Fortunately, tantrums usually lose ground to more efficient and effective verbal strategies in the preschool years. Many successful adults, including teachers, lawyers, clergy, entertainers, and authors, threw numerous and intense tantrums long before they learned to use words to get their points across.

CONCLUDING REMARKS

In many early childhood books, the toddler years are addressed in the shortest chapters. So much of the developmental groundwork is laid during infancy, and the preschool and primary years are full of more abstract and complex academic, social, and movement content. Toddlers seem to exist in a narrow band of time, a brief and marvelous metamorphosis from infancy to childhood. Perhaps it is the swiftness of the passage and the magnitude of the changes they undergo that makes toddlers so adorable; their energy, enthusiasm, curiosity, and anticipation of life's possibilities are truly wonders to behold and one of the greatest joys of working in early childhood.

Vignette 3.4: *Final Entry in a Toddler's Diary (Written by His Mother)*

September 16   *Tomorrow Dustin will be 3 years old. I love watching and being involved in his growing up, but I hate to see it going by so fast. His little face, his hands, his body are all so innocent and precious. His growing independence is a fascinating and wonderful process, but it hurts, too, that it's arriving so quickly.*

EXTENDING YOUR LEARNING

1. Visit a toddler classroom or day-care center that serves children with and without identified disabilities. Review the developmental patterns you learned about in this chapter, and estimate the approximate ages of the toddlers by observing their social and motor behaviors.

2. Arrange to join a toddler playgroup for a day through your local parks department or community center. Observe the interactions between the children, their peers, and their parents. Write a paper detailing the specific differences in verbal and nonverbal communication.

3. Interview parents of three girls and three boys. Ask if you can monitor the physical growth of their children (height, weight, number of teeth, etc.). Keep track of their progress by creating a chart displaying their development across time. Compare the difference in growth patterns between the boys and girls in your study.

4. Play "telephone" with a toddler. List the vocabulary and how it was used. Identify any comprehension difficulties you may have encountered if you had actually been on a telephone in another room where you could not observe the child's environment.

5. Interview the parents of a bilingual toddler. Find out when each language is spoken and how they resolve any confusion between the two.

6. Observe a toddler with an identified disability (i.e., Down syndrome, autism) interact with another peer or caregiver. Review Erickson's model of childhood development and describe how he might explain the child's social interactions.

7. Arrange a playtime session with a toddler. Observe how he or she plays with various manipulative toys. List the basic cognitive skills you observe (tool use, imitation, cause and effect, spatial relations, etc.) along with any reaching and grasping skills discussed in chapter 2.

8. Select 10 fun "treasures" for toddlers and hide them in easy-to-find places around a room, such as on a couch or under a blanket. Make sure the room has been childproofed before playing the game. Next, have the toddler group go on a scavenger hunt to find the various treasures. Identify the problem-solving strategies the children use to get them (i.e., climbing, reaching, asking for help).

9. Ask a parent or teacher for old drawings from their children. Knowing the typical stages of fine motor development (scribbling) estimate what age the child was when he or she drew each picture. Interview the caregiver to find out if your conclusions were correct.

VOCABULARY

Body image.   Mental picture of one's own body.

Center of gravity.   That point in the body that is at the middle of the weight distribution, above the hips for toddlers because their heads, arms, and torsos outweigh their lower bodies.

Congenital.   Hereditary; present at birth; determined by genetics.

Controlled scribbling.   Drawing curves, dots, and circles with intent to produce specific strokes, designs.

Cylindrical grasp.   Holding a cylinder-shaped object with fingers curled around and thumb on the top.

Egocentric.   A perspective that is limited to one's own experiences.

Expressive language.   A pattern of early word usage characterized by a tendency toward labeling affect, motion, location.

Fundamental movements.   Basic movements used separately, such as walking, running, jumping, throwing.

High guard.   Arms bent stiffly at the elbows, with hands open and palms facing away from the body; protective early walking stance.

Marking time.   Early stair-climbing pattern of using both feet on each stair; raising or lowering one foot to a step and then following with the next on the same step, repeating on each step.

Motor planning.   Coordinated knowledge of physical actions with expected outcomes, using body image and knowledge of spatial relations.

Muscle tone.   Resting tension in the muscles; relative looseness or tightness of muscles.

Pencil grasp.   Holding a pencil with thumb and first two fingers in tripod position.

Pincer grasp.   Grasping small objects by using the tips of index finger and thumb in opposition.

Preoperational thought.   Thought processes that are reliant on immediate and concrete perceptions as a basis for understanding the world (Piagetian).

Random scribbling.   Marking with horizontal motion of entire arm, with an emphasis on the marking action rather than on trying to make drawings.

Referential language.   Language that emphasizes labeling objects, people, and events.

Semantic relationships.   Two- and three-word utterances based on the meanings of words used rather than word order of the language.

Semantics.   Word meaning; concepts represented by word symbols.

Stoop and recover.   Squatting down to the ground and standing back up again without support.

Syntax.   Rules for word order and grammar.

Temperament.   Constitutionally based patterns of reactivity and self-regulation; behavioral style.

Word approximations.   Consistent combinations of sounds used as first words; often idiosyncratic and later replaced by more conventional words.

Wrist rotation.   Using the wrist to rotate the hand, both horizontally (as in opening a jar) and vertically to turn the hand over (palm up/palm down).

INTERNET RESOURCES

Web sites provide much useful information for educators and we list some here that pertain to the topics covered in this chapter. The addresses of Web sites can also change, however, and new ones are continually added. Thus, this list should be considered as a first step in your acquisition of a larger and ever-changing collection.

Autism Society of America
   http://www.autism-society.org/

Early Childhood Care and Development
   http://ecdgroup.harvard.net/

Early Childhood Educator
  http://www.edpsych.com/

Early Childhood Educators' and Family Web Corner
  http://users.sig.net/~cokids/

The Families and Work Institute
  http://www.familiesandwork.org

Kathy Schrocks Guide for Educators
  http://discoveryschool.com/schrockguide/

Northwest Regional Educational Laboratory
  http://www.nwrel.org

101 Things to Do With Your Toddler
  http://www-personal.engin.umich.edu/~ajdrake/toddler/open.html

Special Education Resources on the Internet (SERI)
  http://www.seri.hood.edu/seri/serihome.htm

Special Needs Advocates for Parents (SNAP)
  http://www.snapinfo.org

Zero to Three
  http://www.zerothree.org/

References

Ames, L. B., Gillespie, C., Haines, J., & Ilg, F. L. (1978). *The Gesell Institute's childhood from one to six.* New York: Harper & Row.

Anders, T. F., Goodlin-Jones, B. L., & Zelenko, M. (1998). Infant regulation and sleep–wake state development. *Zero to Three, 19,* 5–8.

Arnberg, L. (1987). *Raising children bilingually: The preschool years.* Philadelphia: Multicultural Matters Ltd.

Azrin, N. H., & Foxx, R. M. (1974). *Toilet training in less than a day.* New York: Simon & Schuster.

Bee, H. (1997). *The developing child* (8th ed.). New York: HarperCollins.

Bjorklund, D. F., & Green, B. L. (1992). The adaptive nature of cognitive immaturity. *American Psychologist, 47,* 46–54.

Bloom, L. (1973). *One word at a time.* The Hauge: Morton.

Bristol, M. M. (1998). *Research in autism: Implications for treatment.* Paper presented at the *Child With Special Needs: Pre-conference on Autism.* Anaheim, CA: Contemporary Forums.

Brittain, W. L. (1979). *Creativity, art and the young child.* New York: Macmillan.

Chess, S., & Thomas, A. (1984). *Origins and evolution of behavior disorders: Infancy to adult life.* New York: Brunner/Mazel.

Erikson, E. (1963). *Childhood and society* (2nd ed.). New York: Norton.

Fischer, K. W. (1980). A theory of cognitive development: The control and construction of hierarchies of skills. *Psychological Review, 87,* 477–531.

Flavell, J. H., Miller, P. H., & Miller, S. A. (1993). *Cognitive development* (3rd ed.). Englewood Cliffs, NJ: Prentice Hall.

Gallahue, D. L. (1989). *Understanding motor development: Infants, children and adolescents.* Indianapolis, IN: Benchmark.

Goldberg, S., & Divitto, B. A. (1983). *Born too soon: Preterm birth and early development.* San Francisco: W. H. Freeman.

Goldfield, B. A., & Reznick, J. S. (1990). Early lexical acquisition: Rate, content, and the vocabulary spirit. *Journal of Child Language, 17,* 171–183.

Hale-Benson, J. E. (1986). *Black children: Their roots, culture and learning styles.* Baltimore, MD: John Hopkins University Press.

Kagan, J., Reznick, J. S., & Snidman, N. (1990). The temperamental qualities of inhibition and lack of inhibition. In M. Lewis & S. M. Miller (Eds.), *Handbook of developmental psychopathy* (pp. 219–226). New York: Plenum.

Klin, A. (1998). Asperger syndrome: Overview of clinical features, assessment and intervention, and highlights of current research. Paper presented at the *Child With Special Needs: Pre-conference on Autism.* Anaheim, CA: Contemporary Forums.

Lewis, M., & Brooks-Gunn, J. (1979). *Social cognition and the acquisition of self.* New York: Plenum.

Lowrey, G. H. (1986). *Growth and development of children.* Chicago: Year Book Medical Publishers.

Melzoff, A. N., & Moore, M. K. (1983). Newborn infants imitate adult facial gestures. *Child Development, 54,* 702–709.

Mesibov, G. (1998). The TEACCH approach. Paper presented at *Child With Special Needs: Pre-conference on Autism.* Anaheim, CA: Contemporary Forums.

Nelson, K. (1973). Structure and strategy in learning to talk. *Monographs of the Society for Research in Child Development, 38.* (Serial no. 149).

Piaget, J. (1954). *The construction of reality in the child.* New York: Basic Books.

Pipes, P. L. (1981). *Nutrition in infancy and childhood* (2nd ed.). St. Louis: Mosley.

Rothbart, M. K. (1996). Social development. In M. Hanson (Ed.), *Atypical infant development* (2nd ed.). Austin, TX: Pro-Ed.

Rothbart, M. K., & Ahadi, S. A. (1994). Temperament and the development of personality. *Journal of Abnormal Psychology, 103,* 55–66.

Rothbart, M. K., & Mauro, J. A. (1990). Questionnaire approaches to the study of infant temperament. In J. W. Fagen & J. Colombo (Eds.), *Individual differences in infancy: Reliability, stability and prediction* (pp. 411–429). Hillsdale, NJ: Lawrence Erlbaum Associates.

Rutter, M. (1987). Continuities and discontinuities from infancy. In J. D. Osofsky (Ed.), *Handbook of infant development* (2nd ed., pp. 1256–1296). New York: Wiley-Interscience.

Saunders, G. (1988). *Studies in bilingual development.* Hillsdale, NJ: Lawrence Erlbaum Associates.

Stevens, J. H., & Baxter, D. H. (1981). Malnutrition and children's development. *Young Children, 36,* 60–71.

Thomas, A., & Chess, S. (1977). *Temperament and development.* New York: Brunner/Mazel.

Trawick-Smith, M. J. (2000). *Early childhood development: A multicultural perspective* (2nd ed.). Columbus, OH: Merrill-Prentice-Hall.

Werner, E. (1990). Protective factors and individual resilience. In S. Meisels & J. Shonkoff (Eds.), *Handbook of early childhood intervention* (pp. 97–116). New York: Cambridge University Press.

PRESCHOOLERS: FROM PLAYGROUND TO PEER GROUP

The future of the world is in very small hands.

Ellen Galinsky

▼ Chapter Objectives

After reading this chapter, you should be able to:

- ▼ Describe physical growth of children during the preschool years.
- ▼ Summarize sequences of gross and fine motor development for children ages 3 to 5 years.
- ▼ Explain how preschool children apply fundamental motor skills in social, self-care, and preacademic activities.
- ▼ Describe cognitive development during the preschool years from Piagetian and information-processing perspectives.
- ▼ Identify important aspects of language development and emergent literacy for children ages 3 to 5 years.
- ▼ Summarize the nature of friendships during the preschool years.
- ▼ Recognize variations in preschool growth and behavior across motor, cognitive, and social domains, and draw conclusions about the impact on development.

As you think about and apply chapter content on your own, you should be able to:

- ▼ Relate your knowledge of developmental achievements during preschool to information presented in previous chapters about infants and toddlers.
- ▼ Consider a broad range of motor, cognitive, and social variation in your application of developmental information to your work with preschoolers.

Vignette 4.1: *Moving Day*

"I'm sad," 3-year-old Malia sighs to her mother, and in fact the preschooler appears lethargic and unhappy. She stands looking at the floor, holding her teddy bear with one hand and dragging her special blanket, neither of which has been out of her bed for weeks.

"Honey, what's wrong?" Malia's mother puts aside the box she is packing and hugs her daughter. It has been a difficult week; they are getting ready to move, and the house is filled with boxes. At first Malia had thought moving meant taking the entire house, yard, and all the contents to a different town. Just yesterday, her mother had explained that she was packing boxes for a big moving truck to move their possessions to a different house. Malia's bedroom furniture and belongings would be last, to keep her familiar environment intact as long as possible.

Malia starts to cry. "I were scared in my room alone. I don't want to move to a new house, and I can't have any fun without my toys. And my bear will be lonely without me, and I'll miss him and Daddy, too. And who will take care of Jared?"

Malia's mom explains that they will indeed be taking her toys and her bed and her toy chest and her baby brother. "We will take everything with us that is important: All your furniture will go in the big truck, and we will set up a room for you in the new house. You and I and Jared and Daddy will all be together in a new place, so you won't be alone. You can take your bear and your blanket with you in the car, so you can have them all the time; we won't even pack them in a box."

The preschooler returns to her room, much relieved. In a few minutes she returns to inquire brightly, "Lisa can take her new doll when we move?"

When her mother explains that Lisa isn't moving with them, Malia is despondent again and more than a little angry. She walks around, stopping now and then to kick at the moving boxes, stomp on the bubble wrap, and throw plastic packing peanuts. "You said I could take everything important!! Lisa's my most important friend," she repeats over and over. Her mother's reassurances that Malia will make new friends seem to go entirely unheeded.

On moving day, Malia climbs happily into her car seat without a backward look. She carries her bear and blanket and favors her family with a big smile, seemingly excited for a new adventure. Her mother, on the other hand, cries as they leave. "It's okay, Mama," Malia asserts solemnly, "We will miss our house, but we can make new friends."

Malia's struggle to understand what it means to move is an effective introduction to a number of important developmental topics during the preschool years. As you read about motor, cognitive, and social achievements of 3- to 5-year-olds, keep in mind the following organizing themes:

- Preschoolers begin to use fundamental motor skills as a foundation for social expression and participation (as demonstrated by the reflection of anger in Malia's language and motor behavior).

- The thinking of 3- to 5-year olds is based in concrete perception and personal experience rather than in abstract concepts (reflected in Malia's difficulty in understanding the concept of moving, something she had never experienced).

- Peer relationships begin to become important to preschoolers, and their concept of self is refined (as demonstrated by Malia's friendship with Lisa and her self-confidence about making new friends).

Appearances can be deceiving when it comes to preschool children. They look less like babies and more like their primary school counterparts but enjoy only the simplest of games. Three- to 5-year-olds talk in long, complex sentences but often seem unable to grasp the central point of a conversation. They develop an interest in peers but are still closely tied to their primary caregivers. Preschoolers vacillate between credible impersonations of middle childhood and regressions to behaviors of toddlerhood. They seem to learn new skills overnight and then not know how to use them.

The term *preschooler* technically refers to any child too young for mandatory school attendance but is most often used in early childhood literature to refer to children between the ages of 3 and 5 years. Another connotation of the word is that children of this age are likely to be enrolled in programs in which adults plan and manage group activities, more school-like early education environments that emphasize preacademic or school readiness content. Readers of this text might well be preparing for early childhood careers in such settings. The focus in this chapter is on universal patterns and individual differences of development in young children between the ages of 3 and 5 years; implications for curriculum development are addressed in detail in another book in this series, *The Early Childhood Curriculum*.

FAMILY CONTEXT

Infants are first incorporated into the routines of family life through regular activities of nurturing activities and physical care. The self-directed activity of toddlers requires close supervision by parents and other caregivers as little ones become mobile, independent, and communicative. Preschoolers tend to become more directed than infants and toddlers in their activities and take on specific roles within family routines. They can take care of themselves to some extent and help with household chores; there may be younger siblings who need companionship and guidance in the ways of family life. Preschoolers learn concepts that advance their understanding of right and wrong, self and relationships. They think about themselves as brother, sister, and friend, and bring their most sophisticated abilities to those roles. Parents, extended family members, and older siblings become role models for preschoolers, as they expand their self-concepts to include gender, ethnic, and racial identities.

For a variety of reasons, preschoolers in industrialized countries are more likely to be cared for out of their homes than are infants and toddlers. By the age of 3, most children are beginning to prefer playing with others their age. They are active, mobile, curious, and communicative, making separation easier for both children and caregivers. Parents who have been providing primary care at home often return to the workforce, either from choice or economic necessity. In the United States, child-care and early education resources are more readily available for preschoolers than for infants and toddlers (Cost, Quality and Outcomes in Child Care Centers, 1995). The tendency for preschool children to enjoy and prosper in the company of their peers is also reflected in community-based activities at churches, libraries, parks, pools, gyms, and informal neighborhood play groups.

Of course, preschoolers are also cared for at home by family members in many families. Those with adequate financial resources may choose to hire sitters or nannies to be with their preschoolers at home or to maintain a primary caregiving role themselves.

Many preschoolers have younger siblings, and take pride and pleasure in being a guide and companion within the family.

Young children living in multigeneration families are often cared for by grandparents, aunts, or uncles. Parents working for minimum wage, especially those with more than one preschool child, sometimes discover that the cost of child care exceeds their earnings, forcing difficult choices about how to best support their families.

PHYSICAL GROWTH AND MOTOR DEVELOPMENT DURING THE PRESCHOOL YEARS: MASTERING FUNDAMENTAL MOVEMENTS

Three- to 5-year-old children the world over use *fundamental movements* as a basis for social games and for generating their own learning opportunities. They run, jump, climb, crawl, throw, kick, spin, chase, roll around, poke, prod, draw, bend, stretch, push, and pull with great exuberance, alternating between large muscle exercise and more quiet manipulative activities using their hands. Preschoolers begin to combine motor and social activity with an understanding of rules, concepts, and conventions, resulting in gross motor games such as tag and fine motor pastimes such as drawing. Movement becomes so well integrated by the end of the preschool years that the emphasis in motor activity shifts altogether from development of fundamental motor skills to their application in athletic and academic pursuits.

Physical Growth

Preschool children continue to grow at a rate of approximately 2 inches per year, weigh in anywhere between 30 and 50 pounds, and measure from 3 to 4 feet in height (Lowrey, 1986). During this period, children's torsos, arms, and legs become longer relative to their total height, and their body profile is flatter and leaner. With a center of gravity near the middle of the body, they appear progressively steadier and more in control of their movements.

The heads of preschoolers do not grow as much as their bodies, so 5-year-olds are proportioned more like adults than are 3-year-olds, whose heads still appear large. Brains grow to 90% of adult size during the preschool years (Tanner, 1978). Increased elaboration of existing brain cells between the ages of 3 and 5 results in specialized functions for different regions of the brain (Teeter & Semrud-Clikeman, 1997). One result of more specialized brain function is that preschoolers generally develop *hand dominance*, or a preference for using either the right or left hand, with nearly 90% being right-handed (Tan, 1985). Contrary to previous opinion, left-handed preschoolers are not more prone to motor or academic difficulties than their right-handed peers.

Although most children do show a clearly dominant hand by the time they are 5, it is not that uncommon to see preschoolers who use both hands equally well or switch from using one hand to using the other (Bryden & Saxby, 1985). Failure to establish hand dominance is sometimes associated with fine motor difficulties (Tan, 1985) but may just indicate a higher than usual level of ambidexterity. We knew a 5-year-old who would draw, paint, and write from left to right on the paper, switching hands at the midline and doing equally with right and left hands. He finally settled on left-handedness toward the end of kindergarten but is still quite skilled at using both hands for cutting, throwing, and playing the drums. Having a dominant hand makes for more concentrated practice of activities such as feeding and drawing that require use of one hand, which in combination with smoother and more controlled visual scanning (Davidoff, 1975) explains observed advances in hand–eye coordination during the preschool years.

Assuming adequate nutrition and good health, physical growth seems largely controlled by maturation and heredity (Garcia-Coll, 1990). Minor differences in physical growth and stature between genders and among racial and ethnic groups begin to become noticeable during the preschool years. It is important to keep in mind, though, that maturation alone cannot account for the development of motor skills; the complexity of motor activity demonstrated by typically developing preschool children requires integration of perceptual, motivational, and organizational capacity as well as physical growth and maturation (Thelen, 1989). It is likely that both heredity and experience play important roles in determining the level of activity preschoolers exhibit and the types of skills they master.

Gross Motor Development: Coordinated Motor Play

Preschoolers develop strength and stamina for sustained movement as well as speed, timing, balance, and coordination. One reason they prefer the company of their peers is probably that adults begin having a hard time keeping up. By the time they enter kindergarten, children have mastered a wide range of locomotion, nonlocomotion, and manipulative gross motor skills (Malina, 1982). *Locomotion* includes moving the body through space, for instance, walking, running, skipping, and hopping. Fluid changing of postures with stationary feet is considered *nonlocomotive movement*, such as the bending, turning, and pulling motions in a tug-of-war game. *Manipulative movements* are those that involve use of an object: kicking and throwing, as well as writing and eating with utensils. Preschool children combine locomotive, nonlo-comotive, and manipulative movement patterns, often in social play. Experience with movement activities and opportunities for practice are important aspects of gross motor development for preschoolers.

Playground apparatus reflects the appeal of movement activities and encourages development of skills in the gross motor domain. Slides, ladders, swings, balance beams, sliding poles, climbing structures, tricycles, and balls provide countless hours of entertainment. Although most 3-year-olds require assistance and supervision from caregivers, most youngsters are quite independent by the time they are 5. On the swings, for instance, 3-year-olds usually need to be pushed and may occasionally become frightened, but 5-year-olds are more likely to pump the swing themselves and devise creative competitions for swinging high and jumping out.

Three-year-olds are still perfecting fundamental movements and can be observed watching and imitating specific motor skills like jumping, throwing, and catching. Jumping is a locomotion skill that usually begins when children lead with one foot coming down from a low step, then jump up and down with both feet together, and later with forward momentum (Fig. 4.1). Jumping involves coordinating the timing of lifting the feet with either upward or forward motion of the body or both through space and regaining of balance on the landing, no small feat for small feet.

Ball Play

Balls are favored objects for motor play in many cultures. Toddlers play with balls by rolling and throwing indiscriminately; preschoolers learn more complicated fun-damental skills used in games. The catching skills acquired between the ages of 3 and

FIG. 4.1.   Jumping. Youngsters first jump down with a hesitant stepping motion, then jump up and down in place, and later leap forward.

5 generally begin with youngsters standing still, arms straight out and together, hands open. (It is not unusual to see 3-year-olds bent over with their arms straight down toward the ground.) In this posture, children essentially provide targets at which adults attempt to throw slowly and gently enough for the ball to be captured by little arms against bodies. With practice and prompting, youngsters get the idea that they need to open their hands and bend their arms to actually catch something. After experiencing the thrill of actually trapping the ball in their hands, preschoolers learn to move their arms into position as the ball approaches.

Infants and toddlers like to throw things, but in the preschool years throwing is a manipulative skill of aiming objects at targets. Throwing begins with a stiff and unpredictable release, sometimes resulting in the ball going straight up in the air or even backwards as the entire body is thrown off balance. The first controlled releases are often underhand tosses that make it easier to stay balanced but may not initially have much power. With practice, however, preschoolers learn to open the hand just as it is pointed at the target, and through trial and error are able to judge the amount of force needed to propel the object across the proper distance.

Kicking is another manipulative skill that progresses in small steps and requires practice to master. Three-year-olds often lose their balance when they first attempt to kick but then learn to balance on one foot and move the other. Initial kicks sometimes resemble a prodding and stomping with the whole foot but eventually develop into a smooth swinging motion with the toe making first contact.

Active Play

Preschoolers seem destined to run, and do so with great stamina and enthusiasm in every culture (Ridenour, 1978). Running games illustrate nicely the progression of motor skills in a context of progressively more complex social games. Three-year-olds love being pursued and chasing after others. Four-year-olds often incorporate running and chasing into imaginary play, sometimes taking on elaborate roles: "Let's say there's a troll under the slide, and it's a hungry troll. So when you get to the bottom you have to run away fast or it'll eat you!" The movement sequence for this game is: slide, run (often accompanied by screaming and narrow escapes), climb, slide, run, and climb. Even children not familiar with the scenario are exhorted to "Run! Or the troll will get you!" when they get to the bottom of the slide. One of the preschoolers may play the role of troll, or it may be an imaginary creature, invisible to adults.

Running games like these eventually evolve into games with very simple rules (tag, duck-duck-goose). Other early locomotion games involve stopping and starting (red light-green light, freeze tag), hiding (hide and seek), and naming or requesting specific movements (Simon says, Mother may I?). Younger preschool children are clearly more skilled at the movement components than at following the game rules, as novice teachers discover when duck-duck-goose dissolves into chase or Mother-may-I becomes a mad dash.

With the advent of imaginary play, preschoolers gracefully blend a variety of fundamental movements to represent vehicles, animals, people, and dangerous situations

Preschoolers seek out the company of peers and seem to be in constant motion, readily combining coordinated movement and imaginary play.

that require exceptional skills: "I'm an airplane; I can fly high in the sky" (spinning, dipping, diving, running, climbing, and jumping); "Let's drive our race cars and no crashing" (running, turning, stopping, steering); "I'm the monkey and I took all the bananas! You can't catch me" (running, jumping, twisting, climbing); "We have to carry this medicine to our friend. Don't step off the board. The hot lava will burn us up!" (walking, balancing, climbing).

Chasing and role-playing often involve moving in synchrony or anticipation of other children's movements (Keogh, 1977). Bumping or crashing into one another often develops into contact activities such as wrestling, spinning and falling, rolling about, pretend fighting, and dueling. Although caregivers often worry that rough-and-tumble play will escalate out of control, close observations show that left to their own devices, preschoolers most often regulate such play so that rarely does anyone get hurt (Pellegrini & Perlmutter, 1988). Although it is difficult to believe, most children are less active as preschoolers than as toddlers (Eaton & Yu, 1989). Perhaps preschoolers seem so active because they master so many different types of movement and play more often together.

Fine Motor Development: Proficient Use of Hands

At the same time that preschoolers are becoming skilled performers of a variety of large muscle movements, the small muscles of the hands and fingers are also becoming more coordinated. Three-year-olds are quite skilled at grasping, releasing, pushing, pulling, poking, pointing, squeezing, and rolling motions. Progressive precision of hand and finger control between the ages of 3 and 5 allows preschoolers to use their hands with confidence for a great diversity of self-care, creative, and preacademic pursuits. Depending on the materials and toys available in their environments, younger preschoolers apply their fine motor skills across a wide range of objects and activities: exploring and manipulating toys, creating works of art, constructing and building, scribbling, feeding, and dressing, to name just a few.

Manipulating Objects

As preschoolers continue to use their hands to manipulate objects, control of the fingers becomes more precise and coordinated, and the types of tasks they attempt become more complicated and demanding. Preschool children use controlled grasp-and-release skills to build elaborate block structures indoors and for construction with sticks, leaves, stones, and dirt outdoors. They shape clay and mud into recognizable shapes, operate switches, dials, knobs, and buttons. No longer do preschoolers use trial and error to find the correct fine motor movements for each item; the intent to perform certain actions seems more obvious than the effort required.

Three-year-olds in many families are becoming more independent and press fine motor skills into service for self-care. They begin using refined, careful movements of the fingers to undo fasteners: untie, unbutton, unzip, unsnap. Unfastening is often the most difficult, if initial, step in undressing. Three-year-olds sometimes master all the motor aspects of undressing before learning the social rules about when and where undressing is allowed! Many 5-year-olds learn to tie their shoes, button their shirts, and zip their coats and pants independently, skills that generally take quite a bit of practice. Some youngsters will practice for long periods on their own; others are content with Velcro fasteners, elastic waistlines, and pullover shirts.

Preschoolers also practice opening all sorts of containers requiring strong, sustained pincer grasps and simultaneous wrist rotation, pulling, or pushing motions. Opening containers is a handy skill for getting at collections of blocks, toys, and markers without adult help but is not always appreciated in the kitchen or art supply cabinet. Opening and closing doors and drawers and turning faucets off and on are additional examples of complex, precise small muscle movements.

In homes and early childhood centers where children have access to manipulative materials (pegboards, form boards, puzzles, beads and string, pattern blocks), preschoolers demonstrate increasingly competent application of fine motor skills for fitting objects together and into defined spaces. Coordination of visual input and hand movement becomes more automatic; planning is integrated into movement as the child picks up a piece, evaluates the spaces available, and puts the piece into place in one smooth movement. By the age of 5, children who have had opportunities are putting together simple puzzles with large multiple pieces.

Preschoolers are quite skilled at combining objects in fine motor play, such as dressing dolls and using props for pretend cooking, eating, dressing up, and working at various occupations. Commercially available representational play materials also reflect increasing sophistication in combining and fitting objects together. The sets available for 3-year-olds tend toward a single large setting piece (barn, bus, garage, school) with related people and sometimes animals or vehicles. The pieces are hand-sized and people are often shaped like pegs that fit into corresponding round holes. The sets most popular with 5-year-olds, however, include multiple pieces that require assembly, furniture, tiny articles of clothing for dressing characters, tools, weapons, utensils, decorations, and other accessories that require the most exact of movements to place into the smallest of plastic receptacles. It is often at this point that preschoolers begin to become less meticulous about picking up all the pieces.

Using Tools

Using objects as tools is a more difficult task than those just described, because the tool is intermediate between the action and the outcome. Handling an item for the sole purpose of creating a separate effect begins with using a spoon for many toddlers. Piaget's contention that preschool children have a solid understanding of using means to obtain separate ends is illustrated in the many ways they apply fine motor skills to use tools for a variety of purposes. By the time children are 5, the use of tools allows mastery of many self-care skills and often introduces creative and preacademic activities.

The easiest applications of tool use involve the preschooler's own body, promoting independence in self-care activities. At home, preschoolers progress from using spoons to using forks, practicing wrist rotation with the former and a pushing or stabbing motion with the latter. They will also wash themselves with washcloths and clean up their messes with sponges, easy tools that conform to the child's hand. More difficult is brushing teeth and combing hair, because the motions these activities require aren't visible to children. Serving food and pouring during mealtimes are often introduced in homes and centers during the preschool years.

Tool use is also a requirement for successful mastery of preacademic activities such as drawing and cutting. If provided opportunities, models, and instruction, preschool youngsters will use paints, crayons, markers, glue sticks, and scissors for art and prewriting practice. In fact, an increasing number of early childhood professionals consider drawing and painting important prerequisites to success in writing (Anselmo & Franz, 1995) as well as in creative endeavors.

Drawing and Writing

In chapter 3 we discussed the evolution of scribbling from banging the marker to controlled scribbling. Controlled scribbling is characterized by close attention to the marker and more distinct lines, shapes, and curls and more deliberate, fluid hand motions (Brittain, 1979), although many young preschoolers still hold their crayons in their fists. Three-year-olds who draw frequently start to take pride in their creations but at first, "See my picture" seems to refer only to the fact that they have produced something. Four-year-olds typically begin to hold markers between their thumb and fingers and place their nondominant hands flat on the page to stabilize the paper. Control of hand movements allows children of this age to copy simple shapes (circles, squares, crosses) and to use lines, curves, and circles to copy letters (Lamme, 1984).

FIG. 4.2.   Scribbling and drawing.

Perhaps because adults often ask, "What is it?" preschoolers begin to see their drawings as representing familiar objects, people, and events. Most children start naming their drawings between the ages of 4 and 5 years, although at first the motor act of drawing seems entirely separate from ascribing meaning to the picture. Gradually the preschooler's artwork reminds him more often of something familiar, and the act of drawing converges with ideas as he works (Fig. 4.2). At this point, the child can't always say ahead of time what she is about to draw but will name the resulting picture (Brittain, 1979).

By the age of 5, children generally draw with the intent to represent something they are thinking of rather than something they see (Piaget & Inhelder, 1963). *Early representational drawings* appear primitive to the adult eye, with shapes and lines representing rather than accurately depicting figures. Stick people composed only of a circular head and lines for legs, for instance, are often the subjects of early representational drawings. The objects portrayed during early representational drawing appear to float randomly on the page rather than being oriented accurately in space.

A single object is more likely to be drawn multiple times rather than to be positioned relative to a setting, such as a landscape or house (Brittain, 1979). The drawings of typically developing preschoolers become more complex and full of detail with practice, although some youngsters become intensely interested in "writing" and forsake artwork for more literary pursuits.

Variations in Preschool Motor Development

Although preschoolers worldwide seem to develop similar skills in both gross and fine motor movement, the activities they engage in vary immensely from culture to culture and family to family (Whiting & Edwards, 1988). Preschoolers in some families take on responsibilities for household chores and care of younger children; others play out their motor activity on playground equipment, games with peers, and taking care of themselves. Parents in industrialized countries tend to promote fine motor and manipulative play as precursors to school success, but not all families have the resources to accumulate collections of paper, markers, puzzles, and sets of miniature representational toys.

Motor development during the preschool years can be adversely affected by poor health, compromised physical status, general developmental delays, and specific disabilities. Some young children may be acquiring gross and fine motor skills at a slower pace than their peers. Preschoolers with Down syndrome, for example, generally have been walking and running for less time than other 3-year-olds and will probably also take longer to learn and use a variety of fundamental motor skills. Children with delayed motor development also may need additional instruction and practice in using their hands for manipulative play, self-care, and drawing and writing. Occupational therapists can suggest adaptive equipment for eating and strategies for dressing and toileting.

Youngsters with cerebral palsy exhibit a wide range of motor abilities, from using wheelchairs for locomotion to participating actively with only minor problems in balance and coordination. Some children with motor disabilities are relatively confident in large muscle play but have difficulties with fine motor activities. Others may have good use of their hands but lack the strength and agility to participate fully in active play. A good approach is to try to find ways for all children to participate in gross motor play unless doing so presents a clear danger.

Young children who don't see well are often more cautious in active play, because moving quickly, climbing, jumping, and the like are threatening without visual information about the surrounding space. Parents, physical therapists, and other specialists are excellent resources for ideas about adapting playground and manipulative equipment. Mobility specialists can suggest specific playground modifications or specialized materials, most often the addition of tactile and auditory cues, for children with vision impairments. Switch-operated toys, adaptive grips for markers, and selected commercially available toys can all be used to provide opportunities for children with disabilities to participate in fine motor activities.

Caregivers are often uncertain about supervising preschoolers who don't hear well, fearing that the child who can't hear directions might need closer physical supervision. Parents and teachers of children who use sign language find that learning the signs for playground equipment, action verbs, and rules of safety increases their confidence in monitoring active play. Given proper supports, the play of children with sensory impairments is quite similar to the play of their sighted and hearing peers (Esposito & Koorland, 1989).

Preschool children with poor health or fragile physical conditions are also at risk for delayed gross motor development. Repeated surgeries, casting, and hospitalization to correct congenital heart problems and orthopedic impairments, for instance, can hinder the development of strength, stamina, and coordination for active play. Young children are amazingly resilient following surgery, though, and often surprise adults with the speed of their recoveries. Preschoolers who have chronic and recurrent illnesses also may have lower overall activity levels than their peers, oftentimes needing to limit their physical activity to conserve energy while fighting off an illness or recuperating. Parents are the best sources of information about changing restrictions on children's levels of activity, and some preschoolers are able to adjust their own gross motor behaviors according to how they feel. Caregivers need to remember that the physical condition of preschool children can change quite rapidly and be aware of warning signs of overexertion for those who live with chronic illness.

Youngsters with identified disabilities are at risk for frequent or serious bouts of the upper respiratory infections common among all children. Extremely low or high muscle tone associated with Down syndrome and cerebral palsy can inhibit the ability to cough effectively, increasing the chances that a cold will develop into a more severe infection. Young children with Down syndrome are prone to ear infections, obesity, congenital heart disease, and orthopedic problems (Roizen, 1997), all of which can have a detrimental impact on motor play. Anticonvulsant medications sometimes cause lethargy and slow reaction times as side effects; a child with a seizure disorder may have to avoid climbing to high places to prevent injurious falls if the child should have a seizure on the playground. Preschool children who have limited movement abilities or need to restrict their physical activities for any reason often develop interest and skill in drawing, writing, and manipulative activities, including computer games that allow small motions of the hands on the mouse or joystick to be translated onto a screen as running, jumping, and climbing.

PRESCHOOL COGNITIVE DEVELOPMENT: "I THINK IT, THEREFORE IT IS"

Anyone who knows preschoolers knows that they are always thinking. They carry on conversations, express strong opinions, relate past events, memorize songs and stories, and astound adults with their explanations about the workings of the world. On the face of it, preschoolers seem only a step away from the cognitive sophistication of their primary-age peers who read, write, and use ideas as a basis for interaction and learning. A closer examination of preschool cognitive development, however, reveals that 3- to 5-year-olds are still making a transition from knowledge based on action and perception to knowledge based on thoughts, ideas, and abstract reasoning.

For decades, Piagetian theory has provided a foundation for understanding early cognitive development, although a number of researchers have challenged Piaget's conclusions as underestimating the capabilities of preschool children and emphasizing deficiencies rather than abilities. Many developmental psychologists dispute the notion of an inborn, invariant stage structure, suggesting instead that experience and instruction play greater roles in acquisition of skill hierarchies (Bee, 1997). Nonetheless, Piaget does seem to have captured and described well some of the unique ways that the cognitive processes of 3-, 4-, and 5-year-olds differ from those of older children. The sequences of change that Piaget proposed have also held up well to laboratory study.

Other descriptions of cognitive functioning, most notably information-processing theory, provide alternative explanations for the ways in which young children think and learn. We describe the cognitive development of preschoolers from a Piagetian perspective here and then using information-processing theory in chapter 5.

Preoperational Thought

Piaget (1952) described the thought processes of preschool children as being preoperational, meaning that 3- to 5-year-olds are not yet able to reason using abstract mental operations. Instead, for most of the preschool years, children continue to exhibit *egocentric* and *perceptually based thinking* rooted in their own experiences and centered on the physical characteristics of what they see, hear, and touch. Although it is clear that preschool children use thought to generate questions and hypotheses and to solve problems, their logic is quite concrete, leading to conclusions that are both amusing and unique. It may often seem that preschoolers have missed the point or misunderstood an idea completely, but further investigation usually reveals that their thinking follows quite predictable patterns.

Vignette 4.2: Clouds and Tea

Four-year-old Tolan and his father are walking in the park on a cloudy day. Looking at the sky, Tolan says, "I like sun better than clouds. Where did those clouds come from?" His father thinks for a minute and then replies, reminding Tolan of the steam that rises from the teakettle when water boils. He explains that the clouds are formed in much the same way, when water evaporates and rises into the air. Tolan seems to understand and be satisfied with this explanation. The next morning is sunny, and Tolan is happy until his mother puts the teakettle on to boil. "Don't!" Tolan exclaims vehemently. "If everybody makes tea, the clouds will come back!"

Tolan's interpretation of cloud formation illustrates both the strengths and the limitations of preoperational thought. First, Tolan demonstrates good memory skills in the park when he can picture the workings of the teakettle and again the next day when he recalls the conversation from the park. He also shows an understanding that there are specific causes for the things that happen when he wants an explanation for why it is sometimes sunny and other times cloudy. Tolan understands language quite well and uses it both to share and to obtain information. He understands basic concepts of number, space, and size, figuring that more teakettles boiling mean more clouds rising up into the sky.

The thought processes of preschool children follow predictable patterns based directly on their own perceptions and experiences.

Let's consider some of the characteristics Piaget described as governing the thought processes of preoperational thinkers: literal interpretations, egocentrism, transductive reasoning, irreversible thinking, and animism. Although subsequent research has raised legitimate questions about some of Piaget's specific conclusions, the terms he used do capture a perspective on the world that is familiar to those of us who interact on a regular basis with preschoolers.

Literal Interpretations

Because preschool children attend primarily to the concrete aspects of whatever they see, hear, and touch, the resulting interpretations of events are usually quite literal. Tolan took his father's explanation about the teakettle as the exact cause of clouds instead of as an example of a similar phenomenon. If a word or phrase can have more than one meaning, 3- and 4-year-olds are apt to take the most concrete interpretation. A question such as, "What's your new baby sister like?" is likely to elicit a concrete answer, "Her bottle," from a 4-year-old rather than a response that describes the infant. The image of the baby nursing from the bottle represents something the older sibling has seen; descriptions of the baby's mood or activity level would require more abstract interpretations of the sister's behaviors.

Three-year-olds are famous for asking questions, and the most favorite question is typically, "Why?" When youngsters keep asking "Why?" chances are good that adult responses are either too complex or don't make sense given the intent of the original question. The way Tolan interpreted his dad's explanation of clouds might lead us to surmise that the real question had to do with a concrete notion of location ("Where were those clouds before they came here?") rather than the more abstract process of formation. Tolan interpreted his father's explanation in the context of the more literal question and concluded (using rules of preschool logic) that the clouds were in teakettles before they were in the sky above the park. Realizing that his father was answering a different question altogether and knowing how to rephrase the initial query, however, requires skills that most preschoolers have yet to acquire.

Egocentrism

If the answer to a question doesn't make sense, most adults and older children suspect that they had been misunderstood. Knowing that two people can interpret the same thing in two different ways requires taking the perspective of the listener as well as of the speaker, a cognitive maneuver too complicated for most preschoolers. Piaget characterized preschoolers as continuing to be egocentric in their thinking, able to understand only that which they have experienced. So it does not occur to Tolan that his father might be answering a different question than the one he asked.

Another reason Tolan draws the conclusion he does from his father's explanation is that he does not particularly like clouds and has a vested interest in preventing their return. Also, Tolan does understand about moving from place to place and can understand a change in location; he has not had the experience of changing form, so the entire concept of evaporation is not likely something he will understand.

Transductive Reasoning

Piaget (1952) used the term *transductive reasoning* to describe the manner in which preschool children use specific, concrete ideas to construct theories of cause and effect. Tolan, for instance, did not understand evaporation as a general principle that explained both cloud formation and the steam from the teakettle. Instead, he reasoned from one specific idea directly to another, concluding that the steam from teakettles rises up to become clouds.

Similarly, younger preschoolers tend to think that natural and social happenings are caused by their own actions, causing guilt and fear at times (Garbarino, Dubrow, Kostelny, & Pardo, 1992). For example, if a 4-year-old throws a tantrum and her parents have an argument while she is still calming down, she may think that her tantrum caused the argument. The rules she uses to draw this conclusion are quite concrete: The events are similar in form (people are angry) and occur close together in time.

Irreversible Thinking

Three- to 5-year-olds are making a cognitive transition from thought processes based solely on concrete perceptions to mental manipulations of abstract ideas, so preoperational thought tends to be governed by what the child sees, feels, and hears at any given time. Perceptually bound thinking makes it possible for preschool children to disregard the distinction between reality and appearance and limits their abilities to understand certain constant properties of objects. We discuss the experiments Piaget used to test his hypotheses about perceptually bound thinking in chapter 5 as well as criticisms of the tasks he used and the conclusions drawn. You may recognize, however, some classic examples of irreversible thinking. Tolan, for instance, was unable to imagine a process whereby water turns to water vapor, makes clouds, and then reverses back into water in the form of rain. Another example follows.

Vignette 4.3: *Selena and the Gorilla*

Selena is turning 5 years old and having a party with family and friends at a local pizza restaurant. Her aunt has arranged a special party event: A man dressed up as a gorilla will bring balloons and a present! Everyone, especially Selena, is enjoying the food, the company, and the presents. The plan is for the gorilla to hold Selena on his lap while the guests sing "Happy Birthday" and serve the cake. But when the gorilla enters and picks up Selena, the little girl begins to cry loudly and kick, afraid that she is being abducted by a monster of some sort. The gorilla takes off the headpiece to his costume and assures Selena that he only wants to help her have a fun party; everything seems fine. When the mask goes on again, however, Selena (along with most of her friends) seems just as frightened as she was initially; the children adamantly refuse to leave their parents' sides to sit on the gorilla's lap. Selena's aunt feels just awful, but all the adults present are surprised that the gorilla costume frightens the children.

Piaget would say that Selena was unable to mentally reverse the image of the gorilla and imagine the man inside, as he had appeared holding the mask. So when it looked like a gorilla, it was a gorilla; when it looked like a man, it was a man. Similarly, she might think that there was more birthday cake after it was cut, because she could count more pieces but could not mentally reverse the cutting process to reason that no cake had been added. Selena's perceptions determined reality.

Animism

Another phenomenon you may recognize is a type of thinking Piaget called *animism*, the preschooler's tendency to think something is alive if it moves or makes noise. Animism is the source of many fears during the preschool years, especially at night when familiar objects take on different looks and sounds. If the bushes outside the window cast moving shadows on the wall, preschoolers are more likely to focus on how the shadow looks and moves (like a horde of menacing aliens) than they are to take seriously the relevant properties of light and wind.

One of our children was convinced that there was a monster behind the curtain covering his walk-in closet at night. Inspecting the closet with the light on before bedtime did nothing to alleviate his fears, as in his mind, "He only comes when it is dark." Further investigation revealed that a pet guinea pig in the adjacent room was making scrambling noises that sounded like a monster in the closet, and passing cars threw shadows that looked like there was something big in motion behind the curtain. Moving the pet's cage and closing the shades on the window were successful strategies for getting rid of the closet monster, whereas numerous demonstrations and explanations about headlights and the guinea pig's movements were futile. In this boy's mind, if it looked like a monster, and sounded like a monster, it was a monster. A couple years later, however, he was able to say, "Remember when I thought the lights and the guinea pig were making a monster in the closet?"

The terms Piaget used to define preoperational reasoning provide one useful approach for explaining differences between the thinking processes of young children and those of older children and adults. Many early childhood professionals, however, are uncomfortable with Piaget's contention that the rate of development is consistent across a wide variety of mental tasks, resulting in qualitatively different cognitive structures that emerge in coherent, invariant stages. An alternative approach compares cognition to the operation of a computer in processing information, emphasizing both biological and experiential aspects of cognitive development.

Language and Literacy

Is a certain level of cognitive development required for children to learn language, or does the acquisition of language depend on separate and specific neurological structures? Does language support the development of more sophisticated concepts or simply allow children to express the things they know? Developmental psychologists and psycholinguists still debate the exact relationship between the development of language and cognition, and a review is beyond the scope of this chapter.

By the time children are 3 years old, we expect them to be quite competent in using language as a tool for communication; even strangers can understand almost everything they say, and preschoolers comprehend most of what is said to them in the course of daily life. During the preschool years, typically developing children are working on the pronunciation of difficult sounds, continuing rapid acquisition of vocabulary, refining use of the rules of grammar, and beginning to use language as a tool for learning. By the time typically developing children are 5 years old, language provides a basis for social interactions with peers and adults, a tool for learning new information and becoming literate, and a structure for organizing thought and memory.

Phonology and Syntax

Even though most 3-year-olds are readily understood when they speak, they are constantly learning to produce and comprehend increasingly sophisticated sounds, words, and sentences. They tend to speak in short sentences of between four and five words, confuse certain sounds, and may temporarily seem to lose the ability to put their thoughts into words during emotional or exciting interactions. Younger preschoolers often seem to have complete and important ideas to share but can struggle to express themselves clearly and fluently. A strong desire to reclaim a prized toy might be expressed in the heat of the moment, "I want . . . I . . . I had . . . she . . . she had . . . she took . . . it's Mine!" In this case, even simple vocabulary and sentence structure are likely to be replaced with pointing, stamping, and other gestures characteristic of toddler communications, and adults automatically use contextual cues to determine the exact source of the child's obvious indignation and anger. More experience with using language over the preschool years results in more efficient retrieval of vocabulary and use of standard word order without interruption of the thoughts being expressed. The tendency of 3-year-olds to lapse into incoherence or forsake talking for gesturing when they are excited or upset disappears for the most part by the time children enter kindergarten.

Three-year-olds are generally understandable despite pronunciation errors in the production of certain sounds, because the errors they make are regular and predictable (Menn, 1989). Easier sounds formed with the lips and tip of the tongue (/p/,

/b/, /d/, and /t/) are often substituted for more difficult ones (/g/ and /k/) produced in the back of the mouth. Fricative sounds (/s/, /f/, /th/) requiring a slow release of breath are also replaced with simpler sounds. The following memorable utterances from our field notes illustrate the types of endearing articulation errors of younger preschoolers:

- "Oh, doodie doodie! Dere's da frire twuck!"
          for
  "Oh, goodie goodie! There's the fire truck."

- "Pwees, dimmne dat."
          for
  "Please give me that."

- "Yets do ober dere."
          for
  "Let's go over there."

The number of phonological errors generally decreases during the preschool years, but many children are perfecting pronunciation of difficult consonants and *consonant blends* (/sch/, /fl/, /str/, /fr/, /gr/) into the primary grades. The one child who said "yets" for "Let's" persisted in making this one error long after he began using /l/ in every other utterance.

During the preschool years, the expressive language of typically developing children increases both in the length of utterances and the variety of parts of speech used. Three-year olds generally have begun inserting simple prepositions (in, on), articles (a, the) and auxiliary verbs (is, be, can, will, do) between the subjects, verbs, and objects of three-word utterances (Nelson, 1973; Owens, 1994). "She jump bed" becomes, "She is jumping on the bed," for instance. Younger preschoolers also use a few regular *morphemes*, grammatical markers such as /ed/ for past tense, /s/ for plurals, and /ing/ for ongoing action. They use "no" in a generic way at the beginning of sentences to indicate nonexistence ("No more juice"), to reject ("No drink juice"), and to protest ("No go bed"). Younger preschoolers also begin to ask questions, first by using a rising inflection at the end of a sentence and then by expanding "why" to incorporate /wh/ words like "when" and "where." Preschool children seem to connect the /wh/ words with questions before learning the standard word order that adults use. A 3-year-old might ask, "Where we go?" instead of "Where are we going?"

Between 3 and 5 years of age, children's utterances become longer and much more complex. Four-year-olds begin to use conjunctions (and, but, because, if) to tie ideas together and begin to ask questions using auxiliary verbs (are, is, can, do) and customary word order: "When can I go to Sadie's?" Auxiliary verbs are also used to construct a variety of different types of negative statements, such as, "I don't want any juice"; "There's no more juice"; and "I do not want to go to bed now." Preschoolers also add subject and object prepositions and indirect objects, collapsing two simple sentences into one longer one: "My aunt brought the present. It's my new puzzle" becomes, "My aunt gave me the new puzzle for my birthday." By the time most children enter kindergarten, monolingual English speakers have mastered almost all the major rules for the language (Dale, 1976), including use of personal pronouns, regular and irregular verb tenses, contractions, and passive voice.

Preschool children who are learning English as a second language may substitute sounds and grammatical forms from their primary language when they speak English (Arnberg, 1987). Other youngsters are simultaneously learning two languages and may take longer than their monolingual peers to sort out the rules of grammar for each language. A Head Start teacher who works with Spanish-speaking preschoolers reported cases in which her students sometimes add /o/ to both English and Spanish verbs to form the past tense, a correct rule in Spanish but not in English: *Empujo* is a correct past tense, but *I pusho* is not. Likewise, students who speak dialects such as Black Vernacular English (BE; Labov, 1971) or Ebonics (Phillips, 1994) may apply rules for word order and grammatical forms that are correct usage in the dialect but not in standard English. Differences in the use of the auxiliary verb *be* illustrate this phenomenon: "I be going" is a construction that follows the rules of Ebonics but not English. As preschoolers become more skilled at both language and categorization and classification, they become more proficient and consistent at separating phonology, syntax, and vocabulary of two languages or dialects (Arnberg, 1987).

Semantics and Pragmatics

The vocabularies of preschool children typically continue to expand from hundreds to thousands of words by the time they enter kindergarten. It is likely that they comprehend even more words than they produce, especially in the presence of contextual cues. Preschoolers master entire new categories of words more abstract and conceptual than the nouns and action verbs that characterize the language of toddlers. Prepositions indicate location (in, on, out, between, behind); polar opposites describe physical properties of objects along a continuum (hot–cold, big–little, tall–short, dark–light, good–bad, first–last); preacademic concepts address subcategories within concepts such as color, shape, size, time. Consistent with Piaget's description of cognitive development, preoperational children are becoming more abstract and symbolic thinkers. From an information-processing perspective, increased experience with language forms and usage results in a greater number of available strategies for organization and recall of new knowledge.

The concrete and literal nature of preschool language also reflects Piaget's descriptions of preoperational thought, making it difficult for 3- and 4-year-olds to understand *idioms, similes*, and *metaphors*. Common idioms such as "work out" are often interpreted literally as "working outside," and phrases such as "go to the doctor and get a shot" might connote a doctor with a gun to a preschooler. Using one idea to stand for another, for instance, saying that "You are a ball of energy today" can confuse preschoolers or draw a protest, "I am *not* a ball; I'm a boy!" Youngsters this age may not understand that the same word can have more than one meaning, so they often share jokes that follow the rules for set up and punch line but lack the double meanings that are the basis for adult humor:

Child 1:   "Knock, knock."
Child 2:   "Who's there?"
Child 1:   "Anna!"
Child 2:   "Anna who?"
Child 1:   "Anna crossed the road!"
[Hysterical laughter from both children.]

Another characteristic of preschool vocabulary is the tendency to both overgeneralize and overrestrict application of concept labels. *Overgeneralization* occurs when a child uses a word for a broader category of concepts than it actually represents (Nelson, 1987), for example, when a 3-year-old generalizes a specific term such as *tomorrow* to mean any time in the future, from *later* to *my fourth birthday*. *Overrestrictions* include the use of a general term to refer to a specific example of the category (Pease, Gleason, & Pan, 1989), such as when a preschooler understands the word *bear* to refer only to her own teddy bear and no other. By the time children are 5 years old, they usually have enough experience and knowledge about categorization and classification to organize and apply vocabulary at appropriate levels of specificity, knowing for instance that the word *animals* includes all animals that come from the farm, the jungle, the woods, and household pets and that cows, tigers, deer, and dogs belong to each category, respectively.

Development of language and cognitive skills during the preschool years allows children to share jokes and experiences, organize imaginary play scenarios, and form friendships.

Certain pragmatic aspects of language seem to escape 3-year-olds, as they are often observed to talk at and talk over each other, interrupting or addressing separate topics. They don't always respond to questions immediately (or at all) and are known for making blunt statements and impolite requests. By kindergarten, however, children have learned about the finer points of using language in conversation and for more sophisticated social purposes. They begin to alternate roles as speaker and listener consistently, taking turns and exchanging ideas about the same topic. Older preschoolers generally know to answer when they are asked questions and use questions themselves ("What do you mean?") to clarify information and repair communication breakdowns in ongoing conversation. Four- and 5-year-olds adjust their vocabulary and syntax, taking into account the sophistication of their communication partners, and nonverbal aspects of communication such as facial expressions and body language most often match the content and tone of the overall communication. They can also use language to express their feelings, make polite requests, and negotiate cooperation from both peers and adults.

Emergent Literacy

We have discussed language as a shared symbolic verbal form of communication usually acquired between the ages of 1 and 3 years. *Literacy* is also a shared symbolic form of communication based on print and written information (Literacy Definition Committee, 1992). Although language for the most part involves immediate and direct interactions between or among people, literacy preserves communication in written forms that are accessible to wider audiences across time and distance. In many ways, literacy is a less interactive and more indirect type of communication, often involving long lapses in time between the sending of the message by the writer and its reception by the reader. And whereas children in virtually all cultures of the world learn to speak at least one language, reading and writing are not universal forms of communication. Acquisition of formal literacy is the foundation of school curricula during the primary grades in Western cultures.

The preschool years can be viewed as a critical period during which young children acquire skills that provide a bridge between language and literacy. Cognitive development supports an understanding of print concepts that in turn facilitates subsequent acquisition of reading and writing skills. Cognitive skills in symbol use, sequencing, memory, classification, and categorization provide a framework for learning many important facts related to literacy: Writing is separate from drawing; letters are different from numbers; each letter represents matching sounds; letters make up words; sentences are made up of words (Dyson, 1990). Experience with books and print in the environment also allows opportunities for preschoolers to learn about print conventions: Print conveys information; words stand for ideas; books tell stories; words and pictures can tell the same story; the story moves from page to page, front to back in the book; we read from left to right with spaces between words.

During the preschool years, children begin to use language skills to learn abstract concepts that will become important for success in school and later life: space, time, speed, size, color, shape, temperature, gender, race, and culture. The songs, finger plays, stories, and activities that 3- to 5-year-olds like best are those that use familiar life scenarios to combine action and language, put ideas into words, and promote social interactions. Preschoolers further expand their use of symbolic communication to include graphic symbols, understanding, for example, that golden arches mean fast food; a smiley face means happiness; and a yucky face means poison, don't eat or drink. Drawing and painting are also early ways to represent life experiences on paper.

Children who are told stories will become very sophisticated listeners at this age, learning that stories have a certain sequence, characters, and settings. Those young-sters who are read to will begin to associate words and letters with the spoken language they already know. Preschool children combine their preacademic and conceptual knowledge with a developing sense of self. Of major importance in these years is that children's culture and native language are acknowledged, respected, and appreciated as an integral aspect of who they are and what they are learning about the world (Saunders, 1988).

During the preschool years, children learn a vast number of concepts, including those associated with formal literacy. If all goes well, young children have a solid foundation of social interactions, language experience, and print concepts by the time they enter kindergarten.

Variations in Preschool Cognitive, Language, and Literacy Development

For most children, the preschool years signal a shift from immediate activity to more abstract thinking, including learning a variety of concepts and becoming proficient in language usage. Concerns about language development are the most common reason that 2- and 3-year-olds are referred to special services. Caregivers or professionals often notice that preschoolers are not speaking, do not seem to understand language, or cannot make themselves understood. Further assessment by a team of early childhood specialists is necessary to determine both the cause and the severity of delays in language development.

There is a wide range of variation in acquisition of the more difficult English phonemes, and a speech and language evaluation will often ease fears about children who are difficult to understand. A speech and language pathologist can also determine if stuttering and other disfluencies are irregular and severe enough to warrant therapy services. Other members of the evaluation team will assess youngsters' cognitive, social, and motor development.

Children with cognitive delays are likely to have a limited number of strategies for play, communication, and problem solving in comparison to their peers. They may require more practice and longer times to develop new behaviors or learn new information and are likely to have trouble mastering the symbolic aspects of language. The very nature of mental retardation, for instance, includes slower than typical development of new skills and difficulties with abstract concepts. Some preschoolers with cognitive delays will still be working to master knowledge of spatial relations, cause and effect, tool use (means–ends) and critical sensorimotor skills such as imitation.

Preschool children with hearing impairments are often learning American Sign Language (ASL) or some other form of manual communication. ASL is generally accepted to be a language with manual phonology (finger spelling), manual signs that represent words, and unique rules for syntax and conversational usage (Isenhath, 1990). Becoming fluent in ASL during the preschool years provides the same bridge to literacy for children who are deaf as verbal language does for hearing peers (Strong & Prinz, 1997).

American Sign Language is not a written language, so deaf children who learn to read and write in English are essentially learning literacy in a second language (Mayer & Wells, 1996). Experts in deaf education also consider deafness to be a cultural difference, with unique expectations for alternative methods of communication (Drasgow, 1998). Teachers of preschool children with hearing impairments need to be particularly aware of assessment information about the extent of hearing loss, family preferences for communication strategies, resources for interpreters and classroom materials, and similarities and differences between conventions for use of manual and spoken languages.

Important differences exist among all cultures concerning the rules that govern conversation, and children between the ages of 3 and 5 tend to use the rules they have learned at home in all settings. Professional expectations for social uses of language are based on observations of children in the majority culture who use pragmatic rules shared by the majority of preschool teachers. "Our way" of using language, however, is by no means the only way. When preschoolers have different cultural or linguistic backgrounds than teachers and the majority of children, care must be taken not to confuse appropriate use of language by family standards with delay or disability (Slentz, 1997).

In some communities children learn to be silent in the presence of adults unless spoken to; in other families conversational partners speak simultaneously rather than taking turns (Slonim, 1991), and preschoolers are expected to participate accordingly or be excluded from the conversation. In certain families, silence during conversation indicates consideration and reflection on someone else's statements; in others, silence can be used as a form of disapproval. Although eye contact is often viewed in Western cultures as a sign of attention to the speaker, in some cultures youngsters show respect and deference for adults by looking downward. Some children learn to use relatively fewer words and contact that is more physical during conversation; others learn specific postures or rules for body language (Slonim, 1991). In some cultures smiling is used to avoid conflict and can indicate upset and distress rather than comfort and happiness (Irujo, 1988). It is important that preschool teachers seek to understand variations in social uses of language that exist across cultures rather than assuming differences are indications of problems in development of communication skills.

There are also cultural variations in the activities that provide a framework for emergent literacy skills. Early childhood professionals in Western cultures who focus exclusively on drawing, painting, books, and shared reading may overlook valuable activities that preschoolers from other cultures experience at home. Some Alaskan native cultures, for instance, use knives to create stories using a shared system of traditional markings (DeMarrais, Nelson, & Baker, 1994), providing opportunities for the young children who observe adult models to learn correspondence between ideas and symbols. In cultures with strong oral traditions, story telling is much more common than reading (UNICEF, 1990). Preschool-age youngsters begin to memorize the stories they hear repeatedly and to reproduce important words and phrases in much the same way that preschoolers remember and fill in the sequence of words in their favorite books. Rhymes, songs, word, and sound games also provide valuable preliteracy opportunities for young children (Notari-Syverson, O'Connor, & Vadasy, 1998), including activities that are relevant across the wide range of social experiences preschoolers bring to the classroom.

PRESCHOOL SOCIAL-AFFECTIVE DEVELOPMENT: SELF AND OTHERS, FRIENDS AND FAMILY

As preschoolers become less egocentric (in Piagetian terms) and more efficient and sophisticated at making sense of their perceptions about self and others (in information processing terms), their social landscapes become much more complex, and more stable patterns of individual differences emerge. Parents, teachers, and older children begin more often to describe young children using terms that connote a continuum of stable *personality traits*:

- "She's so outgoing. He's so shy."
- "The twins are both scared of so many things and very cautious; their older sister was much more sociable and less often worried."
- "He's such an affectionate child once he gets to know you. She likes to share everything, even her favorite toys and food."
- "All our children have been artistic from an early age. She is so curious about every new thing. He is so thoughtful and reflective for his age."

In fact, developmental psychologists who study personality use the same terms to describe important differences in the personalities of preschool boys and girls as parents do (Havill, Allen, Halverson, & Kohnstamm, 1994) and have identified five major dimensions along which young children and adults alike differ:

1. How *agreeable* they are in their interactions with others (affectionate, generous).
2. The extent to which they are *conscientious* in carrying out daily activities (reliable, organized, planful).
3. The amount of *emotional (in)stability* they show (anxiety, doubt, worry).
4. How *extraverted* they usually are (activity, energy, enthusiasm).
5. The degree of openness to a variety of activities (imaginative, curious). (Hartup & van Lieshout, 1995)

These five characteristics seem to account for many important individual differences, and studies show that they remain stable from early childhood to adolescence (John, Caspi, Robins, Moffitt, & Stouthamer-Loeber, 1994). You may well be reminded of the discussion of *temperament* introduced in chapter 3, and there seems to be some recent agreement among researchers that the five dimensions of personality listed here are related in some way to temperamental characteristics of infancy and toddlerhood (Ahadi & Rothbart, 1994; Kagan, 1994). The remainder of this chapter is introduced with a brief look at Erikson's psychoanalytic perspective and emotional development and then is divided into sections on the continued development of self and peer interactions.

Preschool as a Period of Initiative

Observation of 3- to 5-year-olds confirms Erikson's (1963) characterization of the preschool years as a period of *initiative*. These youngsters are clearly very busy boys and girls, approaching even the most spontaneous activities with a marked sense of purpose. Preschoolers seem to have goals for themselves as they go about their daily lives and become thoughtful in evaluating their own accomplishments. They use the autonomy of toddlerhood as a springboard for blossoming creativity, increasing control over events in the environment, and engaging in progressively sophisticated social interactions.

As preschool-age children initiate participation in a wide range of activities and react to people and events at home and school, they generate numerous opportunities to learn about the rules and consequences of social interaction. They move quickly and with confidence into areas that are off limits or dangerous; they apply preschool logic to problems and come up with solutions that are self-serving. Behaviors that may look like bad judgment on the part of 3- and 4-year-olds are more likely reflections of incomplete understanding of rules of conduct. Erikson warns that caregivers need to nurture exploration and investigation while providing adequate guidance and limits, so that preschool children do not experience an overabundance of negative consequences as they are learning to associate environmental events with their own behaviors. A quick jaunt into father's closet with the scissors is likely to result in a reprimand that has little to do with a little girl's goal of cutting something besides paper. And the youngster who takes a younger brother's bottle to be a "baby" will probably be jarred by a correction unrelated to imaginary play. Erikson's theory posits that children who are allowed to initiate new and more complex behaviors within safe and supportive environments will emerge from the preschool years assured of their ability to initiate constructive activity. Conversely, preschoolers who become overwhelmed with rules and negative consequences are at risk for feeling guilty about the outcomes of their activity and are less likely to move ahead to industrious accomplishments in the primary grades.

Emotional Development

Preschool-age children begin to exhibit both primary and self-evaluative emotions more predictably as they learn about expected rules of conduct and consequences for complying or disobeying. Three-year-olds can be observed to demonstrate pleasure

and pride in solving problems and will call an adult's attention to their accomplishments with toys, peers, and movement activities. Four- and 5-year-olds will consistently strive to better their own performance and take pride in being "first," "fastest,"
or "most," demonstrating a perspective on their own performance relative to that of
their peers, consistent with their understanding of comparisons. At this point, however, they show little shame if they don't meet their performance goals. Preschoolers
exhibit a wide range of emotions and seem to do so based on both intrinsic motivation and social approval (Stipek, Recchia, & McClintic, 1992).

Preschoolers display emotion and evaluate themselves in a rather black-and-white
fashion. If a parent is angry with them, they may express the belief that *no one* likes
them. Violating one rule may cause them to describe themselves as "bad" children,
and failure at one task translates immediately into, "I can't do anything!" A 4-year-
old who is very angry with a caregiver can certainly appear to have forgotten about
previous positive interactions and emotions, regarding his or her immediate emotional reaction as an enduring state of affairs.

An acquaintance of ours described an interaction in which a preschool child was
quite upset about not being allowed to keep a puppy that had followed her home.
After hours of explanations, discussions, crying, and pleading, the mother gave warning that she was about to end the conversation. The daughter's retort was, "Fine. I hate
you because you are mean. I'll always hate you because you're mean, and I hate that
ugly new haircut, too!" Preschool classrooms are often the arenas where young children learn that they are easily frustrated in physical activities but confident in creative endeavors and that they can like someone but still be angry with them.

Knowledge of Self

Preschool children amass a great deal of specific information about themselves
across a number of dimensions. When preschoolers describe themselves, they cite a
number of visible characteristics of appearance, possessions, and preferences for
activities (Damon, 1983): "I am Anira. I have black hair and dark brown eyes. I have
a baby sister and I like my two birds. My favorite color is orange and my favorite food
is curry rice." Four- and 5-year-olds tend not to describe themselves using traits such
as friendly, happy, hard worker, or active but can identify traits with some accuracy
if forced to choose between statements such as, "I'm usually happy," or "I'm often
unhappy" (Eder, 1990).

Researchers also believe that 4- and 5-year-olds demonstrate the existence of private and public selves (Robinson & Mitchell, 1992). These children know that their
thoughts are their own and not necessarily shared or accessible to others. Even 3-
year-olds have been known to purposely mislead peers and adults, although parents and teachers will most often attest to the fact that preschoolers are not very
good at deception. A frequent deceptive strategy is to blame the ubiquitous
"nobody" as the culprit responsible for transgressions that preschoolers prefer not to
admit. Most adults are not fooled, but preschoolers seem able to overlook evidence
like crayon marks on the wall, a puddle of juice on the floor, wet clothes, or an empty
cookie box.

Between the ages of 3 and 5, typically developing young children come to realize that the self is actually a multifaceted composite of different roles and preferences. There is the family self: brother or sister, sibling or only child, oldest or youngest, grandchild, niece or nephew. A middle child might see himself as competent and caring in the role of older brother yet be worried or jealous in the company of older sister and her friends. In a preschool classroom, a student self might be the tallest but not the fastest runner; she might easily understand print concepts whereas numbers remain difficult; a leader in dramatic play may be content to be a follower in active play.

Gender Identity

During the preschool years, children become increasingly aware of their and others' physical attributes. Knowledge of concepts and classification schemes allows them to compare specific characteristics of people's appearance. Two of the first categories children seem to attend to are age (as age relates to size) and gender. Preschoolers seem to know that they are little, and neighbors and siblings who are "big kids" are often sought after as companions. Older children are physically bigger, more skilled, and often possess highly prized items such as bicycles and electronic games that are alluring to their younger peers. Young children have at least a rudimentary concept of time and often aspire to the activities and possessions associated with being older or bigger sometime in the future. Many preschoolers are motivated to learn new skills that reflect being "a big boy or girl." They begin to take an interest in babies, seeming to like the role of relative competence in providing care and structuring play. Three-year-olds proudly point out the fact that they used to wear diapers and drink from bottles but are now bigger and older, wearing "big kid" clothes and drinking from cups.

By the time most children are 3 years old, they seem to have a solid understanding of *gender identity*, as demonstrated by the ability to accurately label their own and others' genders. Research studies and observations confirm that gender identity is initially determined by consistent physical cues like the length of someone's hair, the clothing associated with males and females, or differences in pitch and tone of adult voices (Levy & Carter, 1989).

There is much more to know about gender, however, than just being able to sort people accurately into categories and label them correctly. The following dialogue from our class notes illustrates both the concrete nature of initial knowledge of gender concepts and the more subtle understandings that develop over time. Students in a class on early development were interviewing a 3-year-old subject about gender:

Student 1:	Ben are you a boy or a girl?
Ben:	*[With a decidedly scornful expression]* I'm a boy. You know that.
Student 2:	How do we know you are a boy?
Ben:	*[Thoughtfully]* Well, I got a boy haircut yesterday. And *[proudly]*, these new shoes are boy shoes.
Student 3:	What about your mother and father? Are they men or women?
Ben:	*[With a cagey look]* One is a women and one is a men.

Student 3:	Okay. Which is which?
Ben:	Mom is a women and Dad is a man.
Student 4:	How do you know that?
Ben:	Mom wears skirts to work and Dad wears work boots and jeans. Mom has long hair and Dad has short hair, like mine.
Student 5:	How about your Aunt Kris and your sister Lauren?
Ben:	Both girls. *[Laughing loudly]* Otherwise they would be my uncle and my brother! *[Afterthought]* And Kris talks like a girl.
	[By now, the students are starting to doubt that there is anything about gender that Ben doesn't know. But they press on with the assignment]
Student 6:	Ben, what if your Dad wore a dress? Would he be a man or a woman?
Ben:	*[Resolutely]* He doesn't ever do that.
Student 6:	But what if he did?
Ben:	*[Glaring]* He won't. I guarantee it!
Student 7:	How about when you were a baby? Were you a boy or a girl?
Ben:	*[Starting to look confused]* I was . . . I think . . . I was a baby.
Student 8:	When you grow up, do you think you will be a man or a woman?
Ben:	*[Fidgeting with his new shoes]* I'll be . . . I'm not sure.
Student 8:	Ben, are you not sure because you haven't decided? Or because you don't know what you'll be?
Ben:	I don't know why I don't know. I just don't know. Can I go now?

Ben clearly has a lot of knowledge about gender, his own and others', but he is still working to refine the concept. Specifically, Ben hasn't yet learned the concepts of *gender stability* or *gender constancy*. Gender stability refers to the notion that a person's gender remains the same across the life span, and if Ben is like most preschoolers, he will master this knowledge by the time he is 4. Gender constancy is the understanding that gender is an unalterable personal attribute that remains constant despite alterations in outward appearance. Research across a variety of cultures with a distinct variety of gender-specific hair and clothing styles indicates that young children achieve gender stability at about age 4 and gender constancy at about age 5 or 6 (Munroe, Shimmin, & Munroe, 1984).

The meaning of gender is inherent in the expectations for the roles males and females assume in daily life and thus highly dependent on family structure, cultural norms, and the times in which children grow up. Existing research makes it clear that young children observe and make sense of differences in sex roles. By the age of 3 years, children show clear gender-based preferences in choice of toys and types of play interactions (Maccoby, 1990), with girls using more verbalizations and choosing more often to role-play domestic and caregiving activities and boys more often selecting construction and active play. Three- and 4-year-olds are also able to categorize jobs and activities to accurately reflect culturally normative gender roles.

Ethnic Identity

There are far fewer studies on the very early development of ethnic identity than on gender, perhaps because concepts of gender and age are more obvious to preschoolers. Existing evidence indicates that young children develop concepts of race and ethnicity somewhat later than concepts of age and gender but do begin to pay attention to race and ethnicity during the preschool years. Based on what you have learned about cognitive development, you could predict that preschoolers would notice differences in the color and texture of skin, eyes, and hair as well as differences in clothing, languages, and foods and begin to compare themselves to other people. *Ethnic identity*, or the ability to accurately label racial and ethnic groups, seems to emerge somewhat later than gender identity, with 4-year-olds being able to consistently identify members of their own ethnic groups (Aboud, 1987), and 5-year-olds able to identify people who share their own racial or cultural background (Aboud & Doyle, 1993).

Not until children are 6 or 7 are they able to consistently categorize other people by ethnic characteristics (Phinney & Rotheram, 1987). Nonetheless, some preschool-age children seek out play partners from their own ethnic groups, although children of color are more likely to play together across groups than are Caucasian youngsters (Howes & Wu, 1990). Perhaps this indicates that preschoolers understand ethnicity and race in two primary categories based on skin color: light or pale and darker tones. As they become more proficient at classification based on more numerous and subtle qualities, children can begin to see that certain skin colors, hair textures, and facial features often occur in combination. Race may be the easiest aspect of ethnic identity to recognize because of the physical dimensions. Ethnicity is, however, a much broader and more complex concept than race or gender, including language, customs, traditions, geographical origins, and shared histories, so it stands to reason that concepts of ethnic identity take longer to learn.

Peer Interactions

A quick look back at the early pages of this chapter sets the stage for a discussion of peer relationships. Active motor play, games of all sorts, imaginative play, art, science, and construction projects—preschool activities provide a boundless variety of interactive venues for youngsters to interact with one another. A number of conditions promote the formation of friendships among preschoolers:

- Natural curiosity of young children about their peers.
- Growing independence from adults.
- Confidence in initiating new activities.
- Competence in formal communication.
- Increased ability to take the perspectives of others.

The vocabularies of preschoolers contain many words pertaining to peer relationships: friends, like, together, alone, nice, mean, play, partners.

Earliest friendships seem to be born of mutually pleasant experiences based on proximity and ease of engagement (Selman, 1980). Preschoolers continue to play together until there is a disagreement or an altercation and then they part ways, regrouping or pairing up with other children. Over time about half of all preschool children show a preference for particular play partners that remains consistent over 6 months or more, often for peers of the same gender or ethnic group (Gershman & Hayes, 1983). Four- and 5-year-olds are more likely than younger children to choose play partners on the basis of shared interests and pastimes (Selman, 1980). For the most part, preschool friendships are formed and maintained with a bond of activity—friends are those who like to do the same things—rather than the reciprocal, interactive relationships primary school children describe as friendships.

Friendships during the preschool years may not be as sophisticated or important in the lives of young children as will be the case later on, but the significance of first friendships for individual children's well-being should not be underestimated. Although research and observations by teachers and parents suggest that friendships in preschool are relatively transitory, we have witnessed many close and enduring relationships beginning in preschool classrooms. It is not unusual for a play partner to feel bereft and isolated when a favorite peer moves away and leaves the class.

The types of prosocial behaviors emphasized by parents and teachers of preschoolers provide a valuable set of skills for friends. Preschoolers are learning to share, to take turns, to use words instead of physical approaches, and to delay gratification, all of which make for more pleasant play interactions than the more immature alternatives. Disagreements and altercations remain common throughout the preschool years, but most youngsters learn the basics of negotiation and compromise by the time they reach kindergarten. Preschool-age children are generally accurate in evaluating their acceptance by peers (Pagioa & Hollett, 1991), reflecting knowledge of themselves in the roles of friends and play partners. Young children with disabilities are often socially isolated from their peers, even in inclusive classrooms (Guralnick, 1999). Many authors believe that the foundations for self-esteem are grounded in a child's earliest perceptions of his or her own value and abilities (Harter, 1990), so being accepted by peers during the preschool years provides an important foundation for more sophisticated relationships in primary school.

In general, increased competence in the social arena allows preschoolers to plan, implement, and evaluate their own accomplishments. They learn much about themselves and others and exercise their most sophisticated skills in movement, cognition, and communication in social settings with peers and adults. Recognition and appreciation of the unique personality and background of each preschooler is an important starting point for teachers who interact closely with children. Knowing every child as an individual first goes a long way toward working successfully with youngsters' diverse economic, cultural, ethnic, linguistic, and developmental backgrounds. By the time they enter kindergarten, most youngsters are beginning to reflect on their own and others' thoughts, behaviors, and characteristics, setting the stage for the complex variety of interactions that form the social panorama of primary school.

Variations in Preschool Social-Affective Development

The preschool years are full of active and imaginary play, social activity, and concept learning. Children at this age are becoming aware of similarities and differences among people, and will begin to take notice if their own appearance or abilities differ from others. Preschoolers are learning about themselves as they come to understand concepts of gender, race, family, and ability, and their evaluations of themselves and others begin to reflect the bias and prejudice that exists in society at large (Tenorio, 1994). The developing initiative of young girls and boys is dependent on a sense of self-assurance, and can be derailed if they feel isolated, ashamed, or rejected. Conversely, preschool children who learn to value diversity and appreciate individual differences are more likely to be confident as they learn about themselves.

More obvious variations in social-affective development occur when 3- to 5-year-olds have identified disabilities such as autism that interfere directly with social and communication development. Preschoolers who cannot interpret social situations to respond and initiate appropriately are at risk for not developing friendships with peers. Young children with behavior problems are often first identified during the preschool years because of disruptions in peer interactions.

Other developmental disabilities can also have a negative impact on social-affective growth. Youngsters with cerebral palsy or other motor disabilities may be left out of active play unless adults make specific arrangements for their inclusion, and children with chronic illnesses often have problems keeping up, also. Three- to-5-year-olds with cognitive delays struggle to understand imaginary play, and have difficulties learning important social concepts about family, friendship, self, and others. Those who can't communicate well because of hearing impairments or an inability to speak and understand language are also at a disadvantage in interacting with peers. Fortunately, it seems that preschool children are most likely be accepting of differences, as long as they have sensitive adult models who are willing to integrate discussions of bias and prejudice into discussion and curriculum (Tenorio, 1994).

IMPLICATIONS FOR CAREGIVERS AND TEACHERS OF PRESCHOOLERS

As described in chapter 1, development is learning that occurs within the context of a particular environment. The environment is considered by some developmental psychologists to be at least as important as heredity in determining the developmental outcomes of young children (Lewis, 1996; Plomin, 1989), highlighting the importance of meeting basic needs of food, shelter, and attention as a critical foundation for early learning. Research results have consistently indicated for decades that by 3 years of age, the effects of chronically impoverished homes are evident in measures of cognitive status (Farran, Haskins, & Gallagher, 1980). Research demonstrated 25 years ago that one of the best predictors of intellectual functioning in 4-year-olds is the educational level of their primary caregivers (Broman & Kennedy, 1975). Early education can be an important factor in promoting resiliency for children whose parents do not have the benefit of a good education, offsetting the negative effects of poverty (Bernard, 1999; Werner, 1990). Almost a quarter of children under the age of 6 in the United States are being raised in poverty (Children's Defense Fund, 1998); improving the chances for children from impoverished homes to succeed in school is the primary mission of Head Start programs.

Studies that demonstrate relationships among income, education, and early cognitive development should not be taken to mean that parents with low incomes are unmotivat-

Preschoolers develop a sense of self that includes concepts of family roles, gender, race, personal preferences, and accomplishment.

ed or incompetent or that children from poor families are born with less cognitive potential than their more affluent peers. In fact, infants from all income groups tend to score similarly on developmental tests, with the effects of poverty becoming obvious in cognitive development during the preschool years (Golden & Birns, 1983). Early childhood professionals, however, should be aware constantly of the negative effects of hunger and poor nutrition, inadequate housing and homelessness, stress, unsafe environments, and insufficient health care on the growth, development, and daily performance of young children in their care. Inadequate nutrition in the first 2 years of life, for instance, has a direct impact on early brain growth (Werner, 1990). Educational services alone are not likely to improve the developmental outcomes for children from low-income families. The importance of comprehensive health, nutrition, and family-centered social services for preschool children from impoverished families cannot be overstated.

Child Care

Janet Gonzales-Mena (1998) synthesized a variety of developmental, educational, and parenting perspectives into a thought-provoking position on the nature of group care for young children. She contends that anyone involved in early care and education should consider themselves partners with families in the rearing of children:

> You can drive your car to work, park it in a garage, and come back and pick it up in the afternoon . . . But you can't park your children. Wherever your children are, they are growing and learning, being changed by their experiences. They are being reared. (p. 130)

This perspective on group care has significant implications for parents and early childhood professionals alike. Because childrearing practices differ in so many ways from family to family, it is obvious that no one approach is sufficient to support early development in just the way each young child's family would prefer. In combination with a nationwide shortage of affordable and available child care (Miller, 1990), the implication is increased diversity among the life ways of the young children in any given program. Diversity is considered a strength and an advantage in early childhood programs, and the field has numerous curriculum resources to support teachers and entice children; nonetheless, the interface between individual family expectations and the logistics of providing group care can generate a multitude of conflicting opinions about daily schedules for eating and sleeping, levels of physical care and activity, rules of social interaction and communication, as well as expectations for curriculum. Hence, a growing aspect of prekindergarten programs is the necessity for caregivers to learn about the family lives of their young charges and to collaborate with parents to identify mutually acceptable goals, routines, and styles.

Teaching Across Languages and Cultures

Children from poor families whose cultural and language backgrounds differ from the mainstream are at particular risk for the "double whammy" of poverty and lack of access to the preschool curriculum delivered in English. We work with one Head Start program that serves children and families from over 15 language groups, many of whom are learning English as a second language. The teachers know that ideally preschoolers would be instructed in their native languages, including American Sign Language for deaf children (Drasgow, 1998) and are constantly searching for meaningful and relevant materials to use in their classrooms. Exposure to books and writing is crucial for early literacy development of all young children, especially those who have fewer opportunities for reading and writing at home (Marvin & Wright, 1997). It is difficult, however, to find and use materials in children's native languages, and interpreters are hard to come by for some of the more uncommon language groups. These teachers understand well the positive effects of making literacy a focus in the design of classroom environments and curriculum and have spent many hours generating effective strategies for creating a print-rich environment that is accessible and relevant to all their students (Fields, Spangler, & Lee, 1991).

Teaching Children of Diverse Abilities

Young children are less likely than adults to have negative stereotypes about race, gender, culture, language, and disabilities, so teachers and parents of preschool children are in an advantageous position to set the stage for inclusion of children with developmental differences. Jeffrey Trawick-Smith (2000) believes that the behavior of adults is more important than the characteristics of children in development of close attachments; successful inclusion is also a process of relationship building that depends on how teachers think and function in the classroom. Preschool teachers who make it a priority to address the developmental needs of each and every student seem to develop a mind-set that fosters creativity and confidence in including a range of developmental variations in physical, cognitive, and social abilities.

Preschool programs most often serve children across an age range within the same classroom, so substantial variations in skill levels is the norm rather than the exception. There is always one child who is the most active, another who needs multiple directions every time, yet another who bounces from one activity to the next, and the one who tires most quickly. Preschool teachers are used to teaching in a way that addresses the developmental needs of each of these youngsters. Sometimes, however, a single child who has a disability is the one who needs the most frequent specific directions, and tires most easily, and needs the most assistance making transitions. All wrapped up into one package, and especially if given a label, behaviors that teachers would feel confident handling singly might seem more extreme or daunting.

CONCLUDING REMARKS

The preschool years mark important developmental milestones for young children with increased competence in concept knowledge, language skills, and social interactions setting the stage for successful participation in school settings. Early childhood educators should not underestimate the importance of their roles in preparing children for the academic and social demands of the primary grades. Preschool teachers are in the privileged position of influencing children's earliest knowledge and appreciation of themselves and others, enlarging and strengthening the foundation of knowledge and skills that youngsters need to be successful in school, at home, and in the community.

Knowledgeable and dedicated early childhood professionals are also in positions to advance the field in general by being willing to try new strategies for addressing the needs of young students with diverse abilities and of those from a variety of cultural, linguistic, economic, and ethnic backgrounds. There are certainly a number of challenges inherent in adapting early educational practices to incorporate and represent the full range of children and families, but the rewards will extend beyond the classroom and be carried forward in the lives of all students whose preschool experience engenders a lasting sense of belonging, confidence in their own competence, and a belief that their contributions are valuable.

EXTENDING YOUR LEARNING

1. Research the preschools in your community. Find out how they meet the needs of students from different cultural and linguistic backgrounds and students with disabilities.

2. Visit a preschool class and watch the children during outside play. Count how many fundamental movements (run, jump, throw, chase, etc.) they use in 15 minutes.

3. Play a game of t-ball with a group of preschoolers. Observe how each child holds that bat, ball, and glove. Look for hand dominance and throwing styles.

4. Interview a speech–language pathologist who works with preschool children. Find out the most common skills they work on with 3- to 5-year-olds.

5. Build a sandcastle with a preschooler. Identify the "tools" they use to help build the castle (i.e., cup their hands, seashell, shovel, rocks).

6. Present a large selection of different types of balls to a group of 3- to 5-year-olds (i.e., baseball, basketball, volleyball, beach ball). Observe the different uses the children come up with for each ball and the fundamental skills they use while playing with them (kicking, throwing, bouncing).

7. Observe a preschool classroom. Count how many children work with friends when they are not specifically asked to. Note the different ways in which the students invite one another to play.

8. Observe preschool children at play, and report on preferences in play partners and favorite activities.

9. Interview parents of preschool-aged children. Find out what activities they do as a family and list the domains (cognitive, gross or fine motor, social, self-care, or language) that the child exercises during each activity.

10. Try some of Piaget's conservation experiments with preschool children and ask them to explain what is happening during daily activities. Note aspects of preoperational thinking, and document examples from your conversations.

VOCABULARY

Animism.   Thinking something is alive if it moves or makes sounds.

Consonant blends.   Multiple consonants put together to make one sound (i.e., /st/, /sh/, /ch/).

Controlled scribbling.   Drawing curves, dots, and circles with intent to produce specific strokes, designs.

Early representational drawings.   Drawings that represent people, objects, and events in a young child's life, primarily containing simple strokes without accurate depiction of reality.

Egocentric.   Thought processes limited by one's own experiences (Piagetian).

Ethnic identity.   Knowledge of the physical characteristics associated with racial and ethnic categories and the ability to identify one's own ethnicity accordingly.

Fundamental movements.   Basic motor movements of locomotion, propulsion, and manipulation; for example, running, kicking, throwing, jumping; refined during the primary grades as transition to sports-related movements.

Gender constancy.   Knowledge that gender is an unalterable personal attribute that remains constant despite alterations in physical appearance.

Gender identity.   Knowledge of the physical characteristics associated with gender categories and the ability to identify one's own gender accordingly.

Gender stability.   Knowledge that a person's gender remains the same during the life span.

Hand dominance.   Preference for using the right or left hand for writing, eating, throwing, and other functional activities; the right hand is more often dominant than the left.

Idioms.   Phrases with common meanings not reflected in the actual words used, for example, *work out*.

Initiative.   Purposeful activity and the ability to follow through with a plan or task (Erikson).

Literacy.   Shared symbolic form of communication based on print and written information.

Locomotion.   Moving the body through space by walking, running, crawling, skipping, hopping.

Manipulative movements.   Movements involving the use of objects, such as kicking and throwing balls, writing and eating with utensils.

Metaphors.   A figure of speech in which a term is used to represent another word through an analogy (i.e., the playground is a disaster area).

Morphemes.   A meaningful linguistic unit that cannot be divided into smaller meaningful parts.

Nonlocomotive movement.   Movement that does not involve moving the body through space, such as bending, turning, pulling, pushing.

Overgeneralizaton.   Using a word for a broader category of concepts than it actually represents, such as calling all construction equipment *backhoe*.

Overrestrictions.   The use of a general term to refer only to one specific example of a category, such as using *man* only as a synonym for *Daddy*.

Perceptually based thinking.   Thought centered on the physical characteristics of what one sees, hears, touches, smells, tastes.

Personality traits.   Individual differences in style of interaction, stability of emotion, levels of activity.

Similes.   A figure of speech in which two unlike things are compared (i.e., hair like silk).

Temperament.   Constitutionally based patterns of reactivity and self-control; behavioral style.

Transductive reasoning. Using perceptual similarities between events as a basis for reasoning and problem solving (Piagetian).

INTERNET RESOURCES

Web sites provide much useful information for educators and we list some here that pertain to the topics covered in this chapter. The addresses of Web sites can also change, however, and new ones are continually added. Thus, this list should be considered as a first step in your acquisition of a larger and ever-changing collection.

Ages and Stages Series
    http://www.nncc.org/childdev/age.stage.page.html

Child Development Milestones
    http://www.nncc.org/childdev/milel.html

Early Childhood.Com
    http://www.earlychildhood.com

Early Childhood Educator's and Family Web Corner
    http://users.sig.net/~cokids/

The ECE Web Guide
    http://www.ccewebguide.com

Growing Together and Preschool Development
    http://www.nncc.org/childev/grow.preschool.html

NAEYC
    http://www.neayc.org

The Perpetual Preschool
    http://www.perpetualpreschool.com/

Special Needs Advocate for Parents (SNAP)
    http://www.snap.org

References

Aboud, R. (1987). The development of ethnic self-identification and attitudes. In J. S. Phinney & M. J. Rotheram (Eds.), *Children's ethnic socialization: Pluralism and development* (pp. 32–35). Newbury, Park, CA: Sage.

Aboud, R., & Doyle, A. B. (1993). The early development of ethnic identity and attitudes. In M. E. Bernal & G. P. Knight (Eds.), *Ethnic identity: 1. Formation and transmission among Hispanics and other minorities* (pp. 46–59). Albany, NY: SUNY Press.

Ahadi, S. A., & Rothbart, M. K. (1994). Temperament, development, and the big five. In C. F. Halverson, Jr., G. S. Kohnstamm, & R. P. Martin (Eds.), *The developing structure of temperament and personality from infancy to adulthood* (pp. 189–207). Hillsdale, NJ: Lawrence Erlbaum Associates.

Anselmo, S., & Franz, W. (1995). *Early childhood development: Prenatal through age eight.* (2nd ed.). Englewood Cliffs, NJ: Merrill-Prentice-Hall.

Arnberg, L. (1987). *Raising children bilingually: The preschool years.* Philadelphia Multicultural Matters, LTD.

Bee, H. (1997). *The developing child* (8th ed.). New York: Longman.

Benard, B. (1999). From research to practice: The foundations of the resiliency paradigm. In N. Henderson, B. Benard, N. Sharp-Light (Eds.), *Resiliency in action: Practical ideas for overcoming risks and building strengths in youth, families and communities.* Gorman, ME: Resiliency in Action.

Brittain, W. (1979). *Creativity, art, and the young child.* New York: Macmillan.

Broman, N., & Kennedy, D. (1975). *Preschool IQ: Prenatal and early development correlates.* Hillsdale, NJ: Lawrence Erlbaum Associates.

Bryden, M., & Saxby, L. (1985). Developmental aspects of cerebral lateralization. In J. E. Obrzat & G. W. Hund (Eds.), *Child neurobiology* (Vol. 1). New York: Free Press.

Children's Defense Fund. (1998). *The State of America's children, yearbook.* Washington, DC: Beacon.

Cost, quality and outcomes in child care centers. (1995). (Tech. Rep.). Denver: University of Colorado, Center for Research in Economic and Social Policy.

Dale, P. S. (1976). *Language development: Structure and function.* New York: Holt, Rinehart & Winston.

Damon, W. (1983). The nature of social-cognitive change in the developing child. In W. F. Overton (Ed.), *The relationship between social and cognitive development* (pp. 103–142). Hillsdale, NJ: Lawrence Erlbaum Associates.

Davidoff, J. B. (1975). *Differences in visual perception: The individual eye.* New York: Academic Press.

De Marrais, K. B., Nelson, P. A., & Baker, J. H. (1994). Meaning in mud: Yup'ik Eskimo girls at play. In J. L. Roopnarine, J. E. Johnson, & F. H. Hooper (Eds.), *Children's play in diverse cultures* (pp. 179–209). Albany, NY: SUNY Press.

Drasgow, I. (1998). American sign language as a pathway to linguistic competence. *Exceptional Children, 64,* 329–342.

Dyson, A. H. (1990). Symbol makers, symbol weavers: How children link play pictures, and print. *Young Children, 45*(2), 50–57.

Eaton, W., & Yu, A. (1989). Are sex differences in child motor activity level a function of sex differences in maturational status? *Child Development, 60,* 1005–1011.

Eder, R. A. (1990). Uncovering young children's psychological selves: Individual and developmental differences. *Child Development, 61,* 849–863.

Erikson, E. H. (1963). *Childhood and society* (2nd ed.). New York: Norton.

Esposito, B., & Koorland, M. (1989). Play behavior of hearing impaired children: Integrated and segregated settings. *Exceptional Children, 55,* 412–419.

Farran, D. C., Haskins, R., & Gallagher, J. J. (1980). Poverty and mental retardation: A search for explanations. *New Directions for Exceptional Children, 1,* 47–66.

Fields, M. V., Spangler, K. L., & Lee, D. M. (1991). Let's begin reading right: Developmentally appropriate beginning literacy (2nd ed.). New York: Macmillan.

Garbarino, J., Dubrow, N., Kostelny, K., & Pardo, C. (1992). *Children in danger: Coping with the consequences of community violence.* San Francisco: Jossey-Bass.

Garcia-Coll, C. (1990). Developmental outcome of minority infants: A process-oriented look into our beginnings. *Child Development, 61,* 270–289.

Gershman, E. S., & Hayes, D. S. (1983). Differential stability of reciprocal friendships and unilateral relationships amongst preschool children. *Merrill Palmer Quarterly, 29,* 167–177.

Golden, M., & Birns, B. (1983). Social class and infant intelligence. In M. Lewis (Ed.), *Origins of intelligence: Infancy and early childhood* (2nd ed., pp. 347–398). New York: Plenum Press.

Gonzales-Mena, J. (1998). *The child in the family and the community* (2nd ed.). Englewood Cliffs, NJ: Merrill-Prentice-Hall.

Guralnick, M. (1999). The nature and meaning of social integration for young children with mild developmental delays in inclusive settings. *Journal of Early Intervention, 22*(1), 70–86.

Harter, S. (1990). Causes, correlates and the functional role of self worth: A life span perspective. In R. J. Sternberg & J. Kollingan (Eds.), *Competence considered* (pp. 67–97). New Haven, CT: Yale University Press.

Hartup, W. W., & van Lieshout, C. F. (1995). Personality development in social context. *Annual Review of Psychology, 46*, 655–687.

Havill, V. L., Allen, K., Halverson, C. F., Jr., & Kohnstamm, G. A. (1994). Parents' use of Big Five categories in their natural language descriptions of children. In C. F. Halverson, Jr., G. S. Kohnstamm, & R. P. Martin (Eds.), *The developing structure of temperament and personality from infancy to adulthood* (pp. 371–386). Hillsdale, NJ: Lawrence Erlbaum Associates.

Howes, C., & Wu, F. (1990). Peer interactions and friendships in an ethnically diverse school setting. *Child Development, 63*, 449–460.

Isenhath, J. O. (1990). *The linguistics of American Sign Language.* Jefferson, NC: McFarland.

John, O. P., Caspi, A., Robins, R. W., Moffitt, T. E., & Stouthamer-Loeber, M. (1994). The "little five": Exploring the nomological network of the five-factor model of personality in adolescent boys. *Child Development, 65*, 160–178.

Kagan, J. (1994). *Galen's prophecy.* New York: Basic Books.

Keogh, J. (1977). The study of movement skill development [Monograph No. 28]. *Quest,* 76–80.

Labov, W. (1971). Stages in the acquisition of Standard English. In W. Labov (Ed.), *Readings in American dialectology* (pp. 1–43). New York: Appleton-Century-Crofts.

Lamme, L. (1984). *Growing up writing.* Washington, DC: Acropolis Books.

Levy, G. D., & Carter, D. B. (1989). Gender schema, gender constancy, and gender-role knowledge: The roles of cognitive factors in preschoolers' gender-role stereotype attributions. *Developmental Psychology, 25*, 444–449.

Lewis, M. (1996). Developmental principles and their implications for infants who are at risk and/or disabled. In M. J. Hanson (Ed.), *Atypical infant development.* Austin, TX: Pro Ed.

Literacy Definition Committee. (1992). *National adult literacy survey.* U.S. Department of Education. Washington, DC: U.S. Government Printing Office.

Lowrey, G. (1986). *Growth and development of children.* Chicago: Yearbook Medical Publishers.

Maccoby, E. E. (1990). Gender and relationships: A developmental account. *American Psychologist, 45*, 513–520.

Malina, R. (1982). Motor development in the early years. In S. G. Moore & C. R. Cooper (Eds.), *The young child: Reviews of research* (Vol. 3, pp. 211–229). Washington, DC: National Association for the Education of Young Children.

Marvin, C., & Wright, D. (1997). Literacy socialization in the homes of preschool children. *Language, Speech and Hearing Services in Schools, 28*(2), 154–163.

Mayer, C., & Wells, G. (1996). Can the interdependence theory support a bilingual-bicultural model of literacy education for deaf students? *Journal of Deaf Studies and Deaf Education, 1*, 93–107.

Menn, L. (1989). Phonological development: Sounds and sound patterns. In J. B. Gleason (Ed.). *The development of language* (pp. 59–100). Columbus, OH: Merrill.

Miller, A. B. (1990). *The day care dilemma: Critical concerns for American families.* New York: Plenum.

Munroe, R. H., Shimmin, H. S., & Munroe, R. L. (1984). Gender understanding and sex role preference in four cultures. *Developmental Psychology, 20*, 673–682.

Nelson, C. A. (1987). The recognition of facial expressions in the first two years of life. *Child Development, 58*, 889–909.

Nelson, K. (1973). Structure and strategy in learning to talk. *Monographs of the Society of Research in Child Development, 38* (Serial No. 149).

Notari-Syverson, A., O'Connor, R. E., & Vadasay, P. E. (1998). *Ladders to literacy: A preschool activity book.* Baltimore: Paul Brookes.

Owens, R. E. (1994). Development of language, communication and speech. In G. H. Shames, E. H. Wigg, & W. A. Second (Eds.), *Human communication disorders.* New York: Macmillan.

Pagioa, L. P., & Hollett, N. (1991). Relations between self-perceived and actual peer acceptance among preschool children. *Perceptual and Motor Skills, 72*, 224–226.

Pease, D. M., Gleason, J. B., & Pan, B. A. (1989). Gaining meaning: Semantic development. In J. B. Gleason (Ed.), *The development of language* (pp. 101–134). Columbus, OH: Merrill.

Pellegrini, A., & Perlmutter, J. (1988). Rough-and-tumble play on the elementary school yard. *Young Children, 43*(2), 14–17.

Phillips, C. B. (1994). The movement of African-American children through sociocultural contexts: A case of conflict resolution. In B. L. Mallory & R. S. New (Eds.), *Diversity and developmentally appropriate practices.* New York: Teachers College Press.

Phinney, J. S., & Rotheram, M. J. (1987). Children's ethnic socialization: Themes and implications. In J. S. Phinney & M. J. Rotheram (Eds.), *Children's ethnic socialization: Pluralism and development* (pp. 274–292). Newbury Park, CA: Sage.

Piaget, J. (1952). *The origins of intelligence in children.* New York: International Universities Press.

Piaget, J., & Inhelder, B. (1963). *The child's conception of space.* London: Routledge & Kegan Paul.

Plomin, R. (1989). Environment and genes: Determinants of behavior. *American Psychologist, 44*, 105–111.

Ridenour, M. (1978). Program to optimize infant motor development. In M. Ridenour (Ed.), *Motor development: Issues and applications.* Princeton, NJ: Princeton Books.

Robinson, J. W., & Mitchell, P. (1992). Child's interpretation of messages from a speaker with a false belief. *Child Development, 63*, 639–652.

Roizen, N. J. (1997). Down syndrome. In M. L. Batshaw (Ed.), *Children with disabilities* (pp. 361–376). Baltimore: Paul Brookes.

Saunders, G. (1988). *Studies in bilingual development.* Hillsdale, NJ: Lawrence Erlbaum Associates.

Selman, R. L. (1980). *The growth of interpersonal understanding.* New York: Academic Press.

Slentz, K. (1997). *Evaluation and assessment in early childhood special education: Children who are culturally and linguistically diverse.* Olympia, WA: Special Education, Office of the Superintendent of Special Education.

Slonim, M. B. (1991). *Children, culture, ethnicity: Evaluating the impact.* New York: Garland.

Stipek, D. J., Recchia, S., & McClintic, S. (1992). Self-evaluation in young children. *Monographs of the Society for Research in Child Development, 57*(1, Serial No. 226).

Strong, M., & Prinz, P. M. (1997). A study of the relationship between American Sign Language and English literacy. *Journal of Deaf Studies and Deaf Education, 2*, 37–46.

Tan, L. (1985). Laterality and motor skills in four-year-olds. *Child Development, 56*, 119–124.

Tanner, J. (1978). *Fetus into man: Physical growth from conception to maturity.* Cambridge, MA: Harvard University Press.

Teeter, P. A., & Semrud-Clikeman, M. (1997). *Child neuropsychology: Assessment and interventions for neurodevelopmental disorders.* Boston: Allyn & Bacon.

Tenorio, R. (1994). Race and respect among young children. In B. Bigelow, L. Christensen, S. Karp, B. Miner and B. Peterson (Eds.), *Rethinking Our Classrooms* (pp. 24–28). Milwaukee, WI: Rethinking Schools.

Thelen, E. (1989). The (re)discovery of motor development: Learning new things from an old field. *Developmental Psychology, 25*, 946–949.

Trawick-Smith, J. (2000). *Early childhood development: A multicultural perspective* (2nd ed.). Columbus, OH: Merrill-Prentice-Hall.

UNICEF. (1990). *Children and development in the 1990s: A UNICEF sourcebook.* New York: United Nations.

Werner, E. (1990). Protective factors and individual resilience. In S. Meisels & J. Shonkoff (Eds.), *Handbook of early childhood intervention* (pp. 97–116). Cambridge: Cambridge University Press.

Whiting, B., & Edwards, C. (1988). *Children of different worlds.* Cambridge, MA: Harvard University Press.

5

PRIMARY SCHOOL:
FROM PEER GROUP TO ACADEMICS

Children need models more than they need critics.

Joseph Joubert (1754–1824)

▼ Chapter Objectives

After reading this chapter, you should be able to:

- ▼ Describe the physical growth taking place in children ages 5 to 8.
- ▼ Tell how motor development affects children's skills in games, drawing, and writing at this age.
- ▼ Use developmental theory to explain how young children achieve literacy and other academic skills.
- ▼ Explain how cognitive and social development are interrelated.
- ▼ Describe the social, moral, and emotional development to be expected in the kindergarten and primary years.
- ▼ Describe the variations that might be encountered at this age in all aspects of development.

As you think about and apply chapter content on your own, you should be able to:

- ▼ Relate your knowledge of this age to the information provided in earlier chapters about younger children.
- ▼ Begin to think about ways to support the developmental needs of both typically and atypically developing children ages 5 to 8.

Vignette 5.1: *Cutting the Cake to Make More*

I had just told an open-ended story to a class of third graders, and the group was struggling with a solution. Essentially, I had asked the children to resolve conflicting issues of sharing, promises, and friendship, three important sociomoral values for children in the primary grades. In brief the story involved a group of two boys and two girls who have ridden their bikes to the park for a picnic. One of the boys realizes he has forgotten his lunch, and two of the children generously share. The fourth child, however, isn't sure what to do. She has two pieces of cake, one of which is supposed to go to the other girl, who helped her make it. This other girl stakes her claim to the cake ("After all, I helped, and besides, you promised") while the boy tries unsuccessfully to be polite ("Well, but I really am very hungry").

I noted that no one suggested a return home to a helpful mother, as children in the first grade had done when I told them the same story. And I wasn't surprised when the class decided, with some relief and self-satisfaction, that the best solution was simply to divide the two pieces four ways, thus making everybody at least reasonably happy.

A surprise was still in store, however. Just as most of the children smiled contentedly, ready to move on, Carla—generally acclaimed the class leader in most things—said, "Everybody could have more if you cut the four pieces in half." Suddenly, most of the class nodded vigorously in agreement. Nonplused, I tried to help the children see that more pieces didn't make more cake. Carla, however, managed to convince almost everyone that her way was preferable, and soon the class was feeling even better about the solution, positive that now the children all would have more cake to eat. (Suzanne Krogh)

Suzanne's experience (Vignette 5.1) demonstrates several points that are discussed in this chapter about the development of children in the final years of early childhood:

- Children in the primary grades are drawn to closer ties with their peers while moving away from their intense closeness to the adults in their lives (as demonstrated by the lack of interest in turning to adults for help and by Carla's influence over the group).
- Sociomoral development is intertwined with cognitive development (as shown by the influence of a mathematical problem on a social decision.)
- At any age, maturation can exhibit temporary setbacks. In the primary years, the new attraction of peer relationships can have an important influence (demonstrated when Carla's persuasive leadership dissuaded the entire class from an accurate mental evaluation of the true quantity of cake).

A second story, which focuses on physical development at this age, completes our introduction to the subjects of this chapter.

Vignette 5.2: *New Rules on the Playground*

It was spring, and as usual for this time of year, the kindergarten children were becoming more competitive physically, some of them trying to imitate the older children's team-oriented games. Relay races, which previously had been demonstrations of happy chaos with no discernible winners or losers, suddenly became the focus of new interest in rules and competition. A few children appointed themselves informal monitors to be sure that participants stayed behind the line until it was their turn to start. The lines they stood in became a bit tidier, and taking a turn out of sequence became cause for outrage.

Observing these changes, their teacher instituted a few basic rules: numbering off for taking turns, required contact with the wall at the far end of the race, and no "jumping the gun." Most of the children understood and accepted the new spirit of following rules. Within a short time, they requested another change and asked to divide into boy and girl teams. The differences between the sexes were immediately apparent. In races involving dribbling or throwing balls, the boys were usually the victors. In the hopping, skipping, or galloping races, the girls proved superior. A brief class discussion concluded with an agreement that the teams should return to a combination of the sexes "because too many of us get our feelings hurt."

The developmental issues raised in Vignette 5.2 include a few that are described in upcoming sections:

- Toward the end of kindergarten, many children begin to understand the structure of adult-style sports (as demonstrated in new interest in rules, lining up properly, and identifying winners and losers).

- As children become more peer oriented, they alter the social focus of their physical games (as these late kindergartners did in becoming more competitive and interested in rules).

- Whereas boys and girls develop physically at about the same speed, they do so with some differences in skills (as the boys showed in their abilities in ball passing and the girls did when hopping, skipping, and galloping).

FAMILY CONTEXT

Your child's first day at school will be a tearful occasion. For you. (Bruce Lansky)

Family life can change significantly when children begin to go to school. Young children's daily schedules change, they typically spend less time at home, and their peer group becomes increasingly important. As youngsters grow more independent and develop other social priorities, relationships with parents may vacillate from affection and dependence to opposition and challenge. Younger brothers and sisters often miss the presence of the older sibling who leaves each day, and school-age children develop interests separate from those of their siblings.

Parents may feel they have less access to information about their children's daily activities and social interactions when their sons and daughters start school. As children venture away from the family for social pursuits, they often gravitate toward other groups. Recess "clubs" are common. Group membership is an important social concept for primary-age children, and their experiences as family members become an important backdrop for peer relationships.

Much of a primary child's rapid social and emotional development is related to a growing cognitive ability to take the perspective of others. Early in the primary years, children begin to understand the variety and interrelationships of social roles. A child can be simultaneously big brother and little brother, son and nephew. Gradually it becomes clear that the child's own mother is also the grandmother's daughter and the

These two friends know each other from school, and are happy to be spending time together on the week-end.

aunt's sister. The teacher is also a son or daughter and even can be a student, and so on and so on.

Some children like to test ambiguous social behaviors (swearing, exaggerating, showing off) in family interactions before risking public feedback. By the end of the primary years, most children can alter their behaviors to fit the social demands of different situations. School becomes central to children's identities as legal requirements ensure that all but the home-schooled spend much of their day in school settings. Teachers universally become important adults in the lives of their students.

Children's development in the physical, cognitive, social, and emotional domains continues to advance independence at home and becomes a major factor in school success. Five- to 8-year-olds are generally more like preschoolers than they are like upper elementary students, but they are making rapid developmental progress through the primary years. We discuss each of the developmental domains in turn, beginning with the physical.

PHYSICAL GROWTH AND MOTOR DEVELOPMENT DURING THE PRIMARY YEARS: THE LATE FUNDAMENTAL AND EARLY SPORTS PHASES

The bodies of young children grow and change in significant ways during the primary school years. With changes in size and stature come new and different ways of moving and thinking about the physical self. Physical development of primary school children is an important consideration in the development of curriculum for both these reasons. As you read about the changes taking place in the 5- to 8-year-old physique and the accompanying advances in motor capabilities, consider the implications for you as a teacher.

Physical Growth

Although observable changes in growth may be less dramatic during the primary grades than in younger years, the impact on overall development is substantial. The rate of growth slows somewhat in the primary grades, and from age 5 and on through puberty, children grow about 2 to 3 inches per year. A 6-year-old, for example, averages 45 inches in height, but 2 inches shorter or taller is quite typical. Boys tend to be slightly taller than girls, carrying this difference through to adulthood. Although children's heights generally echo those of their parents, today final adult height is observed to be 1 or 2 inches taller than that of the previous generation. Improved health care and nutrition since World War II are believed to be major causes of the increase in physical stature (Black & Puckett, 1996).

By age 7, children have increased their weight to seven times their birth weight. Boys may be a bit heavier, with more muscle and bone mass. The average 6-year-old boy currently weighs about 45.5 pounds, and his female counterpart 42.9 pounds. Throughout the elementary school years, girls will gain weight more rapidly and head off to middle school temporarily heavier than the boys.

Until the mid-1990s, most experts believed that the elementary school years were a period of slow, steady, and dependable growth. Parents, however, have long observed that their children often seem to suddenly grow overnight. Research finally has caught up with parental observation and verified rapid periods of growth during the primary years (Lampl, 1993). It is not unusual for children between the ages of 5 and 8 to experience one or more growth spurts that alter the size and shape of their bodies. Husky children may find themselves suddenly slim, or vice versa. Research by Michelle Lampl documented that children might grow over ½ inch in a single day. Rapid growth spurts are sometimes interspersed with weeks and months of no growth at all. Lampl's research also validated parental reports of gloomy moods and increased needs for sleep and food just before rapid growth.

Hands and Eyes

There is a common belief that children's eyesight improves continually until about age 5, yet research indicates that the *visual acuity* of 1-year-olds is similar to the 20/20 vision of adults who see well without glasses (Flavell, 1993). Perhaps the discrepancy lies in the fact that between ages 5 and 7, there is rapid improvement in the ability to focus on moving objects. During the primary years, then, the ability to see clearly is combined with precise coordination in controlling scanning and focusing, the result being sophisticated competence in hand–eye coordination by the end of the primary grades.

Hand dominance is usually established by about age 5, although changes may still be made until age 10. Since most children begin school by their fifth year, the establishment of handedness is often of importance for teachers. Traditional views once held that clumsiness and learning disabilities accompany left-handedness, but these views have been discredited (Tan, 1985). Most important for teachers, left-handedness should not be taken as a sign that something is wrong with a child's development.

Social Aspects of Physical Growth

Gender becomes an important factor in the choice of play partners and knowledge of self during the primary years. Awareness of gender permanence usually is established firmly by the time children are in primary school, as they begin to define gender by enduring biological characteristics (genitals) rather than by the transient physical appearance of clothing or hairstyles. Once children understand that they will remain the same sex as they mature, they often become enthusiastically involved in gender stereotyping. Often tied to gender awareness is an increase in interest in one's own appearance and "looking the part." Racial and cultural identity and individual interests also are reflected in movement activities and appearance.

Self-consciousness related to modesty starts to emerge during this period, and children may refuse to toilet or change clothing in front of others. Kindergarten and first-grade students are still apt to be intrigued with the immediate and concrete health concerns of injury and illness. The bathroom talk and bodily function jokes of preschoolers become less frequent, although they still are used occasionally to shock or insult others. All bodily functions do retain a certain fascination, especially since new situations and distractions can precipitate occasional toileting accidents in the early primary years. Vomiting and bleeding remain major social events for quite a long time. By the end of the primary years, children are taking an interest in their own bodies and the long-term impact of health practices. Nutrition, dental care, and immunizations are aspects of physical development that become important as children begin to participate in maintenance of their own well-being.

Gross Motor Development: Games and Sports

A primary school child is a study in contrasts between stability and motion. The child may change from one posture to another, slumping over the desk, getting up and down, lying on the stomach, standing with arms outstretched. Postures in kindergarten and first-grade children are often tense and asymmetrical, as if it is an effort to maintain the body in one position for long. By the end of third grade, children's postures generally have become more balanced, relaxed, and easily sustained.

Movement often seems involuntary and unconscious as primary school children swing their legs, tap their feet and their pencils, shake their heads, and flex their limbs. In the classroom and at home a child may alternatively "flop around" and seem immobilized. Children quite often violate adult expectations for furniture and its uses, hanging off chairs, sitting on sofa backs, and perching on tables and countertops. Movement is also used to release tension in ways that adults often find unappealing, such as grinding teeth, chewing clothing, or picking teeth and noses.

The kindergarten and primary grades are a time of transition in children's motor development. Even more important than growth in size is the important change in status from one of "little kids" to school-age children. Kindergartners are solidifying their capabilities as part of the *fundamental movement phase* (Gabbard, 1992). As explained in the previous chapter, fundamental or basic movements are general activities such as running, jumping, throwing, and catching, which form the basis for advanced, often sports-related skills. Between the ages of 5 and 8, children typically focus on refining the basic motor movements of locomotion, propulsion, and manipulation mastered during the preschool years.

In the primary years, teachers can expect to see the beginning of the *sport-related movement phase*. During this phase, the fundamental movements that were established during the previous phase are refined, combined, and applied to new situations. The sport-related movement phase is divided into two or three stages that cover the elementary years and all of adolescence. In the three-stage view, children enter the first stage between their sixth and seventh years and remain in this *general* or *transitional stage* until age 10 (Gallahue, 1982). Both large- and small-muscle development are involved.

Between the ages of 5 and 8 years, children in many cultures start using the fundamental movements acquired as preschoolers to play games with rules (Hughes, 1995). Younger children will still need assistance with the fundamental activities of throwing, catching, jumping, and kicking. Kindergartners and first graders usually know how to run and how to kick, for instance, but will need practice to do both at the same time. Rhythm activities and running games such as tag are favorites in the early primary grades, as children extend involvement in simple motor games and the use of outdoor equipment. The introduction of bats and balls, bows and arrows, jump ropes and roller skates facilitates the transition from the playground to games with rules and organized sports, once fundamental movement skills are mastered.

As children develop cognitively and socially, motor abilities are expressed in games with rules, team sports, and creative play activities. In many primary school games, the rules of play are as important as the movement components. Hopping is essential for hopscotch, but one needs to know when to hop on one foot and when to hop on two, when to turn around, and how to pick up the stone without being disqualified. Running is an automatic skill for most 5-year-olds but is used very differently in races than in ball games. Kicking is applied differently in soccer than in kickball. Striking, catching, and throwing are all essential for softball and even for its simpler version, T-ball, but the correct movements depend on the position being played by each child. Better balance is needed for gymnastics and bicycle riding, and walking is taken for granted in just about every activity of life.

Until this phase, gross motor development is fairly well assured as long as typically developing children are provided with a benign and supportive environment in which there are opportunities for exploration and experimentation. By first and second grade, however, practice and training begin to make a difference and may influence a child's later capability in sports; lack of opportunity may set the stage for a life of inactivity. In addition, as we saw in both vignettes at the beginning of this chapter, the influence and attitudes of peers begin to take on significant importance. An ability to keep up physically with the rest of the class can profoundly impact a child's social standing. Since a child's self-concept at this age is based largely on concrete aspects of performance, self-esteem is often reflective of success in physical activity.

Fine Motor Development: Manipulatives and Academics

Once children enter kindergarten, fine motor skills become a crucial foundation for success in schoolwork. From the time they learn to sit steadily and walk independently, youngsters have their hands available for more complex tasks than just maintaining balance and holding toys. By the time they reach kindergarten, most children have learned to eat with dexterity; copy some, or even all, letters; put together a puzzle of several pieces; control crayons and markers as they draw; and maybe even cut with scissors. Some children in kindergarten and first grade are still working to master use of a knife and fork, many prefer tearing paper to the frustration of trying to cut it, and most have yet to master writing neat letters of regular sizes.

Refined fine motor skills are also seen in a primary child's ability to grasp and manipulate academic supplies such as scissors, glue, and pencils. These activities often require intense concentration at first but become more automatic as the child practices and masters a variety of supplies. By the second grade, frustrations in manipulation activities have generally been worked out, and children can add such skills as building with small blocks and sticks, using household construction tools such as hammers and saws, shuffling cards, managing clothes and food packaging, using keys to lock and unlock doors, and folding paper along straight lines (Black & Puckett, 1996).

The ability to engage in coordinated fine motor activities is related to success in the gross motor activities described in the previous section. If children have trouble with more precise skills, it may be helpful for them to focus on the postures they use during writing and manipulative activities. It is common to observe primary school children at the start of a difficult lesson sitting erect and alert, then slumping after a few minutes, then holding their heads in their hands, and finally lying completely over their desks as they struggle to learn something new and difficult. As posture deteriorates, the accuracy of fine motor skill is likely to follow suit.

Of utmost importance for the young school-age child is the ability to write. During kindergarten and first grade, mistakes in writing letters that look alike (w and m; b and d; p and q) may reflect a lack of precision in fine motor aspects of writing rather than deficiencies in perception. This problem generally disappears by the time children have completed the third grade. For most youngsters, writing uppercase letters is the easiest to begin with, because they contain mostly straight lines. With instruction, most children learn to make lowercase letters with relative ease between their seventh and eighth birthdays, staying inside the lines if they are provided, and generally creating entire words and lines with letters of uniform size.

A six-year-old appears very grown up in comparison to the three toddlers who admire his size and abilities.

Perceptual Motor Development

The integration of visual, auditory, and tactile cues with related motor activity is crucial to the successful physical functioning of 5- to 8-year-olds, just as it is to younger children. For example, spatial and directional awareness is not only important to the learning of games but also to writing on the board and beginning map making, music activities that involve rhythm, and a host of other classroom experiences. Tactile abilities are important for cutting, tearing, ball handling, and artistic endeavors. And auditory data must be combined with motor capabilities when the teacher gives instructions for moving about the classroom or lining up to travel down the hall.

What may appear to be uncoordinated and random movement during the early primary grades is in fact an intricate interplay between movement and stable postures. As children grow from 5 to 8 years and learn new motor skills, the constant back and forth between action and inaction provides a foundation for the emergence of the sophisticated coordination, grace, and fluidity characteristic of the intermediate grades.

Variations in Physical and Motor Development

Physical disabilities such as cerebral palsy and muscular dystrophy, chronic illnesses, and sensory impairments can limit children's capacities for mastering more complex and precise movement skills in primary school. As peers rapidly become bigger, stronger, and more coordinated, the impact of physical disabilities becomes more apparent, and it can become more and more difficult for all children to play together. Once children enter primary school, much of their motor play occurs on the playground, with less close supervision and fewer adults available to facilitate inclusive activities.

As a group, primary school children cover more ground and engage in more structured types of play. Modified playground equipment that includes ramps, level surfaces, and supportive structures can go a long way toward providing equal access for all children. Unfortunately, outdoor play equipment is not often high on the list of budget priorities for many schools, leaving students with physical and sensory challenges especially at risk for not being able to participate safely in motor play.

Students who are eligible for special education and related services are more likely to have accommodations available in the classroom for academic pursuits such as writing. A variety of low- and high-technology devices are available for primary school students, including adaptive grips for pencils and pens, laptop computers for students who can type more easily than they can write, and specialized computer-access accessories. Physical and occupational therapists along with parents are excellent resources for solving problems related to inclusion in active play and adaptive equipment for playground and classroom use. Many 5- to 8-year-olds have good ideas for modifications or accommodations that can improve everyone's access to physical activities. A class discussion on equal participation indoors and outside allows input from all children without singling out specific students. In a safe and nonthreatening atmosphere, you might well hear about the concerns of younger, smaller, and shyer students, as well as those who have physical and sensory disabilities.

PRIMARY COGNITIVE DEVELOPMENT: PERCEPTION GIVES WAY TO INFERENCE

During the primary years, most children master several important cognitive skills that serve them throughout their lives. Their way of knowing the world becomes more adultlike. Five- to 8-year-olds use both short- and long-term memory to recall and make use of past life experiences. They become literate and are able to use reading and writing to learn and share new information. Changes in cognitive, language, and literacy development are inextricable from social and physical development in the primary years and are, therefore, central to the primary curriculum. In fact, it is impossible to make sense of the physical and social characteristics of primary-age children without a sound understanding of the way in which cognitive skills develop.

A profound intellectual change occurs within children between the ages of 5 and 9 years. Privileged are the teachers who witness the growth of their students with an understanding of what is happening, for it is during these years that children leave early childhood modes of thinking behind and replace them, bit by bit and step by step, with the more logical approaches of adulthood. In this section, we discuss what these changes are and how, to the best of current knowledge, they take place.

Making the Transition: The Piagetian Perspective

In the decades since Piaget posited his stage theory of cognitive development, theorists and researchers have devoted considerable effort to supporting or refuting, proving or disproving his positions. This is as it should be with any theory, and not surprisingly, the conclusions of these efforts are mixed, and opposing viewpoints survive to this day. Nevertheless, as we have suggested in previous chapters, Piaget's descriptions of the trends in cognitive development in children of this age remain powerful and useful for teachers as guidelines for curriculum development and teaching methods. We discuss Piaget's point of view and then address alternative theories of cognitive development during the primary years.

In Piaget's theory, the movement from preoperational thought to *concrete operations* is the defining characteristic of cognitive development in the K–3 child. For some youngsters, changes in thought processes begin taking place at age 5. For others, preoperational thought remains the standard for thinking until age 7 or beyond. Both time frames are typical, leaving kindergarten and primary teachers with the responsibility of providing a variety of educational activities designed to facilitate learning across a wide range of cognitive levels.

Concrete Operations

The defining difference between preoperational and concrete operational thought is a younger child's reliance on perceptions for understanding versus an older child's ability to think logically about immediate experiences. (It is during adolescence that many children are able to think beyond immediate experience and reason in abstractions, a stage Piaget termed *formal operations*.)

Younger primary children reason, analyze, and draw inferences but still tend to focus on the immediate physical qualities of objects and situations. Often a single physical attribute (size, shape, number, or length) will focus their attention. This aspect of concrete thinking can be seen in the early emphasis on what is "fair." Early in the primary years, children's concept of fair is tied to a single physical indicator. For example, children may choose cookies based on either size or how many there are. Soon they begin to evaluate whether two big ones might be equal to three smaller ones, having acquired the ability to analyze size and number at the same time.

Conservation

As an example, consider the Piagetian task in which two clay balls of identical size and shape are correctly described as equal by both preoperational and concrete operational children. Once one of the balls is flattened, however, the preoperational child perceives that the two no longer contain equal quantities of clay, because the flatter one appears to be larger than the other. The concrete operational child, on the other hand, reasons that although one piece of clay looks larger, it cannot logically have gotten bigger, because no clay was added to it. This same child might be able to arrive at the same conclusion by demonstrating *reversible thinking* and visualizing the flatter one in its previous round form. She has not yet, however, reached the stage of formal operations in which she can simply argue the problem logically without ever having direct experience with the clay balls.

Another example of how thought changes during these years might be demonstrated by asking a child to count the number of pennies in a stack. If the pennies are then spread out, the preoperational child will need to count them to believe that the number is still the same, whereas the concrete operational child uses reason (no pennies were added) to determine that they must still add up to the same number. Both the clay and the penny activities describe the child's developing ability to *conserve*;

that is, to understand that the mass of the clay and the number of pennies remains constant despite changes in appearance.

Conservation is related to math concepts, because knowledge of size, mass, and number are central to concepts such as more–less, counting, and math operations (adding, subtracting, multiplying, dividing). Children begin using number concepts by counting concrete items such as fingers or blocks. Recognizing numerals is the first step in using written number symbols. Children begin to operate on number concepts by adding or subtracting concrete sets of objects and then transferring the manipulations to numerals on paper.

Perspective Taking

Another defining difference between Piaget's preoperational and concrete operational stages relates to egocentrism. Whereas preoperational children see things primarily from their own perspectives, older children begin to understand that others have different views; they also try to figure out what another's perspective might be. Primary-age children begin to evaluate their own behavior based on how they think they appear to other people, especially teachers and peers.

Perspective taking has important social implications, which we discuss later, but it can also be applied quite literally to visual–spatial tasks. The classic Piagetian task involves a large board on which are constructed models of the Swiss Alps (Piaget & Inhelder, 1969). Younger children are unable to describe the view from the perspective of someone sitting opposite them at the table. Concrete operational children are able to take the other person's point of view and describe it. Until children are able to accomplish this task, interpreting or creating standard maps, participating in sports that require an awareness of different players' positions, or dancing in complex and cooperative patterns remain difficult motor skills to master.

Classification and Categorizing

Younger primary-age children focus attention on only one physical attribute of an object at a time, for example, color, or shape, or size. When asked to put the things together that go together, the child will select the most salient feature and sort accordingly. Given a variety of blocks of different shapes, sizes, and colors and asked to sort them, 5-year-olds will generally sort by shape, regardless of size and color; or they might separate the blocks by color, putting all shapes and sizes together in one group of a single color.

Older primary school students demonstrate the ability to form categories based on multiple attributes: "All the big, red ones go here." Eventually, they can form and name categories based on less obvious physical characteristics, an especially amusing pastime for those children who have assembled collections of buttons ("the little shiny ones with two holes"), bottle caps ("the orange ones with pictures"), and the like. The categories that children devise based on multiple characteristics are often revised and rearranged many times for the same collections of objects, giving children experience with number concepts (more–less; many–few) and counting as well as classification and categorization.

These two children can apply cognitive skills of perspective taking, conservation, categorization, and deductive reasoning to solving problems that arise during play.

By the end of the primary years, children begin to understand the concept of class inclusion and hierarchical organization. The boy with the button collection, for example, comes to understand that the total number of buttons always exceeds the number in any given category. And the girl with the collection of bottle caps learns through experience that the fewer categories she devises, the more caps there are in each group.

Transductive to Inductive Logic

At the beginning of the primary years, children think, reason, and try to solve problems by applying information from one situation to another based on perceptual rather than logical similarities. They reason from one specific instance to another, something Piaget called *transductive reasoning*, illustrated in Vignette 5.3.

Vignette 5.3: *Staying Dry at the Beach*

A 5-year-old of our acquaintance often wore a raincoat to keep dry during the rainy Northwest winters. From his lifelong experience with dressing for the rain, he reasoned that "putting clothing on over other clothing keeps you dry." During a trip to the ocean, Jerrel followed this logic and put on two pairs of pants to wade out into the water up to his waist. When it was pointed out to him that he was getting his pants soaking wet, his response was, "Yeah, but I have another pair underneath," quickly followed by, "Oh. But that doesn't work, does it?" (Obviously not, since both pairs of pants were drenched.) Jerrel learned an important lesson, though, and showed his new knowledge the next day when he wanted to keep his feet dry at the tide pools. He looked back and forth between his feet and the water and decided he needed boots to keep his socks dry, knowing without trying that his shoes would not serve the purpose. He also knew that if he was just wading, he only needed to worry about keeping his feet dry. Jerrel had initially focused his attention on one important similarity of rain to the ocean (wet), without being able to think ahead of time about the many differences between walking in rain and wading in the ocean.

Primary school children learn to devise general rules from their own activities. Between the ages of 5 and 8 years, children begin increasingly to use *inductive reasoning*, figuring out general rules and drawing global conclusions based on similarities across their own specific experiences. As children have more and more experiences to draw from, and as they become able to reflect on their own actions, they begin to mentally organize and associate events. An older child would be able to simultaneously consider the nature of the water (rain or ocean), its form in relation to his body (droplets falling or waist-high immersion); the type of clothing available (pants, boots, raincoat); and induce a more effective principle based on numerous experiences with water in different forms.

As children exit the primary years, their strategies for thinking and learning usually have become less physical, more logical and flexible. Abstract concepts can be examined and manipulated with the ease that concrete objects once were. As children become proficient at creating, sorting, and using categories, memories are better organized and more efficiently retrieved. Sophisticated skills in concept use, memory, logic, and sequencing may appear to be entirely different from earlier concrete thinking and learning. Actually, abstract thinking and learning skills develop directly, if gradually, from the concrete operations already described.

Current research supports Piaget's observation that the use of *deductive reasoning* is elusive, at best, for most primary school children (Bee, 1997). Deductive reasoning involves working from a general principle to a specific instance, for example, applying moral teachings to one's own behavior, and requires children to imagine situations they have never yet encountered. Piaget believed that deductive reasoning begins to emerge at about 11 or 12 years of age, as an aspect of formal operations: applying logic or abstract problem-solving strategies to generate and test hypotheses without the need for concrete experiences as a starting point.

Alternate Views of Cognitive Development

Criticisms of Piaget's theory include the fact that he generalized universal stages based largely on observations of his own children. Scholars tend to agree with the general sequences and trends of cognitive development Piaget described but discard the notion of coherent, invariant stages across divergent types of skills (Tomlinson-Keasey, Eisert, Kahle, Hardy-Brown, & Keasey, 1978; Bee, 1997). Some classic research studies also show that the contexts, materials, and questions used in Piaget's tests led to results that underestimated children's abilities. Given relevant situations and familiar materials, young children were able to successfully perform Piagetian tasks in conservation (Gelman, 1972; Price-Williams, Gordon, & Rameriz, 1969), understanding of cause and effect (Bullock & Gelman, 1979); perspective taking (Borke, 1975); and classification (Gelman & Markam, 1986). The results of many similar studies show that preschool and early primary children may demonstrate more advanced cognitive abilities if Piaget's tasks are simplified and familiar but still not be able to explain their responses, an important distinction.

A major criticism of Piaget's theory of preoperational thought is that he disregarded the effect of experience on cognitive development. Many studies make it clear that experience promotes better recall, faster acquisition of information, more efficient and complex organization, and more efficient performance in the specific area of expertise (Chi, Hutchinson, & Robin, 1989; Flavell, 1982).

Despite the many studies that have refined aspects of Piaget's theory, most research results take issue with the pace rather than the sequence with which early cognitive skills are mastered (Trawick-Smith, 2000). The authors of this book find the basic tenets of Piaget's theory to provide the most complete and cohesive single framework for very early cognitive development. There are, however, a number of theorists who have addressed the nature and development of intelligence, and many of these perspectives are especially relevant for an understanding of 5- to 8-year-olds.

Vygotsky's View

Piaget's Swiss upbringing ensured that his theoretical positions would reflect his experience as a member of a Western democratic, individual-oriented society, an important circumstance as we introduce the related views of Lev Vygotsky, a Russian contemporary of Piaget. Vygotsky completed his university education in Moscow in 1917, the same year that the revolution against Russia's tsarist government found success. As a psychologist eager to embrace the widespread hope of a more just society through communist ideals, he posited a theory of development that was less oriented toward the individual than Piaget's and more devoted to the importance of the social group.

Vygotsky's theory of cognitive development implied a very specific and significant role for teachers. Whereas Piaget implied that children must attain a prerequisite level of cognitive development before a teacher's input can make sense, Vygotsky believed that teachers can actively lead children into more advanced thinking. Vygotsky's concept of the *zone of proximal development (ZPD)* was based on the idea that education should take into account children's potential for understanding new ideas rather than emphasize what they already understand. If teachers can identify the next-most-difficult cognitive skills (the proximal zone), they can create experiences that will support learning.

In the mid-1970s, long after Vygotsky's death and before his ideas were widely disseminated in this country, the American Jerome Bruner became known for his educational application of the ZPD (Wood, Bruner, & Ross, 1976). In a process he and his associates referred to as *scaffolding,* "adults provide support to a child who is learning to master a task or problem. When adults scaffold a task or problem, they perform or direct those elements of the task that are beyond the child's ability. . . . Scaffolding can take the form of verbal or physical assistance" (Meece, 1997, p. 159).

This application of Vygotsky's theory is a very practical one for teachers in K–3 classrooms. As an example, three second-grade boys were beginning to discover the attractions of using Cuisenaire rods (small, painted wooden rods of varying lengths) to build even-taller towers. They began playing a game with the objective of building as tall a tower as possible before it toppled over. The teacher observed that some learning in physics was beginning to take place and decided to intervene. First, she simply helped the boys steady the underlying table, a problem they had somehow overlooked. The next day, she provided two or three examples of wider and more complex base structures that would enable the towers to remain stable at greater heights. Soon, the boys were creating new and more efficient structures on their own, and the thrill of achieving new heights became secondary to the interest in more complex designs.

Deciding that the children were ready to move to the next cognitive zone, the teacher stepped in again, demonstrating ways to build bridges. The boys floundered at this for a bit and soon lost interest. Realizing that she had tried to move them beyond their proximal zone, the teacher stopped making suggestions for the time being, letting the boys solidify their earlier learning by repeating and expanding their tower models.

Piaget and Vygotsky also had different explanations concerning the function of *private speech*, or the inclination of young children to talk to themselves. Although this practice begins to disappear in the primary grades, research has demonstrated its importance in learning throughout elementary school (Berk & Garvin, 1984). Piaget's explanation for private speech was that preschool children are egocentric, reflecting a limited sense of audience. As youngsters enter the stage of concrete operations and begin to understand that others have different thoughts and preferences, their earlier self-focused speech is replaced by more social communication skills.

Vygotsky's explanation, on the other hand, was that younger children use private speech to regulate their thinking and behavior. In other words, they aren't engaging in inadequate communication; they aren't even trying to communicate. Rather, they are talking themselves through problem-solving situations. Today, many researchers and educators are more inclined to accept Vygotsky's explanation and prescribe classroom activities that permit children to talk themselves through learning experiences.

Despite differences in their theories, Piaget and Vygotsky bring some similar teaching ideas to the K–3 teacher. Both men, for example, believed the role of peers in fostering cognitive development was essential. According to Piaget, interaction with other children leads to cognitive dissonance, thus forcing some degree of *accommodation* in thought for less advanced children. In his view, such mental activity was a sign of individual construction of knowledge on the part of each child. To Vygotsky, interaction with peers—other members of the child's *collective*—ensured collaboration and joint problem solving. This leads to each child's internalizing cooperative achievements for independent problem solving later. In addition, more experienced peers might function similarly to an adult teacher, perhaps scaffolding more difficult skills and leading less experienced children into their ZPDs.

One first-grade teacher of our acquaintance regularly devotes a rather large part of each day to "choice time." Children may work alone, in pairs, or in larger groups, choosing their activities from a large selection of math and language materials at varying levels of challenge. On some days, the teacher assigns children to small working groups and lets them choose among two or three activities. On these occasions, the students are divided into *heterogeneous* groups to promote the interchange of ideas. This teacher reports that there is always at least one child in each group who easily achieves mastery of the materials and not only teaches the others but may well explore further challenges on his or her own. Conversely, the less advanced children begin to make progress at their own levels and might, in the future, end up teaching others from other groups. Reflecting on what she values as a successful teaching method, the teacher cannot say if she agrees with Piaget's or Vygotsky's theory to explain what is happening, and she is not sure that deciding is essential. She does believe, however, that without the influence of their writings on Western education, she probably would not understand the benefits of her teaching methods and would be more directive and authoritarian.

The Information-Processing Model

The information-processing model of cognitive development uses the computer as a model to describe the workings of the mind and to explain changes in cognition as children get older. The "hardware" of the system includes the biological components of the central nervous system: the brain with its multitude of cells and interconnections in the central nervous system. The "software" component refers to specific strategies (programs) applied to organize and process information entered into the system. Perceptual and motor experiences are seen as analogous to the "data" input into a computer system, and thought processes are viewed as analogous to the coding, categorization, storage (short and long term), and retrieval functions of a computer. Children's behavioral and verbal responses are the resultant output and the indicators of changes in thought processing over time (Case, 1987).

Like Piaget's theory, the information-processing model emphasizes the general processes that form the foundation for thinking and learning as children develop. Piaget's theory indicates that children use qualitatively different cognitive strategies at different ages and highlights contrasting aspects of cognition in infants, children, and adults. Proponents of the information-processing model emphasize the similarities in the thinking of adults and children and explain cognitive development largely as a function of improved speed and efficiency as youngsters acquire information and gain experience using processing strategies (Case, 1987; Kail, 1991).

Many studies of information processing have investigated the development of memory strategies. Given a list of words to remember, children under the age of 5 tend to reproduce only two or three items and do not usually engage in strategies such as rehearsal–repetition to help them remember. If instructed to repeat the list to themselves or to group items into categories or clusters, and reminded to do so, the performance of preschoolers on memory tasks improves (Flavell, 1993; Kail, 1991). Rehearsal and clustering emerge during the primary years as routine strategies when children are trying to remember new information. Experience with using memory strategies seems to help children organize, store, and retrieve more information, which in turn leads to more efficient mental processing and improved short-term memory (Case, 1985).

The information-processing model also offers an alternative perspective on the improved performance of youngsters in solving problems as they get older. Siegler (1983) emphasized attention as a mechanism for organizing input into the system, explaining that younger children focus on concrete, immediate aspects of the environment, a perspective reminiscent of Piaget. As children practice using specific strategies, they become speedier at mental processing, acquire a larger store of prior knowledge from which to operate, and learn to use more than one operation at once (Case, 1985; Beddard & Chi, 1992). For example, a toddler who wants to reach a toy on a shelf might only be able to apply a scanning strategy to look methodically around the immediate environment for a solution. A preschooler faced with the same problem can combine scanning with retrieval of a short-term memory of a similar problem and solution and quickly go to the other room in search of a particular stool. A primary school student probably can scan the room and evaluate the relative height advantages of books, chairs, and containers, efficiently piecing together a solution.

An especially interesting aspect of the information-processing model is investigation of *metacognition*, or the knowledge children have about the strategies they use for mental processes such as memory, problem solving, and decision making. Generalized strategies for planning and organizing information are labeled *executive processes* and seem to first emerge in children between the ages of 4 and 5 years old (Schneider & Pressley, 1989). Executive processes allow young children to describe, monitor, and evaluate their own tactics for learning, remembering, retrieving, and applying information.

One area of common ground between Piaget and information-processing theorists is the notion that children learn new skills in sequences, with each new behavior arising from an earlier form and giving rise to even more complex abilities (Fischer, 1980; Flavell, 1993). Some theorists also acknowledge that the executive processes emerging during the preschool and primary years constitute actual modifications in the way young children think and reason rather than progressive simple refinements of existing processes (Siegler, 1981; Case, 1992), a stance that also reminds us of Piaget.

Howard Gardner's Multiple Intelligences

For a way of looking at cognition that varies considerably from Piaget, Vygotsky, and information processing, we turn to the work of Howard Gardner. A Harvard psychologist well versed in Piagetian theory and its application to education, Gardner eventually concluded that there was more to intelligence than what can be defined by the usual tests of verbal and quantitative capacities, the two elements of development most valued by Western society. Other fields of achievement routinely have been designated *talents* or *skills*, relegated to a lesser form of accomplishment than academ-

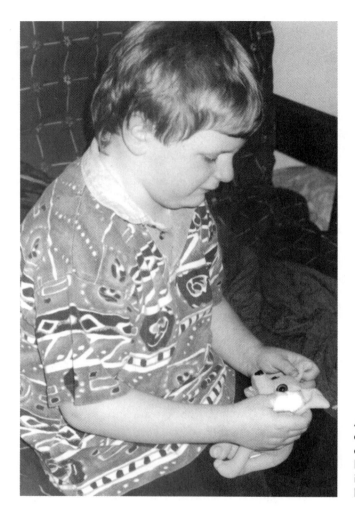

A number of different theories explain the increased capacity of primary-aged children for logical thinking, problem-solving, and sophisticated use of language.

ics in Western cultures. Adopting a larger worldview, Gardner explored the possibility that intelligence was broader than has been typically measured and eventually posited a list of seven "intelligences," with the understanding that others might be added later if they had been overlooked; in recent years he has made tentative steps in expanding the list. Following is a brief description of each of the *multiple intelligences* with an argument for its inclusion in the list (Gardner, 1993).

Linguistic intelligence: As Gardner (1993) points out, linguistic intelligence "is consistent with the stance of traditional psychology." The "gift of language" he said, "is universal, and its development in children is strikingly constant across cultures" (p. 21).

Logical-mathematical intelligence: This second type of intelligence, along with language, forms the basis for IQ tests. Gardner believes it has two important characteristics: scientific problem solving and a lack of need for any linguistic input.

Spatial intelligence: Spatial intelligence is needed in activities from navigation to creating visual art to playing chess, and a particular strength of many children with autism.

Bodily-kinesthetic intelligence: In Western cultures, kinesthetic giftedness is generally regarded as a talent, one that is often accompanied by a lack of "real" intelligence. Gardner argues that body movements are specially adapted to the human species and undergo a clearly delineated developmental schedule in children. Movement is refined and extended through the use of tools and is universal across cultures, providing sufficient rationale for Gardner to consider bodily-kinesthetic capacity as intelligence.

Musical intelligence: Music is another skill that is usually regarded as a talent. However, Gardner points to the finding that "certain parts of the brain play important roles in perception and production of music. These areas are characteristically located in the right hemisphere" (p. 17). In addition, "musical notation provides an accessible and lucid symbol system" similar to those for reading and mathematics (p. 18).

Interpersonal intelligence: This intelligence, says Gardner, "builds on a core capacity to notice distinctions among others; in particular, contrasts in their moods, temperaments, motivations, and intentions" (p. 23). To counter any argument that interpersonal communications must rely on linguistic intelligence, Gardner notes aspects of nonverbal communication and the widely famous interpersonal giftedness of Helen Keller, who had been blinded and deafened as the result of childhood disease.

Intrapersonal intelligence: The person with high intrapersonal intelligence Gardner said, "has a viable and effective model of himself or herself." This is, of all the intelligences, "the most private" (p. 25). Because it is so internal, we must rely on expressions through language, music, or perhaps some other art form to see it demonstrated. Just as interpersonal intelligence helps people understand and work with others, so intrapersonal intelligence makes it possible to understand and work effectively as an individual.

Elevating capabilities seen in Western culture as talents to the status of intelligence provides teachers with a wider appreciation of child development across a range of abilities and promotes greater respect for students' varied ways of expressing their knowledge and skills. No longer is praise reserved only for the early reader and the math whiz. Children gifted in conflict resolution (interpersonal intelligence), the writing of reflective journals (intrapersonal intelligence), dance and gymnastics (bodily-kinesthetic intelligence), singing consistently on key and with feeling (musical intelligence), and drawing a recognizable portrait (spatial intelligence) are as valued as those who may perform more successfully on standard tests of intelligence. Other intelligences are being suggested, for example, *naturalist*, so it will be interesting to see future directions and development in Gardner's work. It is also worth mentioning that many authors have questioned the entire notion of intelligence as an unalterable characteristic.

Perhaps you have noted that some of the intelligences do not strictly fit into this chapter section according to our usual definitions of cognition. Bodily-kinesthetic intelligence could easily be described in the previous discussion of motor development. Interpersonal and intrapersonal intelligence are a part of the upcoming section on social, moral, and emotional development. It is, in part, Gardner's thinking "outside the box" that makes some of his critics a bit uncomfortable with his theory.

Keep in mind that in the introduction to this book we mentioned the arbitrary nature of partitioning children's behaviors into separate domains. It no doubt is obvious by this point that at each age there is great overlap among the various domains. In a very simplified sense, the motor domain provides the means, the cognitive domain provides the meanings, and the social domain provides the motivations for all of children's behavior. Perhaps Gardner's attempt to expand the definition of intelligence is one perspective on acknowledging the overlapping aspects of development. In the next section, we not only look at affective development but also explore connections to cognitive development.

Achievements in Language and Literacy

Adults are able to most reliably study the fascinating thinking processes of young children once youngsters have the language skills to describe verbally what they think and experience. In the previous section, we noted the differences in theory between Piaget and Vygotsky regarding the functions of private speech. Of course, there is much more to language development than this, and both men observed and reported on other aspects as well. In recent decades, increased understanding of the brain's workings and continuing research have enriched our knowledge of language development.

The growing competence of kindergarten and primary children in the area of communication is not so dramatic as during the infant, toddler, and preschool years, but there is still much of importance to observe. Most children enter school already able to manipulate language as an important symbol system. The impressive vocabularies of kindergarten children are refined as conceptual categories are expanded. Perspective-taking is also important for language learning, because a child must master the reciprocal roles of sending and receiving written and oral messages as speaker–listener, author–reader. The complex mysteries of social interactions, conflict resolution, and problem solving also become clearer when viewed from a number of perspectives.

It is, after all, growing competence with language that makes it possible for primary school children to learn to read and to write. It is worth noting here that oral language is a human capability that generally develops as long as there are models from whom to learn, whereas reading and writing almost always require at least a minimum of instruction. It should also be noted that the acquisition of reading and writing skills is the centerpiece of the U.S. K–3 curriculum. Thus, the importance of understanding how children's language develops at this age is underscored.

Language

Language develops during the primary years from a means to communicate what is happening in the immediate context to more complex and abstract use of symbols for many purposes. Primary-age children begin to understand metaphors and the multiple meanings of words that make for puns. Soon they are producing their own jokes and plays on words, recognizable in form even if the punch line doesn't follow the set up. The subtle rules that govern use of formal language are also increasingly understood, with tangential shifts in topics becoming less abrupt across the primary years. Most children discover that certain words and topics work best at home, others at school, and still others with peers.

A review of research by Black and Puckett (1996) reports a list of language competencies for this age group:

Thought and language

- Metalinguistic awareness, or the ability to think about the structures of language, increases during these years so that language can be discussed as a symbol system. Primary children, for example, can begin to define parts of speech and their functions. At least one study has shown metalinguistic awareness in first graders to be a good predictor of reading comprehension in third graders.

- First graders now understand metaphors and, eventually, can create them. If their teacher says, "I think a tornado has struck this classroom," children understand that she simply means it is messy, not that a tornado actually caused the devastation.

- Primary children understand puns and jokes in the more adult sense, not just for the funny sounds of the words or the simple enjoyment of participating in a joke as in earlier years.

- Most first graders begin to understand the meaning and purpose of sarcasm; third graders can detect it in a variety of situations.

Syntax

- Understanding the passive voice remains difficult throughout the primary grades ("The test was given by the teacher" rather than "The teacher gave the test").

- By the end of third grade, children generally use plurals, possessives, and past tense correctly.

- Correct use and understanding of the infinitive form of verbs develops in the primary grades (the "to" form).

Vocabulary

- By age 6, children have a vocabulary of about 14,000 words.

- Increased cognitive development, wider experiences, and formal education all contribute to expanding vocabulary.

- In the primary grades, children move toward using their vocabularies in more conventional, less fanciful ways. *Overextension*, the practice of using one word in related but inaccurate situations, all but disappears.

Literacy

The development of literacy skills begins long before children start learning to read and write. The first steps toward literacy are grounded in early interactions between infants and their primary caregivers: playing turn-taking games, talking and listening, singing, storytelling, and looking at picture books. During the preschool years, children learn a vast number of concepts, including those associated with formal literacy. If all goes well, young children have a solid foundation of social interactions, language experience, and print concepts by the time they enter kindergarten.

Reading and writing do not develop in a vacuum; there are critical cognitive precursors that can be considered steps along the way to formal literacy. The varied experiences of infants lead to cognitive associations and representations during the toddler years, which in turn support symbolic language use during the preschool years. With each of these steps building a solid foundation, children are ready to begin learning to read and write, as illustrated in Figure 5.1.

Children acquire many concepts about printed forms of language and learn to read and write in the primary grades. Using print symbols is yet another step in the continual process of applying and decontextualizing a formal system of language. Most young children understand reading and writing as yet another way to communicate. At first, children find it easier to represent their own thoughts and experiences in print, especially if they have had experience with drawing.

During the time it takes to develop ease with the printed word, children often fall back on concrete contextual cues and strategies. Bigger print and pictures make reading easier, because the word symbols are paired with less abstract cues. In the same

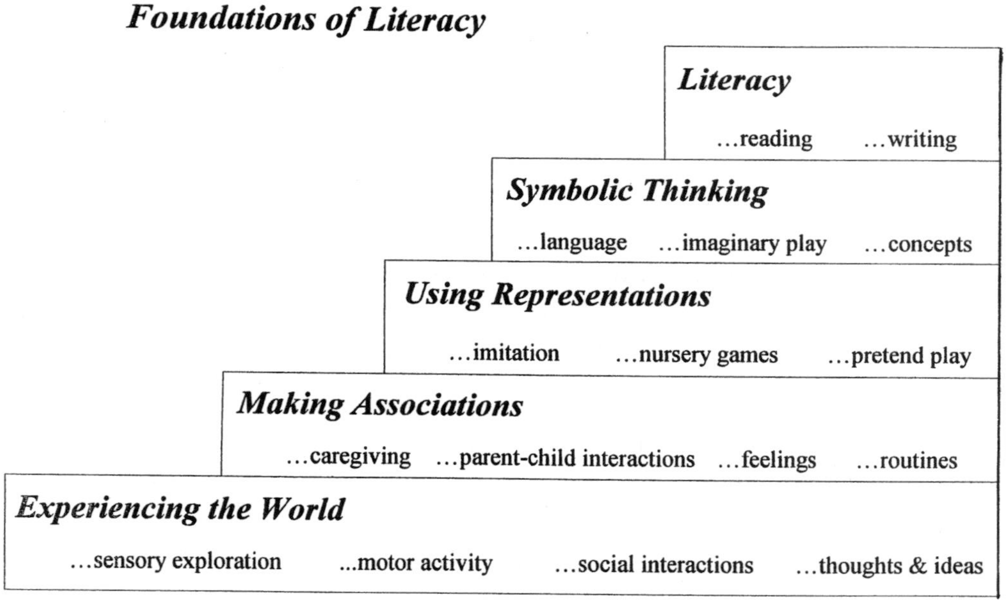

Foundations of Literacy

Literacy
...reading   ...writing

Symbolic Thinking
...language   ...imaginary play   ...concepts

Using Representations
...imitation   ...nursery games   ...pretend play

Making Associations
...caregiving   ...parent-child interactions   ...feelings   ...routines

Experiencing the World
...sensory exploration   ...motor activity   ...social interactions   ...thoughts & ideas

FIG. 5.1.

way, spelling is often less difficult when a computer takes away the physical requirements of forming letter symbols, and oral spelling may be easier for the same reason.
According to Black and Puckett (1996):

- Most children learn to read more easily if the text has meaning to them (as
  opposed to text consisting of broken-up phonetic sounds or lists of single
  words).

- Because short-term memory is still developing and *decentering* is often still difficult, beginning readers may have problems remembering phonics rules, reading without error, sounding out words, and thinking about the meaning of text
  all at one time.

One of the books in this series, discusses in more detail the development of literacy as part of the curriculum. Here, we note the four significant differences between
younger children and those in the primary grades, as observed by Marie Clay.

(a) an older child plans more;

(b) an older child's learning is more often mediated by words;

(c) an older child can deal with multiple features at one time and consider relationships among
features; and

(d) an older child is more able to coordinate thoughts and experiences from multiple settings.

These emerging mental abilities all help children cope with the complexities of reading and writing. (Meece, 1997, p. 279)

Variations in Primary Cognitive Development

In previous chapters, we focused on variations in cognitive development that put children at risk for learning, because these are the most obvious and identifiable differences
among younger children. Programs to support students who need accelerated learning
experiences are seldom available before children are 7 or 8 years old. Also, the emphasis in U.S. public education today is in provision of extra services for children with a
wide array of disabilities rather than in encouraging the development of students with
extraordinary abilities. This may explain why not much effort has been made to define
giftedness in the earliest years or to observe its development from infancy onward.

In addition, the definition of giftedness has made some advances in recent decades,
whereas definitions of disability categories for special education have been refined but
remain fairly consistent over time. Psychologists such as Gardner have challenged the
traditional view of academics as the hallmark of intelligence, choosing to consider a
wider array of capabilities than just mathematics and language skills. Since studies on
an expanded definition of intelligence are still in their infancy, valid and reliable measures are difficult to come by, which presently leaves child development researchers the
difficult choice of waiting for appropriate tests to be developed or resorting to measures of intelligence as the construct traditionally has been defined.

Growing Up Gifted

One group of researchers (Gottfried, Gottfried, Bathurst, & Guerin, 1994) chose the latter route in their longitudinal study of 1- through 8-year-olds. In an attempt to study the emergence of giftedness, the authors selected 150 healthy babies and administered the Bayley Scales of Infant Development at 6-month intervals until the age of 2 years. As the youngsters grew older, tests of intelligence, language, general achievement, and other aspects of development were administered. Nearly 40 tests per child were administered, including inventories of temperament and social functioning, as measures against which intelligence could be analyzed.

The researchers' approach was to test all 150 children in the various categories until age 8, at which point they identified those who scored 130 or higher on tests of intelligence quotients (IQ). They then analyzed the previous 8 years of test scores and observations to better comprehend the developmental course of giftedness. Some of their findings include:

- By age 1, infants later identified as gifted were significantly more skilled in receptive language (comprehension of the spoken word).
- By 18 months, toddlers later identified as gifted were significantly more skilled in expressive language (verbal expression).
- By age 2, youngsters later identified as gifted demonstrated significantly higher scores in general cognition as well as in the quantitative, perceptual, and (as noted) verbal domains.
- As early as infancy and through the primary grades, gifted children demonstrated more goal and object orientation, cooperativeness, positive emotions, ability to work through difficult challenges, and longer attention spans.
- Between the ages of 5 and 8, gifted children were significantly more successful in academic performance and demonstrated more intrinsic motivation for learning, more curiosity and persistence, and less academic anxiety.
- Throughout the primary grades, gifted and nongifted children scored about the same in ratings related to happiness.

In this study, the children identified as gifted showed no social or behavioral problems, although the authors noted that they did not encounter any highly gifted (IQ 160 or higher) youngsters. They do, however, cite other studies that suggest truly exceptional children have physical disadvantages and impaired self-confidence (due to entering school when they are younger and smaller) as well as a tendency toward intolerance of the lesser performance of peers and feelings of social isolation.

A Fuller View of Giftedness

Gottfried and colleagues made an important contribution to knowledge about the developmental course of exceptionally able children, but it was limited in scope if we wish to consider capabilities beyond those measured by traditional IQ and achievement tests. Ellen Winner (1996) identified three characteristics exhibited by gifted children, then made the case for expanding our definition of giftedness. The three characteristics include:

- *Precocity*: Taking steps toward mastery at earlier ages than peers.
- *Marching to their own drummers*: Needing and desiring minimal help and devising novel ways to solve problems.
- *Rage to master*: Motivated to learn to the point of intensity and even obsession.

Winner argued that these three characteristics can be applied not only to children who do well academically but also to those who are artistically or athletically gifted. Some children commonly seen as being talented (as in the arts, social skills, and athletics) rather than gifted (as in language, math, and academics) may well not demonstrate the high scores on tests of achievement and IQ but would score well on tests of creativity.

In one respect, Winner and the Gottfried team agree: The giftedness demonstrated by some children as they enter elementary school is the result of both genetic advantage and a supportive environment. The Gottfried study found that:

- Gifted children receive more enriched environments . . . years before children are identified as gifted.

- Gifted children come from families with higher socioeconomic status and have parents who are more highly educated.

- [Parents of gifted children] were more involved, more responsive, and more nurturing in their children's academic endeavors.

- Families of gifted children endorse more culturally and intellectually stimulating activities by the time the children are 3 years old, and these differences remain through the early elementary years. (Gottfried et al., 1994, 166–168).

Such findings reinforce the ecological theories of development presented in chapter 1, indicating that although exceptional ability is, in part, a biological endowment, the environments in which a child grows can support or hinder expression of their gifts.

Students With Disabilities

Once children enter school, cognitive development becomes almost synonymous with language, literacy, and other academic subjects. Children diagnosed with cognitive delays as preschoolers are often reevaluated for special services and diagnosed with *mental retardation* in first grade. There is very little technical difference between the terms *cognitive delay* and *mental retardation*: *Cognitive* and *mental* both refer to intellectual function, and *retardation* and *delay* both mean slower than some standard. *Mental retardation* definitely has a harsher sound, is associated with more negative stereotypes, and can be more difficult for parents to hear in reference to their children.

Children with mental retardation will, by definition, learn more slowly than their typically developing peers. During the primary school years, curriculum content becomes increasingly abstract, and children are expected to learn by watching and listening as well as by participating in hands-on activities. Children who qualify for special education services have individualized goals and objectives in relevant academic, behavioral, and life skills.

Primary school children may also have difficulties learning in particular subject areas despite an overall level of cognitive development that is typical. Many of these children qualify for special education as having a *learning disability*. Their goals and objectives address the academic area(s) in which they have problems learning. The most frequent area in which children qualify for special education is reading.

Specialized instruction for primary school children may be provided in separate classrooms, in regular education classrooms, or in a combination of these. Students with learning disabilities often go to a resource room for individual or small-group instruction, during the time the rest of the class has reading groups, for example. Students with more severe cognitive delays (mental retardation) may attend *life skills instruction* where modified academic content is taught in a curriculum that emphasizes functional communication, self-care, and social and community access skills.

Specialized instruction in the primary grades is often more structured and more teacher directed than instruction typically is in many regular education classrooms. Students with learning disabilities and mental retardation often miss important points or become confused by activity- and project-based approaches that involve drawing conclusions and testing hypotheses. Special education teachers often present basic academic skills in a very explicit fashion, breaking content down into small steps and monitoring learning very closely. In Vygotsky's terminology, the zone of proximal development is narrower for some students than for others, and the scaffolding required in order for learning to occur needs careful, ongoing attention.

PRIMARY SCHOOL SOCIAL-AFFECTIVE AND MORAL DEVELOPMENT: INTRAPERSONAL AND INTERPERSONAL GROWTH

The primary years are witness to many dramatic changes in children's interactions and understanding of the social world. Youngsters enter school still dependent on their families to organize social experiences and may at first transfer expectations for affection and direction to their teachers. The school environment soon encourages an emphasis on peer play partners and a new set of standards for social behavior. During the kindergarten and primary years, children begin to leave behind their egocentric ways of looking at the social world and focus on the newly discovered importance of long-lasting friendships with their peers.

At kindergarten entry, children tend to be boisterous and active and to wear their emotions on their sleeves. Younger primary children are often talkative, humorous, and even boastful about their own abilities, relying on roles, rules, and bravado as much as on skill to frame social relationships. One of the major developmental tasks for primary-age children is to develop a positive sense of who they are and a pride in how they interact with many other people in a variety of roles.

Affective Development

Affect, or emotion, is the state of consciousness having to do with feelings, and feelings can be pleasant or unpleasant, arrived at irrationally or cognitively. Emotion has to do with how we feel about ourselves as well as about other people, situations, experiences, and places. Kindergarten children are aware of emotions, although when asked to define them, they frequently can only think of two: happiness and sadness. Children in the primary grades, particularly with some teacher guidance, are able to express their feelings with more sophistication.

The subtle complexities of the social world begin to emerge as children's evaluation of social and emotional roles changes from a dichotomous (good or bad; sad or happy) to a more finely graded understanding. For a preschooler, it was enough to be a "good child"; now it becomes necessary to see and evaluate oneself in a variety of roles: student, family member, athlete, friend, helper.

During the primary years, many children seem to become more reflective and contemplative, listening to and analyzing social interactions among peers, older children, and adults. They develop sensitivity to the impact, positive and negative, that their own behavior has on other people. Awareness of feelings is closely related to the child's developing sense of self.

Self-Concept and Self-Esteem

We all can provide both physical and psychological descriptions of ourselves that may or may not be the way others see us. These descriptions are our definitions of ourselves, or our self-concepts. Self-esteem, on the other hand, has to do with the value we place on our self-concept, and this can be positive or negative or, more likely, a mixture of the two. Primary-age children know a lot about themselves; self-esteem develops as they evaluate how they feel about themselves. In kindergarten and particularly in the primary grades, self-concept and self-esteem are intimately related to children's views of their competence in new academic and social settings. The ability to interact well with newly important peers and perceived success in beginning efforts at sports are also important contributors to their emerging sense of self.

As children exit kindergarten and enter first grade, their self-concept becomes more stable. This, in part, is due to the acquisition of the concept of gender, racial, and cultural group permanence (Meece, 1997). Each child's sense of self grows from shared pursuits. Everything from appearance to choice of play partners, materials, and role models can reflect group identification in the primary years. It is a critical time for the development of self-concept, since external forces and role models strongly influence how positively children come to value their own racial, gender, cultural, age, and interest groups.

As they find their own places in the world, primary-age children can develop strong biases and stereotypes or a true appreciation of diversity and individual differences. As children ages 5 to 8 years achieve stable self-concepts, their experiences in and out of school affect their sense of self-esteem. One explanation of the development of self-esteem is provided in the theory of Abraham Maslow.

Maslow's Hierarchy of Human Needs

For humans to achieve self-actualization, or the full development of their abilities and ambitions, a set of needs must be met along the way, according to Maslow (1968). As we see in Fig. 5.2, the most basic need that must be met is that of food and water, and as we know, some children come to school lacking even these. In Maslow's model, reaching the upper levels is dependent on having met the needs of all lower ones. Thus, as can be seen, children who lack proper physical nourishment are at particular risk for success in all aspects of life.

Almost as important as food and drink is the feeling of safety that children have from knowing that food is available, that there are rules to follow and to protect them, that they can learn without fear and anxiety, and that the environment is a stable one. The more chaotic their lives are elsewhere, the more children need dependable adults and predictable routines in school. The third level is reached when children feel accepted and loved in school and at home. They know they have a safe affiliation within which to work out their growing sense of self.

When these first three levels are attainable, children are able to focus on issues of esteem. When youngsters feel wanted, valued, and self-confident, the need for self-esteem can be met. In Maslow's model, self-esteem is achieved from real accomplishment, not from simply talking about feeling good about oneself or from hearing hollow or meaningless praise—an important point for teachers to consider as they reinforce children's good behavior and academic efforts.

At the top of the hierarchy is the need for self-actualization. When the first four levels of needs have been met, humans are able to focus on their long-term ambitions, development of talents, and pursuit of interests related or unrelated to careers. Some

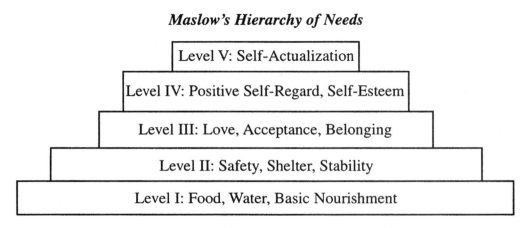

Maslow's Hierarchy of Needs

Level V: Self-Actualization

Level IV: Positive Self-Regard, Self-Esteem

Level III: Love, Acceptance, Belonging

Level II: Safety, Shelter, Stability

Level I: Food, Water, Basic Nourishment

FIG. 5.2.

children in the primary grades may already be laying the groundwork for the fulfillment of this top level. Probably most will achieve the previous level, given a positive and supportive environment and healthy personal development. For some children, school is the most organized and supportive environment they experience, so social-emotional development of primary school students is an important knowledge base for teachers.

Industry and the Development of Self-Esteem

Most books describe the primary-age child as industrious. This characteristic is seen clearly in the child's growing interest in assembling little objects into complex creations, using real tools correctly, playing cards, and continuously expanding and reorganizing collections of small treasures. The importance of completed products is consistent with the young child's growing ability to plan, identify standards of performance, and use tools.

The emphasis of younger children on activity for its own sake becomes focused on projects of a real nature. Games give way to sports, and primary school children take great pride in the enthusiastic design and production of dramatic events; the construction of models and other lasting products; elaborate imaginary play scenarios; and collections of cards, bottle caps, miniature cars, totem poles, and so forth. Through such industrious activity, children' s individual interests and abilities are constantly being defined, expressed, and redefined.

It is easy to see why Erikson (1963) emphasized the primary-age child's strong interests in achieving goals and the risk of repeated failures in his theory of psychosocial development. In kindergarten, youngsters are content to participate in dramatic play in which they pretend to sweep floors, feed babies, or build houses from blocks. By age 6, they become more focused on reality, often preferring to clean the room only if it needs it, to feed babies only if they are real, and to use blocks for academically oriented construction projects. This preference for reality over imaginary play is a gradual development and may be related to cognitive advances in understanding the difference between appearance and actuality. Some authors believe that imaginary play "goes underground" once children start school, because Western cultural values of goal orientation and a work ethic are inherent in classroom settings (Trawick-Smith, 2000). Whatever the explanation, industry is a hallmark of the elementary grades, and before long the entire class will have become seriously and enthusiastically industrious.

Motivation

Children come to kindergarten convinced, for the most part, that they can learn and that they will enjoy doing it. Children whose parents have encouraged them to explore and try new things, reassured them that mistakes are learning opportunities, and have high but reachable expectations have a special advantage (Benard, 1999). Children from the middle classes also are advantaged in that school as an institution is largely oriented to middle-class values. Nevertheless, a majority of K–3 children are possessed of an intrinsic desire to learn that begins, for many, to wear off in the upper elementary grades.

The fears and anxieties of five-to-eight year olds sometimes surface during new activities, and they can relate the frightening experiences of others to their own lives.

Two explanations that have been offered for young children's expectations of success even in the face of disadvantages include optimistic self-perceptions and the view that one can get smarter by working harder (Meece, 1997). For example, interviews with kindergartners have shown that most think they are the smartest in their class. In addition, they believe that ability or intelligence is tied to effort. After several years in school, they begin to realize that some people work very hard but don't succeed, whereas others put forth very little effort yet have high success. By later elementary school, children understand that effort and basic ability are differentiated, a premise often reflected in the reporting of progress in the primary grades.

Fears

As they enter kindergarten, children most likely carry with them the specific fears they developed as 4-year-olds: scary noises, imaginary creatures, dogs, storms, ghosts and witches, going down the bathtub drain, or being sucked into the toilet. By the end of the kindergarten year or in the first grade, fears become less specific and more generalized: being left alone, injury and sickness, ridicule and criticism, failure, being different from one's peers, disasters such as hurricanes or war, rejection by parents or teacher, or the death of a parent (Black & Puckett, 1996; Charlesworth, 1996).

On the face of it, 5- to 8-year-olds seem to have exchanged their preschool fears and strong attachments for new and more mature social activities. In reality, the primary-age child is likely to still have a special blanket or teddy in bed at night and to have more specific, less overt, fears. By third grade, children can relate the frightening and dangerous experiences of others to their own lives and understand enough about global issues like war, famine, and natural disasters to know that the world can pose very real threats.

During the K–3 years, children outgrow the strident exclamations of fear from their younger years and try to repress, or at least mask, their anxieties. Parents and teachers now must observe more closely as youngsters bite their nails, have trouble paying attention, change their eating or sleeping patterns, become more emotional, and increase their dependency. It is often difficult to determine whether a stomachache is an indication of physical illness or emotional stress.

Social Development

The development of what Gardner (1993) called interpersonal intelligence is a life-long undertaking that begins at birth. For children between the ages of 5 and 8 years, peers, as we have said, become increasingly important in determining self-perception and self-esteem. Recall too that cognitive development in primary grades supports the understanding that others have independent and sometimes differing ideas, that problems must sometimes be considered from more than one's own point of view. It follows that interpersonal relationships between children and their peers are now sometimes more important than relationships between children and their teachers or even parents. It is also worth reiterating that social, emotional, and moral development during the primary grades is closely related to and supported by children's advances in cognitive development, most particularly the ability to think more abstractly and to understand the perspectives of others.

Interpersonal Development: Friendship

The degree of success children have in achieving positive peer relationships directly affects their own worth and is thus an important aspect of teaching during the primary grades, as shown in Vignette 5.4. Intrapersonal and interpersonal growth are truly and strongly related for the K–3 child and remain so for the remainder of the lifespan.

Vignette 5.3: *Making Friends*

Paulo and Chip both entered kindergarten about a month into the school year and within 2 days of each other. Both boys come from middle-class families, and their parents are supportive of their development and well-being, volunteering immediately to provide help with field trips and other special class events. In other words, the boys came to school with their basic needs met according to Maslow's hierarchy.

*Within a short time, it became apparent to their teacher that the two boys were involving them-
selves in peer interactions quite differently. During free play on his first day, Paulo stood quietly
to the side of the block corner, watching several of the children construct a model of the grocery
store the class had just visited. Paulo said nothing, and the teacher wondered if he should intervene. He decided instead to observe and see what developed as Paulo watched the other children.
After about 10 minutes, one of the girls dropped a couple of blocks outside the area; Paulo deft-
ly picked them up and handed them back. She thanked him but did not invite Paulo to join in, and
he watched quietly a while longer, then busied himself with materials in the math area. The second day, Paulo stood at the side again, this time offering an occasional suggestion when construction problems arose. It finally occurred to the children to invite him into the block area and
he participated from then on, at first staying somewhat in the background, then eventually taking
his place as the acknowledged leader, a position he in no way seemed to solicit.*

*On Paulo's third day, Chip enrolled and was immediately attracted to the same block area. "Hi
you kids!" he yelled. "I want to play too," and he climbed over a short wall, knocking a few blocks
askew as he did. "Hey, watch it!" one of the boys yelled back and replaced the fallen blocks. From
then on, it seemed that Chip could please no one. He expressed his desires and opinions loudly
and imperatively, continuing to knock things over while trying to achieve his goals. After 3 or 4
days, the children refused to let him play in the block area (Paulo remaining carefully neutral).*

*Knowing that experiences in kindergarten can establish friendship patterns and behaviors for
many years to come, the teacher determined that he must intervene in some way for Chip. He
pulled the child to one side privately and asked if he would like help making friends. Chip
responded affirmatively, and the teacher began to engage him in one-on-one role playing, showing ways he might ask if he could play and suggesting positive follow-up behaviors. The two then
walked to the block area together, and the teacher told the children that Chip had something to
ask. Chip's request was a model of polite deference, and the children reluctantly agreed to allow
him in. The teacher then watched Chip's behavior, occasionally pulling him out for more instruction and role playing when the others became annoyed.*

*Chip needed continuing assistance from the teacher for much of the school year. He never
became as popular as the socially gifted Paulo, but he did graduate to first grade with sufficient
interpersonal skill that the teacher felt he could safely embark on the peer-oriented journey
through the primary grades and beyond.*

K–3 children who have teachers knowledgeable about the importance of peer relations have a distinct advantage in their social development. It is during these years
that children's perspective-taking skills emerge, not only regarding physical situations as we have discussed previously, but in social situations as well. Now, although
children prefer to see an issue from their own point of view (and don't we all!), they
also come to understand that others have important views too. Some children, like
Paulo, step into this understanding early and gracefully; others, like Chip, may need
adult intervention.

Loyalties among friends begin to develop toward the end of kindergarten or in the
first grade, refining the perception that a friend is someone in your proximity who
will share toys with you. By third grade, friendships are understood to be reciprocal,
based on mutual interests and support. Belonging to a group becomes important,
although the actual groupings tend to be fluid and unstable throughout the primary
years. Experiences within groups help children learn the importance of give and take,
the values and dangers of both leading and following, negotiation skills, and decision

making away from the authority of adults. Children who are not accepted into group play are denied the practice necessary to attain these social lessons, suggesting the importance of such adult intervention as Chip's teacher provided him.

Interpersonal Development: Sibling Relationships

Paulo's popularity quickly led to invitations to visit other children's homes after school. After a time, he developed a best friend in Mick, and they visited back and forth frequently. Both the boys had older brothers whom they admired, followed around, and fought with. One day, they decided to play "brother." For more than an hour, they interacted and role played in an idealized model of brotherhood. Gone was any envy, competition, friction, or rejection. Instead, both boys demonstrated acceptance, empathy, cooperation, helpfulness, and affection. Their tones of voice were amusingly sugar-sweet, their care and consideration of each other worthy of newly-weds.

Before dinner, Mick went home, and Paulo's 8-year-old brother arrived on the scene. Paulo told him of his game with Mick, and the two brothers decided to play "brother!" The same idealized behaviors and sweet voices characterized their play for a time. Before long, however, a disagreement broke out and the older brother announced, "Game's over!"

Over the next several weeks, Mick and Paulo, or Mick and his brother, played "brother" for varying lengths of time. During these sessions, the boys demonstrated a clear understanding of the most positive behaviors that emerge among siblings (and friends) during the primary grades. Acceptance, empathy, cooperation, helpfulness, and affection can grow during these years, as children begin to mentally step into another's shoes when differing ideas or disagreements arise. At the same time, rivalries at this age often indicate "the child's emerging sense of identity. Primary school children compare themselves with others in an attempt to affirm their self-worth" (Black & Puckett, 1996, p. 409).

Moral Development

Being able to distinguish between right and wrong in behavior and character is a value in any society. What constitutes right and wrong may differ, however, among societies and between age groups. Children in the fifth through eighth years have defined the moral issues that pertain to them as friendship, sharing, telling the truth, obeying authority figures, keeping promises, and obeying rules (Schuncke & Krogh, 1982).

Dealing with these sometimes conflicting issues provides children with opportunities to learn to make moral decisions. Classroom experiences such as the one described at the beginning of this chapter provide children with adult guidance as well as opportunities to discuss the issues with their peers. Research begun in the 1970s demonstrates that children's moral reasoning skills are enhanced by these opportunities (Damon, 1977; Selman, 1980). Like sports skills and reading, moral reasoning does not come to young humans automatically and requires adult intervention for successful development.

Most of the research begun more than three decades ago was based on Piaget's initial writings from the early 1930s. In his book *The Moral Judgment of the Child* (1965/1932), he suggested a two-stage model of moral development that reflects his stage theory of cognitive development. In stage 1, during the preoperational years (ages 4 to 7), children are authority oriented and obey rules as defined by adults and larger children. They believe that these rules cannot be changed but also that they must be obeyed only when authority figures or the threat of punishment are present. Punishment for disobeying is at the whim of the authority figures and is related to the consequences of a child's actions, not to the good or bad intentions attached to them. The primary characteristic of this stage is *heteronomy*: subjection to the laws and directions of others.

Piaget argued that the primary characteristic of a maturely moral human being is *autonomy*, independence and self-direction in decision making. His observations indicated that autonomy is a condition associated with formal cognitive operations. Between the heteronomous stage and the autonomous stage, in his theory, is a period of transition that occurs during the concrete operational period of cognitive development. Thus, kindergarten children, for the most part, still are heteronomous whereas youngsters in the primary grades are embarking on the transitional period that takes them to autonomy. As children mature they understand that rules are made by all kinds of people, for many different reasons; apply in many different situations; may be altered to suit the occasion or dropped entirely if appropriate. They come to realize too that someone's intentions may be as important or even more important than the consequences of an action.

After Piaget published *The Moral Judgment of the Child*, he returned to his qualitative research on cognitive development. It was more than three decades later when Lawrence Kohlberg, studying the moral reasoning of high school boys, expanded on the theory, at least in regard to older children. Within a few years, William Damon (1977) and Robert Selman (1980) followed with research involving younger children. Like Piaget, they found the K–3 years a time for outgrowing heteronomy and taking the first steps toward autonomy. In addition, they researched in more depth issues of importance to younger children, such as friendship and sharing. An example of Damon's findings that might be of interest to those teaching primary school students includes:

- Kindergartners generally believe that it is best to share equally among everyone present, with total disregard for any extenuating circumstances.
- Primary children might choose to share more with those who are in greater need—but only if the receivers do some extra work or contribute in some way.

Toward the end of the primary years, children seem to emerge from a preoccupation with self into an interactive and independent movement toward consistent, adultlike social behaviors. Children who successfully negotiate the social milieu of the primary years develop a sense of self that is stable and positive. They face the world able to balance curiosity with contemplation, rules with situational demands, and self-appraisal with self-confidence.

Variations in Primary School Social Affective Development

The direct impact of sensory, motor, and cognitive disabilities can be compounded by problems relating to peers during the primary years. Primary school can be a difficult period of adjustment for children with disabilities. Kindergarten and primary classrooms generally have more children and relatively fewer adults than do preschools, making it more difficult for adults to spend time supporting learning and facilitating social interactions for children with special needs. At the same time, the academic, motor, and social demands of primary school far exceed those of preschool or home environments. The result is that youngsters with special needs usually have less available adult support just when they begin to need it most.

In addition, whereas most preschool programs house children across ages in one group, primary classrooms are generally more *homogeneous*. Primary school children begin to understand personal concepts of race, culture, language, religion, gender, and ability. Myths, fears, and stereotypes about disabilities abound among primary school children, putting children with special needs at risk of exclusion, embarrassment, or poor self-concept. Difficulties keeping up with physical activities and informal classroom banter can further distance children with disabilities from their peers.

For the many reasons described in the sections on cognitive and social development, youngsters with disabilities begin to think about themselves in relationship to other people. Athletic success becomes a defining characteristic in the primary grades. Children who require extra assistance with academic and motor tasks can appear younger and less competent in the eyes of their peers. The responses of peers and teachers to children's special needs can have positive or negative effects on self-esteem and become more obvious to them, their peers, and teachers. Unfavorable comparisons are oftentimes easier to come by than positive interpretations.

Variations in social development can also originate from obvious differences in the behaviors of primary school children. Attention deficit hyperactivity disorder (ADHD) and behavior disorders may be diagnosed early in children's school careers, because the associated patterns of behavior are disruptive to classroom routines and school participation.

ADHD is believed to be caused by altered structures in the parts of the brain that regulate behavior. The condition is characterized by high levels of activity and distractibility that interfere with academic learning, often causing teachers to suggest medical evaluation. Behavioral approaches to classroom management and social skills instruction have been successful in remediating the behavioral and social difficulties experienced by students with ADHD. Special education can minimize associated learning disabilities. Stimulant medication is often prescribed and most often effective in decreasing activity and increasing attention in academic settings. The past few years have seen a dramatic increase in the number of children diagnosed as having ADHD, however, and the prescription of medication is cause for concern among parents and professionals alike (Blum & Mercugliano, 1997).

Children with behavior disorders identified during the primary school years may be generally disruptive in the classroom and at home, or exhibit more extreme antisocial behaviors: aggression, anger, defiance, noncompliance. These students have difficulty regulating their behavior, lose their tempers frequently, fight with peers, yell at teachers, and often do not benefit from instruction because of interfering behaviors. Students who qualify for special services as having behavior disorders may receive behavior consultation in the regular classroom or social skills instruction or both. Children with severely disruptive behaviors who pose threats to themselves, peers, and teachers may be served in self-contained classrooms or school facilities. The chapter on guidance and management in the book in this series entitled Teaching Young Children offers a range of suggestions for preventative, environmental, group, and individual approaches to behavior problems in the classroom.

IMPLICATIONS FOR CAREGIVERS AND TEACHERS OF PRIMARY SCHOOL CHILDREN

The more complicated rule-based games and sports of primary school do not indicate a need for intensive formal athletic training—quite the contrary. Although late kindergarten through the primary grades is a time when children are interested in learning about rules and the structure of games, their understanding is in its infancy. Insistence on following adult guidelines often leads to emotional distress and long-term refusal to be involved in competitive sports. The adult view that practice makes perfect can also have a negative impact. Athletic drills and repetition can be saved for later in life. Through the primary grades, most children develop new motor skills most successfully if they can retain the playfulness of their infancy and preschool years.

Thus, any training provided to primary school children should be informal and playful while offering children plentiful encouragement and positive feedback. Guided practice in game-related versions of the fundamental movements, in noncompetitive situations where possible, helps children of this age work successfully toward the upper elementary grades when sports begin to take on more importance. Classroom teachers should not expect physical education specialists to provide all the guided practice young children need. Few school districts have sufficient funding for physical education classes more than once or twice a week, but young children need activities of this sort every day.

Research indicates that U.S. children have insufficient opportunities for motor activity both at home and at school (Poest, Williams, Witt, & Atwood, 1992). Some suggestions for activities that are fun for children, easy for the teacher, and promote enhanced motor development include walking forward, backward, and sideways on a balance beam (or curb or log); hopping and skipping, in games or in accompaniment to music; throwing balls of various sizes to each other in circles or with partners: running around the perimeter of the playground a few times; standing and running broad jumps; and calisthenics. By the primary grades, children have organized their perceptual abilities fairly well, but some refinement is generally still needed. Thus, it is important for teachers to provide activities that make use of all the senses and of both small and large muscles so that children are able to meet the expectations of the school experience (Black & Puckett, 1996).

Children enter school as concrete thinkers. No longer bound totally by immediate perceptual experiences, they are initially still constructing knowledge of the world directly from reflection and understanding of their own activities. Their strategies for finding out about the world tend to be action oriented. Primary-age children learn best by interacting, the operational aspect being acting. Seeing and hearing will be most effective as learning strategies when children can simultaneously touch, handle, examine, explore, and manipulate.

Teachers and caregivers are uniquely positioned to provide the types of support and encouragement required for children with exceptional abilities to flourish. It is possible that many young children who live in environments devoid of stimulation and resources have a biological potential for giftedness. Perhaps they spend their days in schools or centers with teachers and caregivers like you, who can provide an environment conducive to developing their special abilities. Kindergarten and primary teachers need to be aware of the special gifts that all children bring to school, taking care to avoid the belief that children who are compliant, quiet, and well behaved must certainly be the ones who are academically gifted or that specific disabilities preclude giftedness in other areas. It is also important to realize that special talents and abilities in one area do not necessarily indicate a global set of achievements; children who come to kindergarten as readers may have difficulty in math, and vice versa.

Primary school students become very aware of individual differences among groups of peers. The significance that primary teachers ascribe to social development and the approaches they use to introduce issues of individual difference and social interaction to the class can have lasting consequences, positive or negative, for young students. Answering questions and addressing instances of name-calling immediately and directly can bring issues of race, culture, gender, and ability into ongoing classroom discourse. Social conflict and disagreements among children are good content for expanding problem-solving strategies and advancing social and moral development.

CONCLUDING REMARKS

We end this book with a chapter on primary school children, having outlined the sometimes subtle but significant transitions that occur across all areas of development for 5- to 8-year-olds. All the fundamental motor skills developed in the first 5 years of life are pressed into service in games and academic pursuits, with sports and athletic training just on the horizon as the next adventure in physical activities. Children begin to think logically, making group instruction of academic content possible. They become adept at communicating and learning symbolically, as demonstrated by acquisition of literacy skills during the first 3 years of school.

All areas of development have strong social connotations during the primary years. Children develop a stable identity and begin to evaluate their own behaviors against the expectations of others in a variety of settings. Most advanced motor and cognitive skills are applied in social settings: with friends, teammates, classmates, and family members. By the end of the primary school years, young children are no longer very young, and youngsters are on their way to becoming youth.

EXTENDING YOUR LEARNING

1. Volunteer to tutor at a local elementary school in a primary classroom.

2. Coach a little league or Special Olympics sports team. Observe the children's fundamental movements, and identify what cognitive, physical, and social skills are prerequisites to play.

3. Document the progression of language development by observing children ages 5, 6½, and 8 years old. List the skills involved and obtained at each point.

4. Review and compare Piaget's and Vygotsky's theoretical perspectives on child development. List the similarities and differences.

5. Read more about Gardener's multiple intelligence's or information processing. Think about a group of children you have observed and try to explain their thinking from each perspective.

6. Observe children at play, and report on evidence of friendships, preferences in play partners, and favorite activities.

7. Interview parents of primary-aged children. Find out what activities they do as a family, and list the domains (cognitive, gross or fine motor, social, self-care, language, or social) the child exercises during each activity.

8. Interview one primary school child who has been identified as gifted and another who has an identified developmental disability or delay. Record your impressions of their personalities, likes and dislikes, friendships, daily activities, challenges, and triumphs, using nonjudgmental, people-first language.

9. Select one of the children you interviewed in question 8, and accompany him or her to school. Observe their interactions with adults and peers, and record your observations of the content and schedule of his or her school day.

VOCABULARY

Accommodation.   Modification of thought processes or behavior patterns as a result of new information.

Autonomy.   Independence and self-direction in decision making.

Collective.   One's peer group; a social community.

Concrete operations.   Thought processes that make use of memory, inference, and analysis as a basis for understanding the world (Piagetian).

Conserve.   Knowing that quantity and number are constant, regardless of change in appearance, size, shape.

Decentering.   Ability to think from another's perspective and beyond one's own experiences.

Deductive reasoning. Drawing conclusions on the basis of general principles; reasoning from general principles to specific cases.

Executive processes. Generalized strategies for planning and organizing information.

Formal operations. Ability to think in abstractions.

Fundamental movement phase. Basic motor movements of locomotion, propulsion, and manipulation; for example, running, kicking, throwing, jumping; refined during the primary grades as transition to sports-related movements.

General or transitional stage. Earliest phase in sport-related movement, when a child is 6 to 10 years old.

Hand dominance. Preference for using the right or left hand for writing, eating, throwing, and other functional activities; the right hand is more often dominant than the left.

Heterogeneous. Mixed, varied, diverse.

Heteronomy. Moral judgments based on subjection to the laws and directions of others.

Homogeneous. Similar, uniform, consistent.

Inductive reasoning. Devising hypotheses and rules on the basis of discrete experiences and instances; reasoning from a specific to a general case.

Learning disability. Difficulty learning in specific academic areas, most often reading and written expression.

Life skills instruction. Curriculum centers around skills of daily living, such as functional communication, self-care, social and community access skills.

Mental retardation. Significantly delayed or impaired cognitive functioning and associated impairments in functional abilities.

Metacognition. Knowledge about strategies we use for mental process such as memory, problem solving, and decision making.

Multiple intelligences. An expanded definition of intelligence developed by Howard Gardner; includes many types of knowledge and accomplishments commonly considered talents: linguistic, logical-mathematical, spatial, body-kinesthetic, musical, interpersonal, intrapersonal.

Overextension.   Inaccurate word usage based on similarities in situations rather than on word meaning.

Private speech.   The speech young children use to talk to themselves; speech intended to be heard only by the one who produces it rather than for communication.

Reversible thinking.   Ability to visualize something in more than one form, concentrating on abstract concepts of mass or number rather than appearances of size or shape; characteristic of concrete operational thinking (Piagetian).

Scaffolding.   Providing support for learning by prompting, directing or performing the elements of tasks that are too difficult for a child's current ability.

Sport-related movement phase.   Fundamental movement skills that are refined and applied to new situations.

Transductive reasoning.   Using perceptual similarities between events as a basis for reasoning and problem solving (Piagetian).

Visual acuity.   Clarity and accuracy of vision across distance; 20/20 vision is considered the standard for good adult vision.

Zone of proximal development.   Cognitive content that is close to but more difficult than a child's current level of understanding.

INTERNET RESOURCES

Web sites provide much useful information for educators and we list some here that pertain to the topics covered in this chapter. The addresses of Web sites can also change, however, and new ones are continually added. Thus, this list should be considered as a first step in your acquisition of a larger and ever-changing collection.

Early Childhood Educators' and Family Web Corner
   http://users.sig.net/~cokids/

Education World
   http://www.education-world.com/

Kathy Schrock's Guide for Educators
   http://discoveryschool.com/schrockguide

Northwest Regional Literacy Resource Center
   http://www.literacynet.org/nwrlrc

America Reads Challenge
   http://www.ed.gov/ints/americareads/index.html

National Institute for Literacy
   http://novel.nifl.gov

American Association on Mental Retardation
  http://www.acess.digex.net/~aamr

United States International Council on Mental Retardation
  and Developmental Disabilities
  http://www.thearc.org/council/council.htm

National Center on Leaning Disabilities
  http://www.ncld./org/

LD Online
  http://www./ldonline.org

National Attention Deficit Disorder Association
  http://www.add.org

NIMH–Attention Deficit Hyperactivity Disorder: Decade of the Brain
  http://www.nimh.nih.gov/publicat/adhd.htm

National Association for Gifted Children
  http://www.nagc.org

References

Beddard, J., & Chi, M. (1992). Expertise. *Current Directions in Psychological Science, 1*, 135–139.

Bee, H. (1997). *The developing child* (8th ed.). New York: HarperCollins.

Benard, B. (1999). The foundations of the resiliency paradigm. In N. Henderson, B. Benard, & N. Sharp-Light (Eds.), *Resiliency in Action: Practical ideas for overcoming risks and building strengths in youth, families, & communities* (pp. 5–9). Gorham, ME: Resiliency in Action.

Berk, L., & Garvin, R. (1984). Development of private speech among low-income Appalachian children. *Developmental Psychology, 20*, 271–286.

Black, J., & Puckett M. (1996). *The young child: Development from prebirth through age eight* (2nd ed.). Englewood Cliffs, NJ: Merrill.

Blum, N. J., & Mercugliano, M. (1997). Attention-deficit/hyperactivity disorder. In M. L. Batshaw (Ed.), *Children with disabilities* (pp. 449–479). Baltimore: Paul Brookes.

Borke, H. (1975). Piaget's mountain revisited: Changes in the egocentric landscape. *Developmental Psychology, 11*, 240–243.

Bullock, M., & Gelman, R. (1979). Preschool children's assumptions about cause and effect: Temporal ordering. *Child Development, 50*, 89–96.

Case, R. (1985). *Intellectual development: A systematic reinterpretation.* New York: Freeman.

Case, R. (1988). Neo-Piagetian theory: Retrospect and prospect. In A. Demetriou (Ed.), *The neo-Piagetian theories of cognitive development: Toward an integration* (pp. 267–285). Amsterdam: North Holland.

Case, R. (1992). *The mind's staircase: Exploring the conceptual underpinnings of children's thought and knowledge.* Hillsdale, NJ: Lawrence Erlbaum Associates.

Charlesworth, R. (1996). *Understanding child development.* Albany, NY: Delmar.

Chi, M. T. H., Hutchinson, J. E., & Robin, A. F. (1989). How inferences about novel domain-related concepts can be constrained by structured knowledge. *Merrill Palmer Quarterly, 35*, 27–62.

Damon, W. (1977). *The social world of the child.* San Francisco: Jossey-Bass.

Erickson, E. (1963). *Childhood and society* (2nd ed.). New York: Norton.

Fischer, K. W. (1980). A theory of cognitive development: The control and construction of hierarchies of skills. *Psychological Review, 87*, 477–531.

Flavell, J. (1993). *Cognitive development* (2nd ed.). Englewood Cliffs, NJ: Prentice-Hall.

Flavell, J. H. (1982). Structures, stages, and sequences in cognitive development. *Minnesota symposia on child psychology* (Vol. 15). Hillsdale, NJ: Lawrence Erlbaum Associates.

Gabbard, C. (1992). *Lifelong motor development.* Dubuque, IA: Brown.

Gallahue, D. (1982). *Understanding motor development in children.* New York: Wiley.

Gardner, H. (1993). *Frames of mind.* New York: Basic Books. (Original work published 1983)

Gelman, R. (1972). Logical capacity of very young children. Number invariance rules. *Child Development, 43*, 75–90.

Gelman, S. A., & Markam, E. M. (1986). Categories and induction in young children. *Cognition, 23*, 183–209.

Gottfried, A. W., Gottfried, A. E., Bathurst, K., & Guerin, D. (1994). *Gifted IQ: Early developmental aspects.* New York: Plenum.

Hughes, F. (1995). *Children, play and development.* Boston: Allyn & Bacon.

Kail, R. (1984). *The development of memory in children* (2nd ed.). New York: Freeman.

Kail, R. (1991). Processing time decreases exponentially during childhood and adolescence. *Developmental Psychology, 27*, 259–266.

Lampl, M. (1993). Introduction: Human growth patterns. *American Journal of Human Biology, 5*(6), 601–602.

Maslow, A. (1968). *Toward a psychology of being.* Princeton, NJ: Nostrand.

Meece, J. (1997). *Child and adolescent development for educators.* New York: McGraw-Hill.

Mesibov, G. B. (April, 1998). *The TEACCH Approach.* Paper presented at The Child with Special Needs: Autism. Anaheim, CA: Contemporary Forums.

Piaget, J. (1954). *The construction of reality in the child.* New York: Basic Books.

Piaget, J. (1965). *The moral judgment of the child.* New York: Free Press. (Original work published 1932)

Piaget, J., & Inhelder, B. (1969). *The psychology of the child.* New York: Basic Books.

Poest, C. A., Williams, J. R., Witt, D. D., & Atwood, M. E. (1992). Challenge me to move: Large muscle development in young children. *Young Children, 45*(5), 4–15.

Price-Williams, D. R., Gordon, W., & Ramirez, M. (1969). Skill and conservation. *Developmental Psychology, 1*, 769.

Schneider, W., & Pressley, M. (1989). *Memory development between 2 and 20.* New York: Springer-Verlag.

Schuncke, G., & Krogh, S. (1982). *Helping children choose.* Adding, MA: Addison-Wesley-Longman.

Selman, R. (1980). *The growth of interpersonal understanding.* New York: Academic Press.

Siegler, R. (1981). Developmental sequences within and between concepts. *Monographs of the Society for Research in Child Development, 46*(2, Serial No. 189).

Siegler, R. (1983). Information processing approaches to development. In W. Kesson (Ed.), *Handbook of child psychology: Vol. 1: History, theory and methods* (4th ed., pp. 129–211). New York: Wiley.

Tan, L. (1985). Laterality and motor skills in four year olds. *Child Development, 56*, 119–124.

Tomlinson-Keasey, C., Eisert, D. C., Kahle, L. R., Hardy-Brown, K., & Keasey, B. (1978). The structure of concrete operational thought. *Child Development, 50*, 1153–1163.

Trawick-Smith, J. (2000). *Early childhood development: A multicultural perspective* (2nd ed.). Columbus, OH: Merrill-Prentice-Hall.

Winner, E. (1996). *Gifted children: Myths and realities.* New York: Basic Books.

Wood, D., Bruner, J., & Ross, G. (1976). The role of tutoring in problem solving. *Journal of Child Psychology and Psychiatry, 17*, 89–100.

Author Index

A

Aboud, R., 161, *169*
Ahadi, S., 120, *130*, 157, *169*
Ainsworth, M., 76, *90*
Allen, K., 156, *171*
Als, H., 21, 23, *36*
American Heritage Dictionary, 79, *90*
Ames, L., 99, *129*
Anders, T., 72, 73, *90*, 98, *129*
Anselmo, S., 141, *169*
Arnberg, L., 113, *129*, 151, *170*
Aslin, R., 67, *90*
Atwood, M., 210, *216*
Azrin, N., 124, *129*

B

Baker, J., 156, *170*
Bandura, A., 21, *36*
Bathurst, K., 198, *216*
Batshaw, M., 61, *91*
Baxter, D., 123, *130*,
Beddard, J., 191, *215*
Bee, H., 6, 10, *36*, 84, 99, *129*, 145, *170*, 187, *215*
Belsky, J., 80, 85, *92*
Benard, B., 6, *36, 37*, 163, *170*, 203, *215*
Berk, L., 189, *215*
Birns, B., 164, *170*
Bjorklund, D., 110, *129*
Black, J., 43, *91*, 178, 181, 195, 197, 205
Blehar, M., 76, *90*
Blickman, J., 21, 23, *36*

C

Carolina Abecedarian Project, 84, *91*
Carter, D., 159, *171*
Case, R., 190, 191, *215*
Caspi, A., 157, *171*
Cernoch, J., 44, *91*
Chandler, M., 23, *37*
Charlesworth, R., 205, *215*
Children's Defense Fund, 163, *170*

Bloom, L., 114, *129*
Blum, N., 209, *215*
Boothe, R., 65, *91*
Borke, H., 188, *215*
Bornstein, M., 85, *91*
Borton, R., 65, *92*
Bower, N., 44, *92*
Bower, T. G., 44, 56, 65, *92*
Bowlby, J., 43, 76, *91*
Bowman, B., 16, *38*
Brazelton, T., 21, *36*
Bristol, M., 122, *129*
Brittain, W., 104, *129*, 139, 142, 143, *170*
Brodal, P., 47, *91*
Broman, N., 163, *170*
Bronfenbrenner, U., 24, *37*, 76, 91
Brookes-Gunn, J., 117, *130*
Brown, E., 21, 23, *36*
Bruner, J., 188, *216*
Bryden, M., 136, *170*
Bullock, M., 188, *215*
Burns, T., 6, *37*

Chess, S., 119, 120, *129, 130*
Chi, M., 188, 191, *215*
Chomsky, N., 65, *91*
Christensen, K., 44, *92*
Chugani, H., 47, *91*
Cohen, M., 59, *91*
Cost, Quality & Child Outcomes Study Team, 4, *37,* 134, *170*
Crook, C., 65, *91*

D

Dale, P., 151, *170*
Damon, W., 158, *170*, 207, 208, *215*
Davidoff, J., 136, *170*
Davis, L., 44, *92*
De Marrais, K., 156, *170*
DeCasper, A., 44, *91*
DeLoach, L., 73, *93*
DeVitto, B., 70, *91*, 104, *130*
Dobson, V., 65, *91*
Dormans, J., 61, *91*
Doyle, A., 161, *169*
Drasgow, I., 155, 165, *170*
Dubrow, N., 147, *170*
Duffy, F., 21, 23, *36*
Dunst, C., 9, *37*
Dyson, A., 153, *170*

E

Eaton, W., 139, *170*
Eder, R., 158, *170*
Edwards, C., 143, *172*
Eisert, D., 187, *216*
Emerson, P., 77, 81, *92*
Erikson, E., 17, 18, *37,* 75, *91*, 117, *130*, 157, *170*, 203, *215*
Esposito, B., 144, *170*

F

Farran, D., 163, *170*
Field, T., 82, *91*
Fields, M., 165, *170*
Fifer, W., 44, *91*
Fischer, K., 67, *91*, 107, *129*, 191, *215*
Flavell, J., 44, 64, 67, *91*, 112, *129*, 178, 188, 191, *215, 216*
Foxx, R., 124, *129*
Fraiberg, S., 70, *91*
Franz, W., 141, *169*
Freud, S., 17, *37*

G

Gabbard, C., 180, *216*
Gallahue, D., 101, *129*, 180, *216*
Gallagher, J., 163, *170*
Garbarino, M., 147, *170*
Garcia-Coll, C., 136, *170*
Gardner, H., 192, 205, *216*
Garvin, R., 189, *215*
Gelman, R., 188, *216*
Gelman, S., 188, *216*
Gershman, E., 162, *170*
Gesell, A., 17, *37*
Gibes, R., 21, 23, *36*
Gillenwater, J., 44, *93*
Gillespie, G., 99, *129*
Gleason, J., 152, *171*
Goffin, S. G., 5, 10, *37*
Goldberg, S., 70, *91*, 104, *130*
Golden, M., 164, *170*
Goldfield, B., 113, *130*
Gonzales-Mena, J., 164, *170*
Goodlin-Jones, B., 72, *90, 98*
Gordon, W., 188, *216*
Gorski, P., 8, *37*
Gottfried, A. E., 198, 199, *216*
Gottfried, A. W., 198, 199, *216*
Green, B., 110, *129*
Gross, P., 59, *91*
Guerin, D., 198, *216*
Guralnick, M., 14, *37*, 162, *170*

H

Haines, J., 99, *129*
Haith, M., 44, 64, 65, *91*
Hale-Benson, J., 112, *129*
Halverson, C., Jr., 156, *171*
Hardy-Brown, K., 187, *216*
Haring, N., 59, *91*
Harter, S., 162, *170*
Hartup, W., 156, *171*
Haskins, R., 163, *170*
Hauser-Cram, P., 13, *37*
Havill, V., 156, *171*
Hayes, D., 162, *170*
Heffer, R., 82, *91*
Henderson, N., 6, *37*
Hester, B., 21, *36*
Hofer, M., 43, 44, *91*
Hoffman, L., 84, *91*
Hollett, N., 162, *171*
Horowitz, F., 6, *37*
Howes, C., 4, *37,* 84, 85, *91*, 161, *171*

Hughes, F., 180, *216*
Hutchinson, J., 188, *215*
Huttenlocher, P., 47, *92*

I

Ilg, F., 17, *37*, 99, *129*
Inhelder, B., 142, *172*, 185, *216*
Irujo, S., 154, *172*
Isabella, R., 80, *92*
Isenhath, J., 155, *171*

J

John, O., 157, *171*

K

Kagan, J., 81, *92*, 120, *130*, 157, *171*
Kahle, L., 187, *216*
Kail, R., 190, 191, *216*
Katz, L., 5, *37*
Kearsley, R., 81, *92*
Keasey, B., 187, *216*
Kelley, M., 82, *91*
Kennedy, D., 163, *170*
Keogh, J., 139, *171*
Klin, A., 122, *130*
Knoblock, M., 17, *37*
Kohnstamn, G., 156, *171*
Koorland, M., 144, *170*
Kopp, C., 8, *37*
Kostelney, K., 147, *170*
Krauss, M., 13, *37*
Krogh, S., 207, *216*
Kuhl, P., 65, *92*
Kunc, N., 14, *37*

L

Labov, W., 151, *171*
Lake, R., 60, *92*
Lamb, M., 81, *92*
Lamme, L., 141, *171*
Lampl, M., 178, *216*
Lawhon, G., 21, 23, *36*
Lee, D., 165, *170*
Levy, G., 159, *171*
Lewis, M., 21, *37*, 117, *130*, 163, *171*
Literacy Definition Committee, 153, *171*
Lowrey, G., 98, *130*, 135, *171*
Lozoff, B., 82, *92*

M

Maccoby, E., 160, *171*
MacFarlane, A., 71, *92*
Mahoney, G., 85, *92*
Makin, J., 44, *92*
Malatesta, C., 73, *93*
Malina, R., 136, *171*
Mallory, B., 29, *37*
Markam, E., 188, *216*
Marvin, C., 165, *171*
Maslow, A., 202, *216*
Mauro, J., 119, *130*
Mayer, C., 154, *171*
McAnulty, G., 21, 23, *36*
McClintic, S., 158, *172*
McNulty, B., 13, *37*
Meece, J., 189, 197, 201, 203, *216*
Meltzoff, A., 65, 66, 67, *92*, 107, *130*
Menn, L., 149, *171*
Mercugliano, M., 209, *215*
Mesibov, G., 122, *130, 216*
Miller, A., 165, *171*
Miller, P., 44, *91*, 112, *129*
Miller, S., 44, *91*, 112, *129*
Minde, K., 71, 73, *92*
Mitchell, P., 158, *172*
Moffitt, T., 157, *171*
Moore, M., 107, *130*
Munroe, R. H., 160, *171*
Munroe, R. L., 160, *171*

N

Nelson, C., 152, *171*
Nelson, K., 113, *130*, 150, *171*
Nelson, P., 156, *170*
New, R., 85, *92*
Notari-Syverson, A., 156, *170*

O

O'Connor, R., 156, *171*
Owens, R., 150, *171*

P

Pagioa, L., 162, *171*
Pan, B., 152, *171*
Pardo, C., 147, *170*
Parke, R., 81, *92*
Parmelee, A., 8, *37*
Pasamanick, B., 17, *37*

Pease, D., 152, *171*
Pellegrini, A., 139, *172*
Pelligrino, L., 61, *92*
Perlmutter, J., 139, *172*
Phillips, C., 151, *172*
Phillips, D., 84, *91*
Phinney, J., 161, *172*
Piaget, J., 66, 68, *92*, 107, *130*, 142, 145, 147, *172*, 185, 208, *216*
Pipes, P., 123, *130*
Plomin, R., 163, *172*
Poest, C., 210, *216*
Porter, R., 44, *91, 92*
Postman, N., 2, *37*
Powell, A., 85, *92*
Pressley, M., 191, *216*
Price-Williams, D., 188, *216*
Prinz, P., 154, *172*
Puckett, M., 43, *91*, 178, 181, 195, 197, 205, 207, 210, *215*

R

Rameriz, M., 188, *216*
Recchia, S., 158, *172*
Resnick, B., 113, 120, *130*
Reznick, J., 113, 120, *130*
Ridenour, M., 138, *172*
Robin, A., 188, *215*
Robins, R., 157, *171*
Robinson, C., 85, *92*
Robinson, J., 158, *172*
Roizen, N., 144, *172*
Ross, G., 188, *216*
Rothbart, M., 119, 120, *130*, 157, *169*
Rotheram, M., 161, *172*
Rutter, M., 99, *130*

S

Sameroff, A., 23, *37*
Sander, L., 75, *92*
Saunders, G., 113, *130*, 154, *172*
Saxby, L., 135, *170*
Schneider, W., 191, *216*
Schuncke, G., 207, *216*
Sears, R., 76, *92*
Selman, R., 161, 162, *172*, 207, 208, *216*
Semrud-Clikeman, M., 136, *172*
Schaffer, H., 77, 81, *92*
Shaffer, D., 18, *37*, 76, *92*
Sharp-Light, N., 6, *37*
Shatz, C., 47, *92*
Shimmin, H., 160, *171*

Shonkoff, J., 13, *37*
Siegler, R., 191, *216*
Skinner, B. F., 20, *37, 38*
Slentz, K., 154, *172*
Slonim, M., 154, *172*
Smith, D., 13, *37*
Smith, R., 28, *38*
Snidman, N., 120, *130*
Soper, E., 13, *37*
Soto, L., 15, *37*
Spangler, K., 165, *170*
Steinberg, L., 85, *91*
Stern, D., 80, *92*
Stevens, J., 123, *130*
Stipek, D., 158, *172*
Stott, F., 16, *38*
Stouthamer-Loeber, M., 157, *171*
Strong, M., 154, *172*

T

Tamis-LeMonda, C., 85, *91*
Tan, L., 136, *172*, 179,
Tanner, J., 82, *92*, 136, *172*
Teller, D., 65, *91*
Teeter, P., 136, *172*
Tenorio, R., 163, *172*
Thelen, E., 136, *172*
Thomas, A., 119, 120, *129, 130*
Tjossem, T., 7, *38*
Tomlinson-Keasey, C., 187, *216*
Trawick-Smith, M., 112, 115, 118, 124, *130*, 165, *172*, 188, 203, *216*
Tronick, E., 21, *36, 80, 92*

U

UNICEF, 154, *172*
Upshur, C., 13, *37*
Uzgiris, I., 67, *92*

V

Vadsay, P., 156, *171*
Van Lieshout, C., 156, *171*
VanderBerg, K., 8, *37*

W

Walker, A., 85, *91*
Wall, S., 76, *90*
Walton, G., 44, *92*

Waters, E., 76, *90*
Watson, J., 20, *38*
Wells, G., 154, *171*
Werner, E., 6, 8, 28, *38*, 99, *130*, 163, 164, *172*
Werner, L., 44, *93*
Western Regional Center, 6, *38*
Whitebrook, M., 84, *91*
Whiting, B., 143, *172*
Wiesfeld, A., 73, *93*
Williams, J., 210, *216*
Winner, E., 199, *216*
Witt, D., 210, *216*
Wright, D., *171*

Wood, D., 165, *171*, 188, *216*
Wu, F., 161, *171*

Y

York, S., 15, *38*
Yu, A., 139, *170*

Z

Zelazo, P., 81, *92*
Zelenko, M., 72, *90*, 98
Zeskind, P., 82, *93*

Subject Index

A

Alternative views, cognitive development, 187–194
  information processing model, 190
  multiple intelligences, 191–194
  zone of proximal development, 188
American Sign Language (ASL), *see* hearing
  impairments
Attention deficit hyperactivity disorder (ADHD),
  209
Autism, 122, 163

B

Bandura, A., 21
Blindness, *see* visual impairments

C

Cerebral palsy, 61–63, 82, 143, 144, 163, 182
Child care, 84, 134, 164
Child development concepts, 3–10
Cognitive development, *see also* sensorimotor cognition, preoperational thought, concrete operational thought, alternative views, 63–71,
  105–117, 144–154, 183–200
Concrete operational thought, 184–187
  classification, 185
  conservation, 184
  inductive logic, 186
  perspective taking, 185
Cultural diversity, 14–15, 118

D

Development problems, 25–29
  origins of, 25–28
  screening for, 28
Down Syndrome, 26, 71, 82, 104, 105, 116, 121,
  143, 144

E–F

Erikson, E., 17, 18, 74, 118, 157
Failure to thrive, 82
Family context, 42, 97, 134, 176
Fine motor development, 54–58, 102–104, 139–143,
  181
  drawing, 141–143
  grasping, 56–58, 103, 104
  manipulatives, 140, 181
  milestones, 57
  reaching, 55
  scribbling, 104
  writing, 181
Freud, S., 17, 18

G

Gardner, H., 191–193
Gesell, A., 17
Giftedness, 197–199
Gross motor development, 48–63, 99–105,
  136–139, 179–181
  cephalocaudal development, 49
  climbing, 101

Gross motor development *(continued)*
  creeping, 52
  fundamental movements, 98, 135, 177
  games and sports, 179, 210
  head control, 49
  high guard, 100
  infant milestones, 49, 57
  muscle tone, 61,
  prone lying, 50
  reflexes, 45–47
  rudimentary movements, 49
  sitting, 49, 51
  stoop and recover, 100
  walking, 49, 53, 59, 60, 99

H–I

Hearing impairments, 117, 143, 155
Implications for caregivers, 83–85, 122–126,
      163–166, 210
  crying, 79, 82, 84
  eating, 84, 123
  mealtimes, *see* eating
  safety, 122
  tantrums, 125
  teething, 123
  toileting, 124
Individual differences, 1–15, 59, 211
  cultural diversity, 14
  developmental delay and disability, 13–14
Infants, 40–93
  sensory capabilities, 64–66

L

Language and communication, 79–81, 112–116,
      149–153, 194
  babbling, 80
  bilingual learners, 113, 115, 151
  concepts, 116
  early vocalizations, 79
  first words, 112
  phonology, 149
  pragmatics, 153, 155
  semantics, 114, 153
  syntax, 116, 150, 195
  prelinguistic communication, 79–81
  private speech, 189, 194
  symbolic communication, 80, 114, 195
  vocabulary, 113, 161, 195
  word combinations, 114
Learning disabilities, 200
Literacy, *see also* reading and fine Motor, writing
  emergent, 153
  foundations, 196
Locke, J., 19

M–N

Maslow's hierarchy, 202
Newborns, 43

P

Pavlov, I., 19
"People first" terminology, 14
Physical growth, 45–47, 98, 135, 178
  brain development, 47
  hand dominance, 178
  social aspects, 179
Piaget, J., 23, 63, 67–70, 106–107, 145, 147,
      183–187
Play, *see also* gross motor, games and sports;
      social-affective, peer interactions
  active play, 138
  ball play, 137
  manipulative, 140
  outdoor, 182
  peer, 161
  pretend, 111
  toddler skills, 101
Prematurity, 104
Preoperational thought, 106, 110, 145–147
  animism, 148
  egocentrism, 147
  irreversible thinking, 147
  literal interpretations, 146
  transductive reasoning, 147
Preschoolers, 132–172
Primary schoolers, 174–216
Protective factors, 6

R

Reading, 197
Representational thought, 111
Resiliency, 6
Risk factors, 7
  biomedical risk, 7
  environmental risk, 7
  identified risk, 8
Rousseau, J., 16

S

Sensorimotor cognition, 63–71
  cause and effect, 109
  coordinated circular reactions, 69
  domains, 68
  imitation, 107
  means for obtaining ends, *see* tool use

primary circular reactions, 68
problem solving, 109
reflexive actions, 67
secondary circular reactions, 69
spatial relationships, 108
stages of, 68, 106
tertiary circular reactions, 106
tool use, 109, 141
Skinner, B. F., 20
Sleep-wake states, 71–74
Social-affective development, 71–83, 117–122, 156–
    163, 200–210
  affect, *see* emotion
  attachment, 75–76
  emotion, 157, 201
  fears, 204
  friendships, *see* peer interactions
  moral development, 207
  peer interactions, 161, 205–207, 209
  personality, 156
  proximity seeking, 77
  separation anxiety, 77
  sense of self, 117, 158–161, 201, 203
    ethnic identity, 161
    gender identity, 159
  social games, 121
  social referencing, 78
  social smile, 77

stranger anxiety, 77
temperament, 119–121

T

Theories of development, 15–31
  common ground, 29–31
  emphasizing external factors, 19–21
  emphasizing internal processes, 16–19
  in practice, 29
  interactive, 21–25
Toddlers, 94–130

V–W

Variations in development, 58–63, 70, 81–83, 104, 116,
    121, 143, 154–156, 162, 183, 197–200, 209
  cognitive, 70, 116, 154–156, 199
  cultural aspects, 60
  literacy, 155
  language, 154
  motor, 58–63, 81–83, 104, 143, 182
  social-affective, 81–83, 121, 162, 197
Visual impairments, 104, 117, 143
Vulnerability, 6
Vygotsky, L., 188, 200
Watson, J., 19